THICK AND DAZZLING DARKNESS

THICK AND DAZZLING DARKNESS

RELIGIOUS POETRY *in a* SECULAR AGE

PETER O'LEARY

Columbia University Press
New York

Columbia University Press
Publishers Since 1893
New York Chichester, West Sussex
cup.columbia.edu

Library of Congress Cataloging-in-Publication Data

Names: O'Leary, Peter, 1968– author.
Title: Thick and dazzling darkness : religious poetry
in a secular age / Peter O'Leary.
Description: New York : Columbia University Press, 2017. |
Includes bibliographical references and index.
Identifiers: LCCN 2017007545 (print) | LCCN 2017024983 (ebook) |
ISBN 9780231545976 (e-book) | ISBN 9780231173308 (cloth : alk. paper)
Subjects: LCSH: Religious poetry, American—History and criticism. |
American poetry—20th century—History and criticism. |
Religion in literature. | Religion and literature.
Classification: LCC PS310.R4 (ebook) | LCC PS310.R4 O44 2017 (print) |
DDC 811.009/382—dc23
LC record available at https://lccn.loc.gov/2017007545

Columbia University Press books are printed on permanent
and durable acid-free paper.

Printed in the United States of America

Jacket image: Moses and Bush Icon, Sinai, circa twelfth century

IN MEMORY OF MARK KRUPNICK
AND
FOR MICHAEL HELLER
AND NORMAN FINKELSTEIN

Our understanding is dimmer than *Moses* eye, we are ignorant of the backparts, or lower side of his Divinity; therefore to pry into the maze of his Counsels, is not onely folly in Man, but presumption even in Angels; [there is no thread or line to guide us in that Labyrinth]

—Sir Thomas Browne, *Religio Medici*

CONTENTS

ACKNOWLEDGMENTS

Many of these chapters previously appeared as essays in periodicals and anthologies. Chapter 1 first appeared as "Reversion and the Turning Thither: Writing Religious Poetry and the Case of Frank Samperi," *Logos: A Journal of Catholic Though and Culture* 7, no. 2 (Spring 2004). Chapter 2 first appeared as "Robinson Jeffers, the Man from Whom God Hid Everything," *Chicago Review* 49, no. 3–4; 50, no. 1 (Summer 2004). Chapter 3 first appeared as "Spiritual Osmosis: Geoffrey Hill's Recent Poetry," *Delmar* 10. Chapter 4 first appeared as "Prophetic Frustrations: Robert Duncan's *Tribunals*," in *Robert Duncan and Denise Levertov: The Poetry of Politics, the Politics of Poetry*, ed. Albert Gelpi and Robert J. Bertholf (Stanford, Calif.: Stanford University Press, 2006). Chapter 5 first appeared as "What Lies Beneath My Copy of Eternity? Religious Language in the Poetry of Lissa Wolsak," in *Antiphonies: The Gig Anthology of Canadian Experimental Women's Poetry* (Toronto: Gig, 2008). Chapter 7 first appeared as "Robert Duncan's Celestial Hierarchy," *Harp and Altar* 2 (www.harpandaltar.com), and then later as "Robert Duncan's Celestial Hierarchy," in *Re:Working the Ground: Essays on the Late Writings of Robert Duncan*, ed. James Maynard (New York: Palgrave Macmillan, 2011). Chapter 9 first appeared as "Apocalypticism: A Way Forward in Poetry," *Chicago Review* 55, no. 3–4 (Autumn 2010). In all cases, the essays have been revised and modified, and in one instance considerably, from their original appearance. Nevertheless, I remain grateful to the editors of these journals and anthologies, especially to Eirik Steinhoff, Jeff Hamilton, Albert Gelpi, the late Robert J. Bertholf, Nate Dorward, Keith Newton, James Maynard, V. Joshua Adams, and Joshua Kotin, each of whom had a hand in improving these essays for publication.

Institutional support from the School of the Art Institute of Chicago, in the form of two Faculty Enrichment Grants, helped toward the completion and publication of this book. Furthermore, I'd like to thank Paul Ashley at SAIC for his support of this project, as well as Teena McClelland and Kelly Christian in the Liberal Arts office.

Ongoing conversations with some of the poets who are the subject of this book have been a source of inspiration and keen pleasure. To Lissa Wolsak, Fanny Howe, Nathaniel Mackey, Joseph Donahue, and Pam Rehm, my sincere thanks. To these, I would add my brother Michael, Joel Felix, and Devin Johnston, always ready to talk cosmos and bunk. At a crucial point in revising the introduction, Joshua Corey provided helpful insight and perspective.

The comments of the three outside reviewers of the manuscript of this book have been helpful in revising, preparing, and adjusting it for publication. I thank them for the improvements they have suggested.

Philip Leventhal, my editor at Columbia University Press, has been like an excellent baseball manager through the editorial process, improving my fielding skills with focused drills, helping me work on my batting stance, and then giving unambiguous signs for when to bunt and when to swing for the fences. Owing to his leadership, I am hopeful about our prospects in the playoffs.

Though this book largely involves itself with the Christian imagination, it has its roots in the studies that Jewish American scholars and poets have made of Jewish American literature. If there are guide signs for American poets invested in describing a Christian vision of things, they have been placed for us by the Jewish scholars and poets who have gone before us. For this reason, I dedicate this book to the memory of Mark Krupnick, my mentor and advisor at the Divinity School of the University of Chicago, whose explorations of the deep places in the imagination have led me to my own. And then also to Michael Heller and Norman Finkelstein. Both poets have been mentors and friends to me, unstinting in their kindness and support, true models as hermeneuts and poets for living the life in this art form. My debt to both Michael and Norman is profound.

To my wife, Rebecca, who makes all things possible, my love and thanks. And to our sons, Gabriel and Lucian, may this be a curious container of things I was thinking about when you were boys.

THICK AND DAZZLING DARKNESS

INTRODUCTION

RELIGIOUS POETRY IN A SECULAR AGE

STEPPING BACKWARDS INTO THE DIVINE DARKNESS

Here is the description in the Authorized Version of God's appearance on Mt. Sinai in Exodus 20:21: "And the people stood afar off, and Moses drew near unto the thick darkness where God *was*." These words arrive moments after Moses has first heard God utter the Ten Commandments to him. Richard Eliot Friedman, in his *Commentary on the Torah*, translates: "and Moses went over to the nimbus where God was."[1] Everett Fox, in his translation from the Hebrew inspired by Martin Buber's and Franz Rosenzweig's German, renders it: "and Moshe approached the fog where God was," commenting: "'*arafel*, frequently used in conjunction with *anan*, 'cloud.'"[2] *Darkness*, *nimbus*, *fog*, *cloud*: a language of bewilderment, trouble. Saint Jerome in his Vulgate translation from the fourth century rendered the word as *caliginem*, from *caliga* for *darkness*, *gloom*, and from *caligo*, to becloud, to darken, to make dizzy. In his *Epistles*, Dionysius wrote "Divina caligo lux est inacessa, quam inhabitare Deus perhibitur," which means, "the divine darkness is unapproachable light, in which God is said to dwell." (Dionysius wrote in Greek; this Latin translation is the one Dante would have known.) In reference to this passage, the alchemist Thomas Vaughan, in *Lumen de Lumine*, a work from 1651, comments: "That which is above all degree of Intelligence is a certain Infinite Inaccessible Fire or Light. Dionysius calls it *Caligo*

Divina, because it is Invisible, and Incomprehensible."[3] Thomas's twin brother Henry, aspiring to the indefinite, puts it more directly in "The Night":

> There is in God (some say)
> A deep, but dazling darkness; As men here
> Say it is late and dusky, because they
> See not all clear;
> O for that night! where I in him
> Might live invisible and dim.[4]

Imagine Moses, then, in the act of giving the Law to Israel. The Israelites are terrified. Seismic upheavals have anticipated God's commandments. Their souls are quaking. "And all the people saw the thunderings, and the lightnings, and the noise of the trumpet, and the mountain smoking" (Exod. 21:18). In a fright, the people ask Moses to speak on their behalf, not wanting to confront this potent divinity themselves. Telling them not to be afraid, he suddenly steps into the dizzying "thick darkness," where the Lord speaks to his prophet, instructing him to erect an altar whereon Moses and his kind will make sacrifices. For which God promises to bless them forever after. Moses's contact with God in this moment stands for the symbolic acts of the religious poet: though the atmosphere is gloomy and ominous and the location strenuous to get to, the divine is present, and there is the prospect of law, covenant, revelation, and genuine power.

Thick and Dazzling Darkness is a book about the role religion and a religious worldview play in the work of a handful of modern and contemporary poets working in North America. It's also about writing and reading religious poetry in a secular age. It's commonplace to hear that we live in a secular age, but what does this mean? More to the point, what does it mean for the poets who are the subject of this book—Frank Samperi, Robinson Jeffers, Geoffrey Hill, Robert Duncan, Lissa Wolsak, Fanny Howe, Nathaniel Mackey, Joseph Donahue, and Pam Rehm—to write religious poetry, which is to say, to choose to write religious poetry in a secular culture in which religion has ceased to carry the meaning—both cultural and literary—that it has in the past? The purpose of this book is to discuss the role religion plays in the poetry these poets have written and also to place their religious worldviews in context—one that includes both spiritual and literary-historical meanings. My title serves to prepare the way I'm imagining into this material.

The Rhetoric of Religion, Kenneth Burke's study of religious systems as systems of action in language, begins with the following claim: "Insofar as man is the 'typically symbol-using animal,' it should not be surprising that men's thoughts on the nature of the Divine embody principles of verbalization."[5] Because religious doctrine is verbal, so argues Burke, it will show something about the process of this verbalization. By this, he means that it is possible to assess claims about the "nature of God," for instance, by looking at the thoroughness, clarity, and difficulty of the language used to make those claims. Put another way, you could say a pathway into the thick and dazzling darkness of the divine is blazed in words. You use language to bring you to the hidden radiating core of divine knowledge. The second chapter of Dionysius's "Mystical Theology" begins:

> We pray that we may come into this darkness that is beyond light, and, without seeing and without knowing, see and know that which is above vision and knowledge through the realization that by not-seeing and by not-knowing we attain to true vision and knowledge, and thus praise, superessentially, him who is superessential, by the abstraction of the essence of all things. This is like those who, carving a statue out of marble, abstract or remove all the surrounding material that hinders the vision which the marble conceals and by that abstraction bring to light the hidden beauty.[6]

We attain to true vision and knowledge, and thus praise, superessentially, him who is superessential. This is the negative metaphorical language used to approach the divine, in thought and description. It captures the mystery of such verbalization: A dizzying, self-negating language is required to move into the divine nimbus. I like to think of it as stepping purposefully but backward into the unknown. Or, as Robert Duncan puts it, "The seed of poetry itself sprang to life in the darkness of a ground of words heard and seen that were a congregation of sounds and figures previous to dictionary meaning."[7] Though Duncan is referring to the prerational language of childhood, he is pointing to the precognitive, divine language of creation as well.

Thick and Dazzling Darkness primarily addresses and discusses the ways poets verbalize thoughts and feelings on the nature of the divine, typically in symbolically rich language. It is also concerned with how poets both make and unmake meaning in poetry through their engagement with the religious imagination. Religion is presently a vexing topic in relation to poetry, and secularization has affected and impeded the understanding of religious poetry. Here, I'm thinking of Robert von Hallberg's claim in *Lyric Powers* that the "deepest well of authority [in poetry] is religious"[8] but that a shift in culture toward the secular has made the affirmation of religious authority in poetry difficult for readers and critics to take, even as the lure to write religious poetry has remained. "With this shift," writes von Hallberg, "has come a narrowing of the range of passion: secular, skeptical culture—that of universities—is at a disadvantage in the expression not just of joy but of conviction more generally."[9] This is attributable, in part, to an exclusionary rhetoric that dominates secularity: "From the secular point of view the exclusionary approach presumes that it is precisely the religious that represents the menace to the social order and, therefore, needs to be constrained, institutionally, philosophically, and behaviorally."[10] For the contemporary reader of poetry, religion, especially the expression of religious convictions, can read as a nuisance or a vestigial remnant of a poet's childhood faith. "There is a field of faith that the faithful inhabit," observes Fanny Howe.[11] As a person of faith, she can see this field. But for readers without such faith, it simply looks like an empty field.

As a poet and a scholar, this field of faith that the faithful inhabit is the field in which I've most been interested to pitch my tent. The stakes for my tent are made from my own creative involvement with religious material. As a young poet in Chicago in the early 1990s, I found myself in a community of like-minded poets, writers, visual artists, and musicians who were committed to publishing and exhibiting their works in magazines and at happenings. There were readings, concerts, and exhibitions to attend. My brother Michael and I, along with our friend Joel Felix, were publishing a literary magazine, *LVNG*, which brought me into contact with other young poets as well as older, more established poets whose work we were soliciting. I had also begun an earnest correspondence with Ronald Johnson, whose advice I sought for how to move forward on the path of the life of poetry. This was a time of almost complete immersion in poetry and the arts for me. I decided, prompted by Johnson's sense that a graduate degree in creative writing might not serve my needs, to enroll instead in divinity school, with the purpose of apprenticing myself to the study of a poet's work (Robert Duncan's specifically) and the religious material that informed his work and that of the twentieth century more broadly. In divinity school, I studied religion and literature, Christian mysticism, the depth psychologies of Freud and Jung, and the history of religions, with a special emphasis on myth and the historical study of myth. While pursuing my studies, I remained actively involved in different creative communities, but the encounter with all the religious material I was studying did two transformative things: It provided me with a lifetime's worth of subject matter from which I could quarry my work, and, more potently, it drove me inward to examine my own faith.

Raised in a Catholic family on the east side of Detroit, I was taken dutifully to Mass on Sundays and lived in a bubble in which families were distinguished not by faith but by which parish they belonged to. (St. Clare's, St. Ambrose's, or St. Paul's.) It was the 1970s, so this wasn't the rigid church of the fifties but the newly opened church of Pope Saint John XXIII's *aggiornamento*. For years, my family went to the 9 a.m. folk Mass in the basement of St. Clare's, where the choir consisted of a rock band with tambourine, electric bass, and emphatically strummed guitars. (To hear the "Great Amen" from the folk Mass is for me to dip a madeleine into a cup of tea.) As I moved through high school in the early 1980s, I remained an active churchgoer (reinforced by attending a Catholic high school), despite exposure to new ideas such as Asian religious meditative practices, Western esotericism and black magic, philosophical nihilism, and mind-altering drugs. (All of this placed in my lap thanks to a wholehearted immersion in progressive rock, heavy metal, and Frank Herbert's *Dune*.) These interests persisted during my years in college; my faith in the church and its doctrines waned. And as some interests intensified, others were added: poetry most emphatically but also mysticism generally and systems of mystical contemplation more specifically.

By the time I enrolled in divinity school in 1993, I only ambivalently practiced my faith, though I still found myself driven to engage with and understand systems of hidden meaning, inspired especially by the imaginal esotericism that runs through Robert Duncan's work, which I had discovered in college in 1988 and had been immersed in since.[12] As I began my coursework, I found, somewhat to my surprise, my faith intensifying. I studied for the first time (and despite a lifetime's relationship with Catholicism) the doctrines and history of the church, as well as those of Christianity more broadly, and began an active involvement with its systems of mystical belief, especially those of the Orthodox churches. Mystical Christianity radically reordered my own faith; I found in it a language and discipline for generating new poetry. A question began to form in my mind: how to write a Christian mystical poetry in an idiom of American experimentalism? The examples at the time were only a few: Thomas Merton and Brother Antoninus, both of whose work I admired (Antoninus's especially) but neither of whom provided a model for me, since both were members of religious orders. The discovery of Frank Samperi's poetry proved wildly validating in this regard: I found in his writing something avowedly experimental but so completely involved in Catholic mystical doctrine, I felt total permission to pursue my own similar trajectory. In 2013, Skysill Press in the United Kingdom reissued Samperi's groundbreaking *Trilogy* as a single volume. I was asked to provide an introduction for that volume, in which I wrote: "Here was work in the idiom of the New American Poetry that was not only open to the spiritual but explicitly religious in a way that spoke to another tradition with which I wrestled, Catholicism. The book quickly became a treasure."[13]

Thick and Dazzling Darkness began with the writing of the first chapter on Samperi's work, which inaugurated the questions that drive this book: What does it mean to write religious poetry in a secular culture? How does a poet write Christian or Christian-inflected poetry in an experimental vein? And what challenges lie in reading this poetry in a secular culture in such a way that its religious perspectives are not invalidated by critical stances or by what von Hallberg describes as a "narrowing of the range of passion"? Furthermore, it concerns itself with speculation about how within the field of a religious perspective these poets make and unmake the meaning that they find there in the acts of sometimes extravagant, sometimes mysterious expression they record in their poetry. I offer close readings of these recent poets for whom the verbalizing of their understanding of divine realities defines their work but whose poetry runs the risk of obscurity or neglect because the larger literary, secularizing culture has lost the ability to understand such work without anxiety or, more damningly, has lost the interest in such material altogether.

What does it mean to call any poetry "religious"? More generally, what is religion? For the purposes of this book, I follow Jonathan Z. Smith's definition that religion is "a system of beliefs and practices that are relative to superhuman beings." In Smith's definition, "superhuman beings are beings who can do things ordinary mortals cannot do."[14] It's commonplace nowadays for people (especially in the humanities) who feel squeamish about using the word "religion" to trade it for the word "spirituality." *Spiritual* implies personal beliefs where *religious* signifies institutional, doctrinal adherence. Throughout this study, I am referring to religion and not to spirituality. I don't think substituting spirituality for religion is a fair trade. Where spirituality is as evanescent as one's lifestyle, religion signifies tradition. Tradition comes from the Latin word *traditio*, from *traditus*, which is the past participle of *tradere*, which means "to deliver," specifically in the sense of handing something down. In this specific sense, religion and poetry are two of culture's richest traditions.

For my argument, poetry is religious in two potential senses (often together). It's religious when it draws its material or its outlook from a religious tradition—in the case of the poets in *Thick and Dazzling Darkness*, that religious tradition is Christianity. Frank Samperi's, Geoffrey Hill's, and Fanny Howe's work represent this kind of religious poetry. It's also religious when it performs one or more of the functions or exhibits one or more of the phenomena of religion, even when the poet is not himself or herself expressly religious. In the twentieth century, Paul Celan's work serves as a good example of this second kind of religious poetry: The mystery and revelation of religious ritual seem to be submerged in the mysterious and revelatory properties of the language in his poems. Celan's work powerfully involves itself with religious material, to be sure, especially the hermeneutical, mystical, and thematic properties of Judaism, but also other religious strains as well.[15] Nevertheless, it's the feeling readers get of a religious meaning made and unmade that draws them to Celan's work and accounts for what has made him an unusually strong influence in contemporary American poetry. Consider these opening lines to a sequence of poems in Celan's *Fadensonnen* (*Threadsuns*): "Out of the angelic material . . . "; "The freely blowing light-crop . . . "; "Dress the wordcaves with panther skins . . . "; "The highworld—lost, the insanity-trip, the day-trip . . . "; "The muttering . . . "; "And no kind of peace . . . "; "Nearby, in the aortal archway . . . "[16] The language here suggests even as it invents a mysterious reality the poem is merely beginning to glimpse. For instance, the poem "Out of the angelic material . . ." beginning in German, "Aus Engelsmaterie, am Tag / der Beseelung, phallisch / vereint in Einen /—Er, der Belebend-Gerechte, schlief dich mir zu, / Schwester—",

I'd translate "Out of the angelic material, on the day / breathed into, phallic / united in one /—he, the righteous restorer, slept you into me, / Sister—." In these lines, as much as Celan alludes to the mysticism of Kabbalah (and the *Zohar* specifically), he enacts a dazzling performance of that creation, so that his word "Beseelung" (ensouling, literally) alludes to God breathing life into Adam but in an act of intense arousal (hence the word "phallisch"), sliding into the sexual and creative pun/echo of one ("Einen") in union ("vereint").[17] Several of the poets studied in *Thick and Dazzling Darkness* activate religious meaning in a mode comparable to Celan, including, especially, Lissa Wolsak and Nathaniel Mackey. And then, there are the poets whose work modulates between these kinds of religious poetry, availing religious material and performing religious expression (or verbalization, to use Burke's term again) in the quest for poetic meaning. Robinson Jeffers, Robert Duncan, Joseph Donahue, and Pam Rehm fall into this category.

All of these poets involve themselves in an expression of religious anagogy in their poems. *Anagogy*, a term I will return to throughout this study, refers to mystical, interpretive tactics that open up the hidden meanings of words. Specifically, it refers to an interpretive process of spiritual uplift acquired by reading or even contemplative prayer. It's a word that had a central place in the mystical theology of Dionysius, the Christian mystic who lived in the fifth or sixth century and whose thought continues to inform Christian mystical thinking. In Dionysius's conception, anagogy implies a spiritual hierarchy, which is to say, meaning magnifies anagogically (or mystically) in the midst of a higher order. It's an active function of the imagination, literary or otherwise. Bernard McGinn offers a provocative comparison. "For Dionysius," he writes, "uplifting is really more like 'instressing' (to borrow a term from Gerard Manley Hopkins)."[18] "Instress" is one of Hopkins's invented dynamic poetic concepts, derived from the writings of Duns Scotus. By instress, Hopkins means "stem of stress between us and things to bear us out and carry the mind over."[19] Anagogy is the fourth and deepest of the fourfold polysemous levels Dante elucidates in his letter to Can Grande, who served as one of his patrons while he was writing the *Divine Comedy*. In this sense, it resembles metaphor, which Northrop Frye, for instance, has argued lies at the deepest expressive level of language.[20] Metaphor isn't directly mystical, not even in poetry, but it operates in a manner functionally similar to anagogy, such that words or phrases appearing to mean one thing suddenly mean other things and, scrutinized more deeply, begin to unmean what they signify as well, suggesting all along a higher reality of meaning to which the work at hand alludes. Just as anagogy can carry the mind over, to use Hopkins's description, so too can metaphor. The works of the poets explored in *Thick and Dazzling Darkness* are directly and anagogically religious, providing as they do literary epitomes for religious expression and experience.

SECULARIZATION

In a book that proposes to make claims about religious poetry in a secular age, it's imperative to have as clear a sense of what secularization means as possible. A simple but elegant model for the process of secularization was proposed by the sociologist Peter L. Berger in 1967 in his groundbreaking book *The Sacred Canopy*.[21] Before looking at Berger's model, I should ask: What is the secular age? What does it mean to live in such an age? First, the secular age is almost always understood in relation to Christianity, having arisen historically in Europe in the very early Renaissance. The historian Diarmaid MacCulloch sees Desidarius Erasmus (1466/9–1536) as a secular innovator. Trained as a priest, Erasmus turned his attention instead to secular literature and philosophy, eschewing the roles of hierarchical priest or professor, choosing instead a life as a "roving international man of letters who lived off the proceeds of his writings and from money provided by his admirers."[22] Unbound by any specific ecclesiastical commitments, Erasmus became the exemplary humanist and provides a model for thinking about the shift toward secularism in Western Europe: It's a shift toward humanism, toward learning, toward new possibilities. But that shift is always seen in relation to Christianity. Talal Asad, an anthropologist of religion, is careful to examine the connection between secularism as an epistemological category and as a political doctrine, which is how it is typically invoked nowadays. He points out that you can find aspects of the secular in medieval Christianity, in the various Islamic empires, and elsewhere too. As such, the model of secularism that arises in relation to Christianity is applicable to non-Christian, non-European cultures. Thus, it exists as an epistemological category, one that saturates the present day. Furthermore, Asad argues, the thing about secularism is that it "presupposes new concepts of 'religion,' 'ethics,' and 'politics,' and new imperatives associated with them."[23] Asad invokes the recent work of the philosopher Charles Taylor to puzzle out the meaning of secularism and living in a secular age. Taylor makes a straightforward comparative claim in his book *The Secular Age*, writing, "whereas the political organization of all pre-modern societies was in some way connected to, based on, guaranteed by some faith in, or adherence to God, or some notion of ultimate reality, the modern Western state is free from this connection. . . . Religion or its absence is largely a private matter."[24] To this, I would make one slight modification: in earlier times, political *and economic* organizations were connected to God. I mention Asad's and Taylor's studies not to question them but to provide a more contemporary backdrop to Berger's model. We're still thinking the meaning of secularism through, still trying to model it in our understanding.

In my mind, Peter L. Berger's *The Sacred Canopy* continues to provide the best model for how secularization takes place. Berger proposes in the title of his book a unifying metaphor for understanding the process by which religion enacts world construction and involves world maintenance. The sacred canopy, in Berger's description, is the conceptual aspect that overarches reality. "Society," he writes, "is a dialectical phenomenon in that it is a human product, and nothing but a human product, that yet continuously acts back upon its producer."[25] This dialectical process involves society projecting its qualities and concepts outside of the social reality, where they take on a property of independent reality that, when recognized by society, is reabsorbed into individual selves as an objective, validated reality. Through this process, the built-in instability of the world is settled, if only momentarily. Berger calls this process of stabilization the establishment of the "nomos" of the world, using the Greek word for law. In Berger's understanding of the social order, especially in its incipient stage, nomos is synonymous with cosmos. "Whenever the socially established nomos attains the quality of being taken for granted, there occurs a merging of its meanings with what are considered to be the fundamental meanings inherent in the universe. Nomos and cosmos appear to be co-extensive."[26] Berger points out that in archaic societies, nomos and cosmos are identical; in modern societies, the understanding of cosmos takes the form of scientific propositions, which work to separate nomos from cosmos.

In Berger's estimation, "religion is the human enterprise by which a sacred cosmos is established. Put differently, religion is cosmization in a sacred mode. By sacred is meant here a quality of mysterious and awesome power, other than man and yet related to him, which is believed to reside in certain objects of experience."[27] Here, Berger is identifying in religion some prospect of meaning making (world building and world maintenance) that is otherwise harder to locate, simply because, in a primordial sense, the law of the universe (its nomos) is understood intrinsically to be the universe itself. Religion, claims Berger, "is the audacious attempt to conceive of the entire universe as being humanly significant."[28] He does not mean to argue that religion is impervious to flaw or that it always operates smoothly as a meaning-making system. To adjust his own metaphor, sometimes there are holes in the sacred canopy, and light from another world begins to shine through, or reflect back, into our own. When light from that other world includes radical modes of doubt and disenfranchisement, especially in the circles of political and economic realities, it can be hard for religion to maintain the world with confidence, to say nothing of audacity.

Put another way, there is some deforestation of the sacred canopy. Berger focuses in his book specifically on the effects of Protestantism on the European religious imagination (and in this respect he shows his debt to his sociological precursor Max Weber), claiming that during the Lutheran reforms, Protestantism "divested itself as much as possible from the three most ancient and most powerful concomitants of the sacred—mystery, miracle, and magic," leading to a radical disenchantment of the world such that reality became "polarized between a radically transcendent divinity and a radically 'fallen' humanity that, *ipso facto*, is devoid of sacred qualities. Between them lies an altogether 'natural' universe, God's creation to be sure, but in itself bereft of numinosity."[29] Berger's characterization here is perhaps too simplistic, but his point sticks: at some time during the past five hundred years in the Western Christian imagination, the sacred cosmos became (should one add *merely*?) visible as the natural cosmos, at which point a kind of stabilizing meaning was set aside. "Probably for the first time in history," hypothesizes Berger,

> the religious legitimations of the world have lost their plausibility not only for a few intellectuals and other marginal individuals but for broad masses of entire societies. This opened up an acute crisis not only for the nomization of the large social institutions [by which he means things like governments] but for that of individual biographies. In other words, there has arisen a problem of "meaningfulness" not only for such

> institutions as the state or of the economy but for the ordinary routines of everyday life.[30]

Or, to put it in another way, in the words of Robert Duncan, "people who once had dreams and epiphanies, now admit only to devices and ornaments."[31]

OCEANIC FEELINGS: AMERICAN POETRY IN A SECULAR AGE

How does Berger's notion of the secular illuminate the situation of North American poetry in the secular, twentieth century? And more to the point, how does the poet, as manifesting agent of the sacred canopy and generator of meaning, become the medium through which mystery, magic, and miracles speak? It's a truism that the headwaters of American poetry are the colossal springs of Whitman's and Dickinson's work, both of which fed into the twentieth century and whose technical achievements only underscore their unprecedented, anomalous, and weirdly dissimilar eccentricities. I'd like to call Whitman's credo the "tenacious merge," product of an insatiable curiosity and observational intelligence, amativeness, and affability. Early in "Song of Myself," he claims,

> I am not an earth nor an adjunct of the earth,
> I am the mate and companion of people, all just as immortal and
> fathomless as myself;
> They do not know how immortal, but I know . . .
>
> Who need be afraid of the merge?
> Undrape . . . . you are not guilty to me, nor stale nor discarded,
> I see through the broadcloth and gingham whether or no,
> And am around, tenacious, acquisitive, tireless . . . . and can
> never be shaken away.[32]

Who need be afraid of the merge? That could stand for the creed of Whitman's religion, a cosmic, somatic, insistent commingling of atoms and faith. Dickinson's seems a flintier religion at first reading, but, as Susan Howe demonstrated in her groundbreaking study *My Emily Dickinson*, the poet "audaciously invented a new grammar grounded in humility and hesitation," building "a new poetic form from her fractured sense of being eternally on intellectual borders, where confident masculine voices buzzed an alluring and inaccessible discourse, backward through history into aboriginal anagogy."[33] Dickinson's credo aggressively distorts a Christian Platonism into a dynamo of suffering and revelation. Consider:

The Love a Life can show Below
Is but a filament, I know,
Of that diviner thing
That faints opon the face of Noon—
And smites the Tinder in the Sun—
And hinders Gabriel's Wing—

'Tis this—in Music—hints and sways—
And far abroad on Summer days—
Distills uncertain pain—
'Tis this enamors in the East—
And tints the Transit in the West
With harrowing Iodine—

'Tis this—invites—appalls—endows—
Flits—glimmers—proves—dissolves—
Returns—suggests—convicts—enchants
Then—flings in Paradise—[34]

It's the verbal barrage of the third stanza that opens the verses to revelation, so intense and thoroughgoing, that it seems to eradicate the subject of the poem itself. To what does "this" in the final stanza refer? And what is it that "flings in Paradise"? And from where? The poem is stained with intelligence. *With harrowing Iodine* could be Dickinson's credo to match Whitman's fearless merge.

Let's acknowledge for now that the legacies of Whitman and Dickinson were for the most part ignored, with a few notable exceptions, until the middle of the twentieth century, which saw a revival of the work of both poets as well as a willingness to embrace their poetic, vatic, religious imperatives. Whitman's began with the republication of the 1855 *Leaves of Grass* in 1955, edited by Malcolm Cowley, but more potently and lastingly when Allen Ginsberg wrote "Howl" the same year. (It was published in book form in 1956 and immediately seized by authorities for being obscene.) Ginsberg's genius was to have absorbed Whitman's influence almost completely in that work, a creative merge that sustained all the rest of his poetry. Editorial interest in Dickinson's work changed in 1951 with the three-volume publication of *The Poems of Emily Dickinson*, edited by Thomas H. Johnson, which famously restored the dashes to Dickinson's poems as well as correcting some of the other editorial interventions that had occurred over the previous century (including dozens and dozens of word changes). But it wasn't until the publication of Susan Howe's *My Emily Dickinson* in 1985 that Dickinson's radical religious vision became visible to her readers. Howe showed how completely Dickinson had been misread over the decades, allowing the influence of the poetry to surge forth anew. But these are recoveries and uncoverings that happened in the later twentieth century. What about the early twentieth century?

The religious visions of Whitman and Dickinson were rarely in sight for modernist poets as they are for us now (and have been for almost all of the poets considered in this book). However, there were religious compulsions guiding the work: Frost's stoicism, Pound's Dionysian mysticism, Crane's visionary intensities, or Stevens's platonic theology, to say nothing of Eliot's apocalyptic Christian plaints. But for most canonical modernist poets, religious matters were deflected in their poetry for something "truer": Frost's gloomy sense of place, Pound's cultic hymns to beauty and cubist composite of history and myth, Crane's linguistic euphoria, Stevens's hymns to the imagination. I take Crane to be one of the great visionary poets of the American idiom, but of the modernist poets, it's really only H.D. and Eliot who took religion seriously as a subject matter and theme. For most of the rest of the poets, it was a topic of ridicule or discomfort best left to silence.

T. S. Eliot wrote the most avant-garde poem of the twentieth century, at least in English, in no small part because of its cataclysmic vision of the end times. "The Waste Land" is also one of the great apocalyptic poems in Christian literature, a total assault on the imagination that lives in the hope of some eventual deliverance, some salvation. "A poet's specific task," wrote Northrop Frye, "has something to do with visualizing the Promised Land: on the historical level, he may often be a lost leader, a Moses floundering in a legal desert."[35] Frye takes Eliot's oft-repeated judgment that he had produced only "rhythmical grumbling" in his masterpiece not at Eliot's word but as a sign that he'd somehow misunderstood his poetic calling. Eliot, famously, in the wake of the catastrophic vision unleashed in "The Waste Land," retreated (at least that's how it is often read) into Christianity, specifically a self-professed Anglo-Catholicism. "As Eliot says," Frye observed, "it is the Word in the desert that is most likely to hear 'The loud lament of the disconsolate chimera.' It is difficult to feel that Eliot's view of Western culture is anything more than a heresy in his own sense of the word, a partial insight with 'a seductive simplicity' which is 'altogether more plausible than the truth.'"[36]

"The loud lament of the disconsolate chimera" comes from Eliot's poem "Burnt Norton," which first appeared in 1936 at the end of *Collected Poems 1909–1935*. "Words, after speech, reach / Into silence," writes Eliot, who focuses his eye on the Christian logos: "The Word in the desert / Is most attacked by voices of temptation, / The crying shadow in the funeral dance, / The loud lament of the disconsolate chimera."[37] Temptation alludes to the Gospel of Matthew, 4:1–11, in which Satan tempts Christ in the desert. The Word is the present. The desert is the modern world. Who or what is the disconsolate chimera? The voice of faith? Its lack in the modern writer?

At the beginning of *Civilization and Its Discontents*, Freud's polemic against human culture and aspiration first published in 1930, he describes with obvious envy a spiritual register—"the real source of religiosity"—a friend of his, Romain Rolland, has experienced but that Freud himself conspicuously hasn't. His friend reports that it is

> a feeling that he was inclined to call a sense of "eternity," a feeling as of something limitless, unbounded—as it were, "oceanic." This feeling was a purely subjective fact, not an article of faith; no assurance of personal immortality attached to it, but it is the source of the religious energy that was seized upon by the various churches and religious systems, directed into particular channels and certainly consumed by them. On the basis of this oceanic feeling alone one was entitled to call oneself religious, even if one rejected every belief and every illusion.[38]

Civilization and Its Discontents involves Freud's creative efforts to modify Rolland's notion with his theories of the competing death and sex drives. In spite of this, in this brief statement, Freud provides one of the most lucid descriptions of the religious feeling and spiritual longing since Saint Augustine's plaint to God that though he made us for himself, "our hearts are restless until they rest in thee." What Freud accomplishes at the beginning of *Civilization and Its Discontents* is the creation of a new language for religious inwardness.[39]

It's not coincidental that H.D. was psychoanalyzed by Freud. H.D.'s religious vision, which was Christian, mystical, and richly esoteric, was experientially rooted and integrated with psychological insight (which, despite Freud's disapproval, was frequently connected to esoteric practices and insights). In 1919, she was pregnant with the child of Cecil Gray, a musician in London. At the time, H.D. was married to Richard Aldington, who had encouraged her to initiate an affair with Gray—their marriage was "open." H.D.'s pregnancy, then, was no more scandalous than Aldington having a mistress of his own, but given the sexual politics of the day, Aldington held the upper hand. H.D. begged her husband to recognize the child as his own, but he refused, threatening a lawsuit if the child should bear his name. Perhaps as a sign of her vulnerabilities, H.D. contracted the Spanish flu at the time, becoming perilously ill, endangering the birth and health of her daughter, whom she named Perdita. It was at this moment that Bryher, who would become her lifelong companion, swept in and took H.D. to the Scilly Islands, where H.D. and child recovered. "Bryher's love and care saved H.D.'s life during her severe illness and gradual recovery," writes Susan Stanford Friedman.[40] Bryher, the daughter of Britain's wealthiest ship owner, had the means to support H.D. and her daughter, whom they raised together (despite H.D.'s two subsequent marriages of convenience), traveling widely throughout Europe and the United States.

On the Scilly Islands, H.D. entered into a state of consciousness in which she felt herself merged with her surroundings and her new baby. An oceanic feeling, if you will. Albert Gelpi explains that she "moved into moments of consciousness in which feelings of separateness gave way to a sense of organic wholeness: collapse gave way to coherence and alienation to participation in a cosmic scheme."[41] H.D. herself characterized this as a state of "jelly-fish consciousness" in which an "over-mind" drooped down across her field of vision, "a cap of consciousness over my head, my forehead, affecting a little my eyes." This began what William James would characterize as a noetic, mystical experience, which H.D. elaborated as "a set of super-feelings. These feelings extend out and about us; as the long, floating tentacles of the jelly-fish reach out and about [me]. They are not of different material, extraneous, as the physical arms and legs are extraneous to the gray matter of the directing brain. The super-feelers are part of the super-mind, as the jelly-fish feelers are the jelly-fish itself, elongated in fine threads."[42] H.D.'s oceanic feeling was so metaphorically saturated that it was pervaded with sea creatures whose motions activated altered states of consciousness. The jelly-fish consciousness created an anticipatory awareness of the unison she would feel with her daughter: "For me, it was before the birth of my child that the jelly-fish consciousness seemed to come definitely into the field or realm of the intellect or brain."[43]

And this shift in her consciousness prepared her for another visionary experience she would have in 1920, less than a year later, on the Greek island of Corfu, where in her hotel bedroom she experienced a sequence of shadow visions that signified for her a desire for union with her mother. This was during her first trip to Greece, a place she had already stamped into modernist verse in her revolutionary imagist poems from the previous decade. In the late afternoon, in a state of relaxed receptivity (a state the British psychoanalyst D. W. Winnicott would describe as "unintegrated"), H.D. watched as shadows formed on the wall of her room, unusual shadows. Three forms appeared, in sequence. First, a featureless figure, in three-quarters profile. Then, a cup, "a mystic chalice." And finally, in a way difficult at first to discern, a shape that resolved into a tripod, a primordial vessel that would serve as a religious implement. This sequence of visions formed the core of H.D.'s analysis with Freud, who was himself fascinated by archaic shapes. In the memoir of her analysis, *Tribute to Freud*, she is careful to indicate that these shapes did not appear as shadows flickering on bright walls. Rather, the first shape—an archetypal figure—"was a silhouette cut of light, not shadow, and so impersonal it might have been anyone, of almost any country." The tripod suggested to her something Delphic, the "venerated object of the cult of the sun god, symbol of poetry and prophecy," but also something more ordinary: a device to be used for boiling tea in the afternoons.[44]

H.D. regarded this visionary sequence—a pictographic elaboration of the jelly-fish consciousness she experienced on the Scilly Islands—as a cipher through which to interpret her work but also, somewhat ironically, as a religious summons. Freud, despite his native religious skepticism, seemed to agree. "We can read my writing," she offered,

> in two ways or in more than two ways. We can read or translate it as a suppressed desire for forbidden "signs and wonders," breaking bounds,

> a suppressed desire to be a Prophetess, to be important anyway, megalomania they call it—a hidden desire to "found a new religion" . . . Or this writing-on-the-wall is merely an extension of the artist's mind, a *picture* or an illustrated poem, taken out of the actual dream or daydream content and projected from within (though apparently from outside), really a high-powered *idea*, simply over-stressed, *over-thought*, you might say, an echo of an idea, a reflection of a reflection, a "freak" thought that had got out of hand, gone too far, a "dangerous symptom."[45]

Overthoughts emerge presumably from the overmind. This isn't a Freudian superego; rather, the overmind is a highly generative, dynamic, but nevertheless occult, intellective, and predictive force. In other words, it's the power from which H.D.'s esoteric, Christian mystical poetry precipitated.

H.D. wrote the three parts of her magnificent *Trilogy* between 1942 and 1944, from the traumatic center of the Second World War but still engrossed in the long shadow of her analysis with Freud, which she conducted in 1933 (thanks to the social connections and generous funding of Bryher). This poem, composed of "The Walls Do Not Fall" (1942), "Tribute to the Angels" (1944), and "The Flowering of the Rod" (1944), is for me the apex of H.D.'s literary achievement, a poem whose cryptic content feeds like a great influx into the freely flowing open water of the verse itself, which is limpid and crystalline. It's also one of the great religious poems written in English in the twentieth century, in which Christian mystical, astrological, esoteric, and nakedly psychological elements come together in a mindful intensity. Take these lines from late in "The Walls Do Not Fall":

> I heard Scorpion whet his knife,
> I feared Archer (taut his bow),
>
> Goat's horns were threat,
> would climb high? then fall low;
>
> across the abyss
> the Waterman waited,
>
> this is the age of the new dimension,
> dare, seek, seek further, dare more,

here is the alchemist's key,
it unlocks secret doors,

the present goes a step further
toward fine distillation of emotion,

the elixir of life, the philosopher's stone
is yours if you surrender

sterile logic, trivial reason;
so mind dispersed, dared occult lore,

found secret doors unlocked,
floundered, was lost in sea-depth,

sub-conscious ocean where Fish
move two-ways, devour;

when identity in depth,
would merge with the best,

octopus or shark rise
from the sea-floor:

illusion, reversion of old values,
oneness lost, madness.[46]

The poet hopes for the psychological clarification of the new age, "the age of new dimension," the Age of Aquarius, heralded by the Waterman. H.D. is alluding to the zodiacal ages, conceived of by stargazers because of the phenomenon of the precession of the equinoxes, which denotes "the retrograde movement of the Vernal Point through the constellations," or, in other words, the visible phenomenon in which one constellation in the zodiac is seen to drift across the pattern of another constellation.[47] Technicalities of precession aside, H.D.'s poem includes an anticipation that the Age of Aquarius, which is expected to last two thousand years and whose dawning at the time she wrote these lines was believed to be near. This age, so forecasters believe, will be characterized by features associated with the Aquarian zodiac; it will be "friendly, humanitarian, progressive, persistent, inventive, perverse, creative, tolerant, fond of science and literature, discreet and optimistic."[48] Notice, however, how H.D.'s verses give way to a more ominous anticipation of a frightening oceanic feeling, a possible catastrophic outcome to her jelly-fish consciousness, "oneness lost, madness." Rather, she would merge (that Whitmanian term) with octopus or shark, powerful predators of the depths, unlocking secret doors and daring occult lore. This is H.D.'s vision of a religion for the modern age, if not for many, at least for herself.

Consider in comparison Eliot's more ironically attuned esoteric invocation in "The Waste Land," when Madam Sosostris, the fortune teller, appears with her "wicked pack of cards" in "The Burial of the Dead":

> Madame Sosostris, famous clairvoyante,
> Had a bad cold, nevertheless
> Is known to be the wisest woman in Europe,
> With a wicked pack of cards. Here, said she,
> Is your card, the drowned Phoenician Sailor,
> (Those are pearls that were his eyes. Look!)
> Here is Belladonna, the Lady of the Rocks,
> The lady of situations.
> Here is the man with three staves, and here the Wheel,
> And here is the one-eyed merchant, and this card,
> Which is blank, is something he carries on his back,
> Which I am forbidden to see. I do not find
> The Hanged Man. Fear death by water.
> I see crowds of people, walking round in a ring.
> Thank you. If you see dear Mrs. Equitone,
> Tell her I bring the horoscope myself:
> One must be so careful these days.[49]

The card I am forbidden to see curiously characterizes Eliot's apocalyptic anxiety, in contrast to H.D.'s active visualization of the coming esoteric age. In a footnote to this passage, Eliot confesses, "I am not familiar with the exact constitution of the Tarot pack of cards, from which I have obviously departed to suit my own convenience."[50] What seems like an artful dodge perhaps should be accepted on face value. Eliot doesn't know about the Tarot cards because he can't "see" them (which is to say envision them) particularly well. Northrop Frye notes: "A curious, and to me regrettable, feature of Eliot's critical theory is his avoidance of the term 'imagination,' except in the phrase 'auditory imagination' at the furthest remove from the poetic product."[51] This avoidance is ironically present in Eliot's poetry, argues Frye, insisting that the imaginative world of the poems must be approached through its imagery, which, he suggests, consists of innocence and paradise contrasted to images of experience and torment (or hell). Madame Sosostris is a satirical character whose forecasts are oracles of the mundane, of ennui, which in Eliot, as Frye points out, is "not so much sin as a state of sin."[52] In H.D.'s poetry, Madame Sosostris would simply be the oracle herself, without irony. Both poets are responding in part to the religious anxieties of the age in psychological, esoteric, and apocalyptic language, Eliot in a high ironic style, H.D. more earnestly.

MODERNITY: ASWIM IN THE CURRENTS OF THE OCEANIC FEELING

Perhaps not surprisingly, *Trilogy* remains an obscure poem, despite its place as a major work by one of the major modernist poets, whereas "The Waste Land," a much less approachable poem in comparison, is taught in high schools (though not likely for its apocalyptic content). Among poets of the subsequent generation, only Robert Duncan recognized the requirement to make something himself in the image of H.D.'s poem (while harboring a skepticism toward Eliot's poem, a New American prejudice he cultivated without much hesitation). Duncan's recognition of H.D.'s poetic powers points to the core of the argument for *Thick and Dazzling Darkness*, which is a reading of twentieth-century and contemporary American poetry under the sign of religion. Duncan devoted a solid decade of his writing life in the 1960s to the production of *The H.D. Book*, chapters of which were published in his lifetime but the whole of which came to print only recently, in 2011, almost a quarter-century after Duncan's death. This massive work is many things, but it is especially a religious, sacramental, and esoteric reading of recent literary history, with special emphasis on the conductive role H.D.'s work played in the generation and validation of his ideas. Reading *Trilogy*, Duncan claims,

> Every resonance had been prepared, for I had found . . . a new Master over Poetry in the work of H.D. In these things my mind likewise was stirred to rapture, my heart moved to such pleasure . . . For that winged bright promise that the soul seeks in its beloved appeared to me in the life that the inner sensitive consciousness of . . . H.D., had found for itself in [her] writing, thriving there, hidden from the careless reader, surviving the scorn and even hatred of the antipathetic reader, a seed that would chance somewhere, sometime, upon the ground that awaited its revelation, for the reader who would not misunderstand or revile but who would come to find therein his own kindred life.[53]

Duncan is describing the click of recognition that initiates a religious conversion, the first glimmer of a unifying vision. For Duncan, this was a vision of Poetry, capitalized. "The work itself," he intones in *The H.D. Book*, in a chapter called "Eros," "is the transformation of the ground. In this ground the soul and the world are one in a third hidden thing, in imagination of which the work arises. It is the work of creation then. It is Poetry, a Making."[54] William James, in *The Varieties of Religious Experience*, draws a narrative in which a "divided self" in whom dominant lower tendencies rule over the higher wishes, which therefore lack the "explosive intensity . . . [to] burst their shell, and make irruption efficaciously into life and quell the lower tendencies forever."[55] Most of us, in James's reckoning, spend our lives thus split, our desires to unify our vision regularly suppressed by the avalanche of doubts and duties that consume us. "To be converted," James assures, "to be regenerated, to receive grace, to experience religion, to gain an assurance, are so many phrases which denote the process, gradual or sudden, by which a self hitherto divided, and consciously wrong inferior and unhappy, becomes unified and consciously right superior and happy, in consequence of its firmer hold upon religious realities."[56] So firmly does Duncan's religious vision command his view on reality that through H.D.'s poetry he sees "the inner works of the poetic opus." "The rhymes of this poetry are correspondences, workings of figures and patterns of figures in which we apprehend the whole we do not see."[57] So penetrating is his gaze, he sees in the poetry before him occult vibrations of its archetypal origins: "Our work is to arouse in a contemporary consciousness reverberations of old myth."[58]

Not all religious claims about contemporary poetry are so grandiose, even as Duncan occupies a central place in my thinking about the religious imperative in writing and reading poetry. Like H.D., Duncan is exemplary of the poets addressed in this book because he insists on understanding poetry under a vatic, prophetic, mantic sign. We live in a secular age, there's no question. And most of our art reflects that age, if only by dint of mimetic necessity. The poets I have chosen to study in this book are unified by a kind of religious calling in poetry, drawn along the lines Duncan spells out in *The H.D. Book*. Each presents an individual but connected response to the fact of the secular age, stepping, in Moses-fashion, into the thick darkness where God is, which, often enough, is hidden not in the dazzle of religious revelation but in the obscure drudgery of a world from which forms of sacred meaning have been dutifully drained, like water from unwanted marshland. Frank Samperi, working in almost total obscurity, found himself aroused to a melancholic, angelic vision. Robinson Jeffers, mystic and misanthrope, perched himself in a stone tower built by his own hands overlooking the Pacific to watch in rapt gloom as the Western world declined into darkness once and for all. Geoffrey Hill's later poetry argues for a psychopharmacological spilling of prophetic spleen as omen for a new century. Robert Duncan's prophetic frustrations envision celestial diseases as angelic presences to counteract political insipidity. Fanny Howe's poetry of Catholic conversion glares its spotlight on injustice and destitution. Lissa Wolsak writes a poetry of revelatory fragmentation to serve as heuristic prolusion for a poetry to come. Nathaniel Mackey's Gnostic chants of antiepistemological quest give the lie to spiritual resolution in religious searching. And, finally, Joseph Donahue's visionary projections and Pam Rehm's plainspoken rue ally to provide an apocalyptic way forward for poetry. Speaking for them all, I might have them say, "Our work is to arouse in a contemporary consciousness reverberations of religious intensity." Specifically, the work of these poets suggests that a secular art, even in a secular age, is insufficient for representing reality completely. There must be sacred art. For poets, this means there must be religious poetry written.

1

A MYSTICAL THEOLOGY OF ANGELIC DESPAIR

Writing Religious Poetry and the *Trilogy* of Frank Samperi

Idcirco accidit ut, quantum illos proximius imitemur, tantum rectius poetemur. Unde nos doctrine operi intendentes, doctrinatas eorum poetries emulari oportet.

—DANTE, *DE VULGARE ELOQUENTIA*

[Thus it comes about that, the more closely we try to imitate the great poets, the more correctly we write poetry. So, since I am trying to write a theoretical work about poetry, it behoves me to emulate their learned works of poetic doctrine.

—TRANS. STEVEN BOTTERIL]

FRANK SAMPERI, POET

Frank Samperi belongs in the category of the overlooked talents of American poetry of the last fifty years. He wrote his best poetry in the 1960s and saw it published partially in the 1970s. By the end of the seventies, he had nearly entirely faded from the publishing scene, living in obscurity until his death in 1991. Born in Brooklyn in 1933, Samperi—an orphan and autodidact—as a young man sought out Louis Zukofsky; letters between them date back to the time Samperi was twenty-four.[1] The older poet mentored him, connecting Samperi eventually with Cid

Corman, who became his champion and publisher in *Origin*. Samperi was a fixture of *Origin*'s Second Series, presented with the likes of Zukofsky, Ian Hamilton Finlay, Gary Snyder, Lorine Niedecker, William Bronk, and of course Corman himself. These connections led to the publication of an untitled trilogy of books in the early 1970s by Grossman/Mushinsha. Composed of *The Prefiguration* (1971), *Quadrifarium* (1973), and *Lumen Gloriae* (1973), these books collected eighteen pamphlets and small books Samperi had written in the late 1960s. The trilogy of books, designed and printed in Japan, is strikingly beautiful, featuring rich and unusual stone prints by Will Peterson on the dust jackets, as well as oblong pages (10½" × 5¼"), making for one of the handsomest sets of books of American poetry from this period.

What is at stake in choosing to be a religious poet? The work of Samperi, an obscure poet who wrote out of an explicitly Catholic vision of the universe, demonstrates the risks and challenges the religious poet faces. Samperi's masterpiece is his *Trilogy*.[2] In the introduction to the recent republication of these books in a single volume, I wrote,

> No description, however complete and subtle, can adequately paraphrase the experience of reading Frank Samperi's magnificent *Trilogy*. Not even reading each of the three volumes separately accounts for how firmly the cumulative achievement of this poetry impresses itself on the imagination. At once minimal and theologically dense, obscure and crystal clear, abstract and symbol-laden, joyous and melancholy, Samperi's poetry in his *Trilogy* is ultimately *angelic*, laden with divine messages and abiding in a realm that intermediates the worldly and the heavenly.[3]

Given the grand presentation of the initial publication of the three books in the *Trilogy*, one might presume some attention was paid to the poetry. Samperi's trilogy received only two reviews: one by the poet John Taggart (discussed below) and another by Cid Corman, the latter being less a review and more a praise of the poet. Despite this neglect, Samperi continued to publish poems in *Origin* and *Caterpillar* as well as collecting his poetry in occasional editions published by small presses such as Elizabeth Press and Station Hill. And even after he ceased to publish, he maintained active correspondence with a few poets, chiefly Corman and the Australian poet Clive Faust, and continued to write, producing, along with poetry, a translation of Dante's *Paradiso*. But Samperi's work stands or falls on the *Trilogy*. It is the most complete presentation of his work available, it is reasonably discrete, and it can be read beneficially as a progression, beginning with poetic foretime in *The Prefiguration*, establishing theological and doctrinal principles in *Quadrifariam*, and attaining a formal poetic completion in *Lumen Gloriae*, which is under half the length of either of the other two collections. In appraising Samperi's poetry and in speculating on the plight of the religious poet, I will focus entirely on *Trilogy*.

The challenge of reading Frank Samperi's poetry is the challenge of reading religious poetry. Is Samperi a poet of vision, of singular insight? Or is individual vision antithetical to the doctrine he emulates in his poetry? In the Western tradition, when we think of great religious poetry, we think of Dante, Milton, Blake. Each a poet of vision, of singular insight. Each also a Christian. Samperi emulates Dante, mainly, who looked through the communal vision of a medieval Catholicism, out of which his own vision emerged and was focused. Samperi frequently appeals to the "theological poet" who seeks after "Eternal Form," of which Dante for him is exemplary. Samperi's theological poet is removed from the world, a lonely predator of the adoration. His separation and solitude are essential to an understanding of God's purposes: "true work can only have for its vision the Eternal *the final identification forgone* the abstractive *useless*" (from "Anti-Hero," in *Quadrifarium*).[4] Who is the audience, then, of the theological poet who writes out of the abstractive useless? Samperi's "theological poet" seems an anachronism. By reverting to a medieval imagination and cosmology, he seeks to fortify his poetic vision. Imitating Dante can make for an auspicious beginning and can even sustain great work over the course of a lifetime. (Consider the examples of Pound and Eliot.) But Samperi's work resonates with belief, conviction, and despair in a way that seems both to depend on the work of his modernist forebears and then also to transform it into something else, something I would call a mystical theology of angelic despair.

There is a major tension between any communalistic adherence to religious belief and an individual talent, and this tension is powerfully augmented in poetry. As a poet informs her work with peculiar vision, it individuates and takes on value. The poet who asserts a communal vision acts as a ventriloquist. Her poems are the dummy. Who speaks? Not the poet. Doctrine speaks. Or dogma speaks. Communion, in the sense of the people joined together, is essential to Catholic faith and prayer. You can't believe merely in private. It is only in communion that collective prayer can be offered and felt, through the vehicle of the liturgy. Other forms of prayer—petition, which is private asking; meditation, which is listening to God; or contemplation, which is silent attendance to God's presence—rest on the bedrock of communion. But poetry is not prayer, even when it is offered as prayer or is prayerlike. Poetry is making. It is an emulation of God's enunciation and the subsequent vocables uttered at creation. A grandiose claim. I mean that making poetry arises out of the same original creative urge. (In the Septuagint translation of Genesis from Hebrew into Greek, the word translated in the King James Version as "created"—"In the beginning, God *created* the heaven and the earth"—is *'epoiisen*, which shares the same root as *poetry*, "to make.") And this is not the urge of prayer. Samperi's poems are not prayers, though they involve petitionary claims and often resolve into marvelous contemplations of natural and supernatural forms. But his poems do make powerful religious, even theological claims, wrestling with and then awarding victory to doctrines and visions the Catholic Church has validated over the centuries. His work is especially keenly attuned to a medieval Christian imagination, one he appears to emulate in his work even as he elaborates that imagination into something thoroughly modern.

DEFINING THE SPIRIT

I first encountered Samperi's work in John Taggart's essay "The Spiritual Definition of Poetry," which is a review of Samperi's *Trilogy*. Taggart's essay is expository, in that it describes Samperi as an essentially visionary poet, and it is critical, in that it presents Samperi as a poet who has not lived up to the visionary potential of his own poetry, which is to say that while vision may have informed Samperi's writing, the poet has merely asserted that vision, rather than composing one himself (which is what, according to Taggart, Blake and Dante did). Toward the end of the essay, Taggart proposes a poetic program for obtaining this vision. "There are two ways to secure this definition," he writes, "for poets who would write from the visionary imagination":

> 1) arduous study of and complete immersion in mythic and spiritual literature; 2) a like immersion in language. Poets will have to find their own path in the first area. They may choose to follow Plato through

> Plotinus on to Thomas Taylor and Blake (or follow Blake to Plato). Which text, whether a part of their own culture or not, does not matter. Eventually, they will have developed a sense of the entire literature and will have found what they specifically need, a discovery recognized by sympathy as a vision. That is, the visions encountered do not (and cannot) exactly duplicate the poets', but by their relative degree of congruence compel poets, like metaphor itself, to reexamine their experience, to look again.[5]

When I first read this passage, it struck me as clarion. I copied it into a notebook. It both affirmed my intuited path and gave it a shapeliness I hadn't yet discerned in it. Taggart's essay did more toward articulating a spiritual definition of poetry for me than had any other single source. Even the caution about Samperi's work at the end of his essay—"The failure of these poems is a failure to engage the imagination at sufficient depth and duration in the complex, organized, and dynamic whole that is language"[6]—did not dissuade me from seeking out Samperi's work.

Looking back on Taggart's piece, through a lens of several years reading Samperi, I am moved again by its voice of conviction. Now my admiration of this essay is mixed with some questions about it, particularly in the light of Samperi's verse. Is his imagination really insufficient? Perhaps it is misunderstood or incompletely understood. I cannot elevate Samperi any higher than his poetry will allow. Neither could Taggart. Exegesis cannot replace actual poetic insight or accomplishment. Nonetheless, rereading Taggart's program, there is an almost therapeutic note to his sense of reexamination that attempts to quell the stringencies of a spiritual path. Is the poet compelled to seek out the visionary imagination toward some sort of betterment, whether emotional, psychic, or poetic? As Michael A. Sells has noted, mysticism in the Judeo-Christian traditions is marked by the unusual convergence of the Semitic prophetic tradition with the worldview and cosmology of the Greco-Roman world. As such, powerful speech—the very language Taggart is asserting above—attains the vision of a "Ptolemaic symbolic cosmology and a central assertion of one, transcendent principle of reality."[7] Accordingly, mystical language directly reflects (and deflects, or even shatters) the ascensional directive toward a hidden, emanative, transcendent God. Furthermore, the totality of any mystical vision is subordinated to its actual articulation or pronouncement. The point is that God subverts all personal vision into divine immanence or divine hiddenness. Vision fades. God perplexes. The mystic hangs suspended, impermanent, between these fields, but they have been activated by his language and vision, there to be approached and tested by seekers and petitioners.

I wouldn't call Frank Samperi a mystic, but, like Taggart, he is a mystical poet, one who avails himself of mystical techniques and language in his poetry. Mysticism does not define the limit of his poetry; Samperi's raids on the inarticulate are visional; they are angelophanic (to use one of Henry Corbin's favorite words—which he defines as "divine anthropomorphosis on the plane of the spiritual universe, the human Form or divine humanity of the angelic world").[8] Samperi is seeing things, putting them into words. Nevertheless, he might agree that mystical speech is subordinated to and ultimately unraveled by the divine. The poet fixes his eye on the unfixable, immutable, always hidden God beyond the Ptolemaic universe he imagines himself in and transmits the vision of the cosmos he gazes at in the words he has at hand. Language pales, but it also excites, uplifts.

Taggart's sense of religious language in the passage quoted above is that it can function as a retrospective, corrective prism on experience. The lens of this language, however, is wide-angled, at least according to his prescription that any religious texts, from any culture, will do. Vision—as a thing received—is never pick-and-choose (even when it's something constructed and ramified, as in Taggart's own spectacular poetry). There are many paths, but a single path must be followed. Too many texts, too many traditions, lead to flaccidity. This notion reflects Samperi's own view on religious language. In a late poem in *Lumen Gloriae*, he reduces his view to a set of language equations in fourteen words:

love	knowledge	divided
mysticism	science	divided
union	identity	divided
glorified body	spiritual man	undivided[9]

In our minds, in our lives, love and knowledge are often divided; likewise, mysticism and science, and union and identity. But in the glorified body—the body shot through with divine light, the body of the aspiring spiritual man—all of these things, so the poem proposes, become united. As language fractures, isolates, divides, the spiritual vision unifies, making way for the undivided, unitive power of the glorious light. In the indivisible light of the spiritual, love and knowledge unite; mysticism and science unite. Individual identity is absorbed into the divine communion.

Even so, Samperi's vision in his poetry can be as isolating as the language with which he utters it. Are we, as his readers and his audience, undivided in his poetry, even as we receive it? Can the spiritual man, indivisible with the glorified body of light, be the religious poet? A power of Samperi's poetry arises from its sometimes abject, melancholic stance. Though the work is epiphanic—it frequently resolves in radiant insights—it struggles through melancholic moods, a sense of rote and dreary stations, ones to which the epiphanies stand in sometimes stark contrast. (This description speaks to what I was calling earlier Samperi's "mystical theology of angelic despair.") And the insights when they come often arrive garbed in high-church language, such as "glorified body spiritual man undivided," such that even to a discerning reader, it can be difficult to gauge the degree to which the epiphany is an individual, mystical insight or, perhaps, a Catholic doctrinaire expression. I think this is why Taggart suspects Samperi of failing to engage the imagination at sufficient depth. My own perspective differs from Taggart's. Instead, I suspect that in his poetry, Samperi struggles to capture in words something of the motion that would return his vision to God, consonant with the grace by which he received that vision, thereby transfiguring it into an energy worthy of God, such that both he and his poem become "partakers in the divine nature," in the words of Saint Peter. This is what I believe is at stake in Samperi's work, especially in his *Trilogy*.

PARTAKING

Samperi's is a poetry of spiritual recovery, not of formal creation, nor even of a participation with that creation. The unitive power he aspires to is above and beyond him, not something emanating from him or created by him. It is something he receives and reflects, and in reflection, something he gives. In his poetry, Samperi would restore us to the undivided, glorified body of God. Late in *Lumen Gloriae*, he writes:

> Then the dwelling of the angel in the soul
> or rather the odor
> sign

of the dwelling
continuing
habituating the man
to the daily
drawing out radiance
preparing
rendering
transparent
the surroundings
the universe
the aureole
receiving
truest
ray[10]

To what is the provocative word "odor" attached in the lines above? To the angel? To the perfume of the indwelling of the angel in the soul? The word instantly locates this set of thoughts in the actual, "habituating the man." *Receiving truest ray* might serve as a motto for Samperi's poetic wish, in his surroundings, in the universe, in the angelic aureole. Receptivity to the divine happens in the human sensorium: smell, sight, feeling.

To understand the division and reunion Samperi strives for, doctrinally, in terms of Catholic beliefs, we can turn to the *Catechism* for the Catholic Church, which states:

> The holiness of God is the inaccessible center of his eternal mystery. What is revealed of it in creation and history, Scripture calls "glory," the radiance of his majesty. In making man in his image and likeness, God "crowned him with glory and honor," but by sinning, man fell "short of the glory of God." From that time on, God was to manifest his holiness by revealing and giving his name, in order to restore man to the image of his Creator.[11]

Through creation (and the fall), man is divided from the inaccessible center of God's eternal mystery. Yet this aporia of God's abiding mystery is evident in—revealed through—history. The poet receives glimpses of this revelation, fragmentarily, which he reassembles and restores in his writing. These, perhaps simplified, are the terms of Samperi's theological poet, and in this respect, they are not so different from the terms that describe the purpose of an Andalusian Kabbalist in the thirteenth century or even an Alexandrian Gnostic in the first century of the Common Era.

However, participation is essential to any religious vision. This extends even to mystical participation, whose communions occur with supernatural beings. As the energy of God flows from the Godhead outside of creation into creation, so must it be returned, flowing back to God to complete the circuit. This is what St. Peter means when he understands us, through the Holy Trinity, as "partakers of divine nature." "The divine nature," wrote St. Gregory of Thessalonica, "must be said to be at the same time both exclusive of, and, in some sense, open to participation. We attain to participation in the divine nature, and yet at the same time it remains totally inaccessible. We need to affirm both at the same time and to preserve the antinomy as a criterion of right devotion."[12] The antinomian character of such belief in spiritual poetry is exemplified in Blake, especially the prophetic books. But Blake is never merely lawless: the individual vision must coalesce into a communal vision. For Blake, Jerusalem is a woman who is the emanation of Albion. But she is also the Heavenly City, which is the perfect society. She is both Divine Vision and "the Mystic Union of the Emanation of the Lord."[13] Albion is fallen primordial man, who aspires to return to Jerusalem through the Divine Vision that emanates from her:

> Albion replyd. Cannot Man exist without Mysterious
> Offering of Self for Another, is this Friendship & Brotherhood
> I see thee in the likeness & similitude of Los my Friend
>
> Jesus said. Wouldest thou love one who never died
> For thee or ever die for one who had not died for thee
> And if God dieth not for Man & giveth not himself
> Eternally for Man Man could not exist! for Man is Love:
> As God is Love: every kindness to another is a little Death
> In the Divine Image nor can Man exist but by Brotherhood.[14]

Nor can Man exist but by Brotherhood: Only in union is individual life possible because only in communion can the nature of sacrifice be felt. In elaborating Isaac Luria's Kabbalistic idea of divine withdrawal, or *tsimtsum*, by which God condensed himself into a microscopic point and then withdrew his presence from that point, such that he went into exile within himself, Gershom Scholem identifies a feature of human participation with the Godhead that Christian sources frequently ignore: its tragic consequences, which are also somehow heroic. "But the precarious co-existence of the different kinds of divine light," admits Scholem, "produces new crises. Everything that comes into being after the ray of light from *en-sof* has been sent out into the pleroma is affected by the two-fold movement of the perpetually renewed *tsimtsum* and of the outward flowing emanation. Every stage is grounded in this tension."[15] The tension necessitates human intervention. In this light, God is incomplete without human reversion of divine energy to its source, the pleromatic Godhead, *en-sof*, or God-beyond-knowing. The tension is polar: God on one end, humans on the other: "For Luria," writes Scholem, "this process takes place partly in God, but partly in man as the crown of all created being."[16]

As a religious poet with his own convictions, Samperi works into his writing a Kabbalistic pattern of divine bestowal, divine withdrawal or melancholy, and then the devoted effort of the soul to be reunited with the divine. As we will see, it resonates with other similar patterns in Neoplatonic thought. (Samperi does not appear to have been directly influenced by either of these mystical traditions; instead, his work can be seen to operate analogously to these systems.) Samperi should be thought of foremost as a mystically driven Catholic poet who wrote a typically minimalist, often simply revelatory New American–inspired poetry. To label his work that of a "religious poet," in many contemporary literary contexts, is perhaps to apply one of the most constricting labels of all to his work, at least to potentially sympathetic readers.

This label, presented nowadays to poetry readers averse to religion and allergic to the spirit, raises defensive hackles. These readers don't want to read religious poetry or don't want religious doctrine presented to them in poetry, which they might connect to for reasons other than ones that might be labeled religious. Patrick S. Diehl, in his book *The Medieval Religious Lyric*, identifies three presumptions about modern poetry that make religious poetry unpalatable: First, readers believe poetry should be the expression of an individual and not an institutional opinion; second, poetry should offer experiential not doctrinal truths; and third, poetry should have no palpable design on the reader.[17] Samperi's poetry resolutely pits his meandering, melancholic individual experience against the institutional and doctrinal truths of the Catholic Church, which he sees amplified for him in a glorious light. Samperi uses the beliefs, doctrines, and experiences of the Catholic Church to elevate his personal experiences into another realm of meaning and to exert a divine design on poetry in general. Such a move would seem antithetical to the goals of modern poetry, at least so far as Diehl spells them out. Furthermore, Samperi's vision appears medieval, in that his relation to God, to Christ, and to the intervening angels who drift like beneficent debris through his poems is hierarchical and vertical. And his engagement with the meaning of this hierarchy is communal rather than individual; in the poems, he tends to deemphasize personal interpretation in favor of more universal understandings of his experience, as in these lines from late in *Lumen Gloriae*:

if a man wakes sprightly
the body
not necessarily
diaphanous

if heavily
possibly
earth
by degrees

glorifying[18]

Here, the oppositions between "sprightly" and "heavily"—suggesting something about how a person feels when he wakes up—enables the lovely pairing of "diaphanous" with "glorifying" as a way to understand the depths of the earth by degrees.

In the prose portion of his poem "Via Negativa," Samperi claims: "Personalism does not belong to a spiritual art."[19] In his meditation "Paradiso *Canto Primo*," he insists, "The Commedia is Eternal Form—not medieval art; therefore, any critical evaluation is out of the question."[20] The poet who gestures toward this Eternal Form—through the medieval paragon of Dante, along with the more ancient example of Saint Augustine, probably the figure besides Dante most important to Samperi's poetry—challenges his audience to see his own work in the same light. Is it possible?

I think it is. To engage Samperi is to engage the poetry of Paradise, of spiritual renewal.

SAMPERI'S POETRY

Samperi utilizes two major styles/forms in his writing, each of which bears directly on the theological program and goals of the poetry: The first is a usually lengthy objectivist list but also frequently a short, sometimes uninflected, sometimes lyrical imagist poem. (There's also a corollary abstract form Samperi employs in this mode I would call "theological minimalism.") The second form he uses is a sometimes dense and abstract, sometimes straightforward prose meditation. In this prose mode, Samperi tends to explore theology, literary theory, and, more obliquely, autobiography. Of the objectivist list, I recognize two species: first, a spiritualized list nearly stripped of detail, frequently involving the movement of an angel through the field of the poet's vision; and, second, a seemingly quotidian list, sometimes cataloguing things seen on walks through the park (birds, trees, hills), other times directly expressing the poet's feelings in relation to these things seen. These second lists tend to be more personal but contribute to the overall program of the mystical theology of angelic despair. As an example of the first, spiritualized list poem, consider these lines from "The Triune":

> center
> angels
> water
> objects
> transcendentals
> forms
> undefined
> experience
> individual
> universal
> identity
> eternal form
> supposition

image
shadow
trace
informative
lover
contemplative
speculation
participative
reason
visional
beatific[21]

There are forty-four lists that comprise "The Triune," which is the first book in *Quadrifariam*; each is printed one to a page, with thirty-five lines apiece. In this poem, each word or phrase occupies one line, providing a novel form of prosody. The rhythm of this poem is completely internal—which is to say, internal to the reader, however fast he or she works down the page. The visual effect is that of verticality, acting as "visional" ladders to Paradise. And the words, because they are mostly abstract nouns, provide an opportunity to contemplate the poem (or climb the ladder of its words) at your own pace.

As an example of the second type of list, in which the poet records seemingly quotidian details, here is another section from "The Triune":

Wood
then
up
path
hill right
sea beyond
then
down
rocks
path left
grove
below . . .[22]

Such poems typically go on for the full thirty-five lines, sometimes concluding with an abstract noun or two, "wood/self" in the case of the poem just quoted, sometimes with overtly spiritual abstractions that propose a teleology, as in these four lines from the poem directly following the poem above: "therefore / angel completely / light / cause."[23] As an aside, it's worth noting that since I have created these categories from my experience of reading the poems in "The Triune," they are not hard and fast within the work; nor are they something Samperi himself devised. Frequently, the movement from personal, experiential poem to communal, abstract mystical poem can cause a blur, as in the opening poem of "The Triune," which begins:

> I walked conversing with angels—
> trees to the right
> animals to the left
> the path beyond quiet—
> we moved toward the animals—
> they moved with us toward flame
> the quiet
> then the air changed
> the right reflected the left
> and the movements ceased—
> my spirit vanished beyond the hill—
> birds flew up from the trees above the river
> then night
> wind[24]

The scene is spelled out here compellingly in the opening line, "conversing with angels." After such a provocative beginning, some details of the sensory surround are provided in an orphic scene: animals, trees, a path, illumination, the quiet, the wind. The poet wants us to notice the motion as well as the stillness, to experience the natural scene he is charging with supernatural light.

In the long poem "Via Negativa" in *Quadrifariam*, we encounter Samperi's melancholic rumination:

> 2:30 in the morning
> woke up
> fright
> took a shower
> loneliness

a spiritual necessity
my room
done up
as if holiness
were ambience[25]

My room done up as if holiness were ambience: This is the reflection of someone struggling through a crisis of the dark night of the soul but as if it were commonplace. "Took a shower" suggests to me that this has happened before, an experience belonging to the expression of the abject noun "loneliness," which becomes freighted here with the same personal resonance as the phrase "my room." How is this a "spiritual necessity"? This kind of suffering, in poetic terms, is haunting. Are these lists little daily records of life lived, things seen? Or are they subtler spiritual information, news from an invisible paradise? John Martone has suggested that these lists represent a spiritual agony and atonement, a daily meditative ritual of a personally strenuous but ultimately transformative Stations of the Cross.[26] Whatever they are, they can feel bleak and barren, and they cast Samperi's poetry in the light of an existential crisis, but in a way that constitutes the central magnetic focus of these poems, contributing mysteriously to the grandeur and majesty of their totality. Accumulations, layerings, lacquerings of sensitivity and awareness suggest the larger nature of creation and the generative role the poet moving through that nature plays.

The list-poems represent the form to be found most frequently in *Trilogy*. The other form, the prose meditation, though used less often, is nonetheless more telling in determining Samperi's motivations and beliefs. There are two broad kinds of prose Samperi includes in *Trilogy*. The first of these forms I would designate a rich, unpunctuated, repetitive theological catechism. The following two poems from "Unitiva Via" (the unitive way), in *Quadrifariam*, show Samperi at his most lucid, I think:

   theological poetry Eternal Form because the identification
Use the Gift clarifies the background (the intensification)
species in the Image

. . . .

   the glorified body the individual the universe
the identification the individual the universal formal

individual universal an identification undefined
Spirit the spirit an identification[27]

Typically, these poems utilize a Latinate and church-inflected language (Gift, species, Image) as well as delineating a usually mystical Catholic doctrine. So, for instance, in the first poem, Samperi proposes that theological poetry reflects the species of the Eternal Form, who is God, whose Image is Christ. As Christ clarifies the "background" of God, through an intensification, so theological poetry clarifies the Image of Christ through a further intensification. Thus, the theological poem participates in the Eternal Form of the Godhead. In the second selection, Samperi blurs the distinction between the individual and the universal in the form of the glorified body: this refers both to Christ and to the resurrected body of Paradise. In fact, what he is proposing is that the meaning of the relation between the individual and the universal can only be identified—and thus understood—in the Spirit, part of the triune glorified body. It is the Holy Spirit that makes the identification of the glorified body possible. It's compelling to address the theological diction and mystical concepts of Samperi's work in this mode. But it's just as important, perhaps, to acknowledge the emphatic quality of these selections achieved by plowing through syntactical rules. When "because" appears in the first line of the first selection above, you naturally expect some explanation to appear as part of the subordinating clause "because" introduces. Instead, "because" seems to be functioning like a preposition. "Use the Gift" immediately follows the "because" phrase, shifting the poem into the imperative. But "Use the Gift" functions as an unusual subject for which "clarifies" acts as a verb. "Use the Gift" clarifies "the background," which Samperi seems to apostrophize as "the intensification." Syntactically, these lines might seem superficially confusing, but they hold together in a kind of rushed, excited, even breathless confession that reinforces the intensification the poet is declaring.

Related to what I'm calling Samperi's rushed theological catechism in *Trilogy* is the other prose form he uses, which is an extensive essay, usually on a theological theme but sometimes on an autobiographical or poetic theme instead. Embedded within these essays are phrases that have an aphoristic quality, which can sound like the style of the theological, spiritual form, without the repetitions and grammatical shifts that characterize it. In the other direction, these essays are sometimes transformed into the kinds of lists to be found in "The Triune." In the essay "Morning and Evening," Samperi writes:

> Angelic knowledge despite "species connatural" is still a
> confrontation.
> There can be no audience when a work's vision is total.[28]

These lines are characteristic of the assertions to be found in these essay-poems. On the one hand, they propose that Samperi's poems aspire toward angelic knowledge. (Does he mean knowledge—as in awareness—of the angels or the knowledge the angels themselves possess of God?) On the other hand, Samperi indicates that when a work is replete with hard-won angelic knowledge—which is both "connatural" and conflictive—then the work requires no audience. This is to say that God—in the Species of Christ—requires no audience because the work of God's vision is total, encompassing all. Impressive to say, but can even the most devout poet truly believe this? In "Crystals," from *The Prefiguration*, an essay that entertains spiritual and artistic contemplation, Samperi tells us:

> The new man is always the spiritual man.
>
> . . . .
>
> It all amounts to this: if a man is capable of knowing
> completely, then his companions are the angels.
>
> . . . .
>
> The beatific vision brings the world face to face with the Truth.
> In the meantime, what do we do?
>
> . . . .
>
> The hierarchical orders of the Church can only be valid
> metaphorically; therefore, every movement toward specific
> difference is the church's movement toward its proper
> prefiguration.[29]

"Prefiguration" refers to Catholic typology. Classic Christian biblical typology proposes that parts of the Old Testament are predictive types to the antitypes that appear in the New Testament: so, Abraham prefigures John the Baptist just as Moses (or David) prefigures Christ; the opening of Genesis prefigures the opening of the Gospel of John. Likewise, the type for the Catholic Church is the covenant with Abraham; furthermore, the church prefigures for us on earth the heavenly order of Paradise. Thus, the believer gets a complex series of telescopes and microscopes, in which he or she can perceive God through the lens of history; likewise, through a heavenly lens, God views life in a kind of simultaneity, such that Moses is in fact Christ, is in fact God himself. Just so, the building of the church itself is a metaphorical heaven and a metaphorical narrative of the Life of Christ. And the liturgical arts instruct the congregation in how to live not merely in this life but also in the joyful hope of the coming glory that is their promise. For Samperi, the theological poet does not create these realms but renews them. He gives them new eyes, his eyes.

SAMPERI AS MEDIEVAL MODERNIST POET

Samperi renews the prefigured realms of art, life, and church by activating a thoroughly medieval religious imagination as if it were a completely modernist poetic imagination. By understanding some of the basic principles of medieval belief and poetic composition, particularly in the light of Saint Bonaventure's mystical *Itinerarium* (sometimes called "The Soul's Journey to God"), we can glimpse in Samperi's poems the *lumen gloriae* he intends them to shine out of, in the process of which we might glimpse the way a poet whose theological convictions compel increasing poetic privacy arrives nonetheless at a communal, vitalizing art.

Medieval culture was centripetal, theocentric, and ecclesiological. By contrast, modern culture is centrifugal, anthropocentric, and social. Medieval culture was paradigmatic; modern culture is paradigm breaking. The medieval universe was bounded and elaborately interconnected; its principle of organization was the vertical hierarchy of each being, event, or thing to the Creator. The horizontal plane of history and causation was similarly related to the vertical hierarchy of the Creator. The modern universe is open, elaborately interconnected, but indeterminate. It has a horizontal orientation, determined by material and mechanism, sometimes wobbled by paradigm shifts; knowledge of this universe is an outwardly spreading field that either does not include divine powers (as in the case of some modern science) or includes an orientation toward an inwardly radiating divine presence or power (something like the interior justification of faith, as in Protestant Christianity, which constitutes a private witness).

Chance operations—used rather prophetically in modern art—are the great levelers. The cosmos of the medieval poet was expressive of the will of God, which had once been transparent but following the fall has only been known through a painful spiritual recovery, and then only ever partially. Nowadays, the universe is an unknown whose mystery we are gradually discovering through the exercise of human reason. Humans are one element in this unfolding, rather than the medieval instrument of it.[30]

Samperi's poetry—like that of a medieval poet—is *exemplary* of Christ. Saint Bonaventure, whose thinking parallels the work we find in Samperi's *Trilogy*, can help us understand this exemplarity. "For Bonaventure," writes Ewart Cousins, "the Father is the fountain-fulness, *fontalis plenitudo*, in whom the divinity is fecund, dynamic, self-expressive."[31] Furthermore, the Son intercedes for the Father in his created reality. The Son is the expression of God in creation and is the one who refers back to him. Medievalists call this fact "exemplarism" because Christ is grounded in God and is God's eternal Exemplar.[32] "This is our whole metaphysics," wrote Bonaventure, "emanation, exemplarity, consummation; to be illumined by spiritual rays and to be led back to the highest reality."[33]

Although this may sound passive—that the soul waits to be visited and illuminated—it is more properly speaking gnostic in the intuitive, contemplative sense (rather than in the heretical sense), in that through contemplation, mystical activity, or poetic composition, one seeks to exceed the limitations of the mind or to have the mind transformed by the movement of the will toward God. Bonaventure puts it succinctly at the conclusion of the *Itinerarium*:

> In this passing over, if it is to be perfect, all intellectual activities must be left behind and the height of our affection must be totally transferred and transformed into God. This, however, is mystical and most secret, which *no one knows except him who received it* (Rev. 2:17), no one receives except him who desires it, and no one desires except him who is inflamed in his very marrow by the fire of the Holy Spirit whom Christ sent into the world.[34]

It is in this spirit that Samperi repeatedly challenges and even rejects the notion of audience, as he implies in this poem from "Anamnesis," in *Quadrifariam*:

> therefore
> to withdraw

from the literary world
is a must
this proves
our style no style
ars imitatur naturam
in sua operatione[35]

(The Latin reads: "Art imitates nature in her manner of operation," a quotation from Saint Thomas Aquinas.) Samperi's occasional dismissal of audience for his poetry seems to be as much an anxiety about critical discourse as it is a sense that the true poet requires no audience besides the divine. "What kind of poetry is left?" he asks in another poem, after suggesting neither poetry of place nor person is realistically possible. "It takes courage to go this way / because it is not the way of the world,"[36] he muses to himself and to his potential audience. What kind of poetry is left, then? "Theological poetry" is the only answer he can imagine. Notably, and perhaps curiously, Samperi found his expressive calling for these theological themes not necessarily in the work of these medieval Christian exemplars but in the work of twentieth-century avant-garde poets, Louis Zukofsky in particular. While Zukofsky's work includes religious material, it tends toward a materialist ideology (Zukofsky was a Marxist, after all; in "A"-8, he claims Marx as an artist) sometimes transformed into a poetic mysticism (as in the word counting in "A"-22 and "A"-23, for example). It could be argued, therefore, that while medieval theology catalyzed Samperi's poetry, modernist experimentation enabled it to be expressed.

Samperi aspires to a theological poetry not out of hubris, as Taggart suggests in his review of the trilogy,[37] but out of the sense that his communion as a theological poet is not with the world but with the Corpus Christi, in whom all affection is transformed into mystical knowledge. In "Anti-Hero," Samperi writes:

> It is true that my withdrawal from the literary world is complete, but withdrawal can only mean desire of fame (vanity)—writing is not pride: to write for Humanity *God the Subject* alters every sense of the writer as *personality*: therefore, it is not the writer's job to seek out the latest innovations of the day—the principles of the craft are perennial; he has ancient teachers, and with them he silently converses.[38]

Samperi's withdrawal is a struggle against creative vainglory, against an exaltation of his attention to God the Subject. In the privacy of his withdrawal is company, the ancient teachers. But also silence. There is an ache to this quiet solitude that even Samperi's argument can't mask. We feel his struggle; we maybe even sympathize with it. His conversation with the ancients is another problem altogether. Taggart hears ventriloquism in Samperi's verse, rather than seeing original vision:

> When I look into the "Triune" image [of Samperi's poems], however, I see Blake's "Soul embraced by divine lover" at the end of *Jerusalem*. It could easily have been "When the Morning Stars sang together" or any other of Blake's illustrations for the Book of Job. The fact that I saw these "old" visions and not Samperi's "new" one is indication that his cumulative linear shadow trace is not sufficient to render spiritual vision viable.[39]

Samperi has backed himself into a spiritual corner. When Samperi withdraws from the literary world, his purpose is not to hide from or to alienate his readers. If that were the case, why publish these poems in such elegant books? What is Samperi's appeal, if not to "render spiritual vision viable"?

Samperi's purpose, like that of the writer of the medieval lyric, is to restore a proper relationship with this divine truth and to renew poetic vision through that act of restoration. Diehl makes an observation about medieval poetry that is useful toward thinking about Samperi's work: "Both verse translations and medieval religious lyric produce the sensation that the poem is still half-embedded in its matrix, half-emergent, haunted, or inhabited by its origin."[40] Likewise, Diehl speaks of the typically paratactic, discontinuous, and anacoluthic structure of medieval religious texts. This happens because of the thematic verticality I've been mentioning: meaning aligns in the heavenly realm; the earthly realm merely alludes to that paradise. Diehl explains: "In this structure, ideas and phrases have the air of fragments washed down from higher and older regions, their angles pointing out from the text to some eternal point at which they will meet and marry into meaning, if the reader has the qualification for ascending to that focus."[41] Samperi's curious stance toward his (prospective, yet unrealized) audience can be understood in this light: Like Samperi himself, his readers must aspire to the verse, use the brief phrases like rungs on a ladder to lift themselves into the revelations of that "higher and older region." In "Anamnesis," Samperi elaborates:

can there be a poetry of place
no
people
no
no poetry that seeks to release
even the Material Ideal
can be dramatic
epical
or
lyrical
then what kind of poetry is left
given the Hegelian
the Marxist
there can be no poetry
because the upshot is
the Platonic user
maker
no imitator
therefore
the kind of poetry
we postulate
is the kind that resolves
book
canzone
song
what kind is that
theological poetry[42]

Like an internal dialogue, Samperi poses questions here that he answers: The final answer is that theological poetry is the kind that resolves the book, the canzone, the song into one, into a unitive expression (the resolution of book, canzone, and song had been Dante's goal in *De Vulgare Eloquentia*). Is Samperi's theological poet merely a genuflection at an ideal? In the introduction I wrote for the new edition of *Trilogy*, I asked: "What is the novum in this work? Where does the new energy arise from?" These strike me as the operative questions about this poetry. How, in writing a theological poetry, does Samperi renovate? My suspicion is that his renovation involves "the necessity of witnessing the passage of angels through the world. As they move through the world, these angels form vortexes, out from which the creative imagination emerges."[43] As Samperi writes in "Anti-Hero," in *Quadrifariam*, "The man moves, the angel illuminates, full common society the ground the Holy Spirit the foundation the Way toward final release."[44]

Samperi's poetry is compelling, particularly in its indication of a theological attainment, because it suggests any such attainment is intermediated by the presence and action of angelic beings who seem both messengers of divine love and also harbingers of a melancholic acedia, a spiritual torpor that marks life in the modern world. "You've reached a depth of despair from which no gathering up is possible," he laments in "Morning and Evening," in *The Prefiguration*. "If there's longing for confraternity with the angels," he muses shortly after, "then every movement a man makes to establish such is a movement toward specific difference. The differential world is the glorified body."[45] The angels in *Trilogy* simultaneously mark the poet's despair ("A man going away to sorrow" begins "Morning and Evening") and point toward the differential, glorified realm beyond.

Inhabiting poetry of such theological aspiration is challenging. According to Samperi, the work of the theological poet exceeds his audience, in that revealing God is his goal; the revealed God is the receiver of the gift of his poem:

word it again
the imitator is in relation to
Use in the Gift
if this is so
then the notion of audience
takes its significance from
Spirit the spirit an identification
the final identification forgone
therefore

the theological poet
indirectly reveals
the user and maker
in harmonious relation to
the Holy Spirit
because the true object
of the theological poet
is Eternal Form
Species in the Image
the experiential[46]

In this sense, as his readers, we too should find "Use in the Gift," identifying, presumably, not so much with the theological poet but with the spirit of his work, which must be the very person of the Holy Spirit. Yet this doesn't track, at least not experientially. Reading Samperi's poems, I find myself identifying very much with the theological poet who is so earnestly struggling to articulate these subtle, intransigent, marvelous things. Nevertheless, Samperi releases his audience from the obligation to follow him:

the senses of the audience
unimpeded
each member released
free to journey his own way
it must be so[47]

Samperi's release of his audience is an abandonment of it to God, or to our own *itinerarium* to God. Each reader must make this journey unimpeded. Samperi's verse stands less as a guidebook for that journey than as a statement that he has tried to make it himself. As a record of his own Journey of the Mind to God, it is spare but richly textured (especially with angelic light) and resolutely unidirectional, resonating with the story of God's suffusion of the created world with his glorious light.

REVERSION-TO-SOURCE: THROUGH THE VISIONAL ANGEL

It's useful, in the light of all this theological speculation and mystical aspiration, to keep in mind some facts overlooked so far in my consideration of Samperi's poetry. Namely, he was a man living in New York City in the twentieth century, writing an experimental American poetry he had learned in part from Zukofsky, which he published obscurely in pamphlets and then rather sumptuously in Japan, in books that few other poets over the years have taken the time to read. Is this neglect an accident, or might there be something purposeful to it? Not every reader—not even every Catholic reader—can be expected to recognize medieval theological imperatives in his verse. His work becomes available to us, then, through its principal innovation: to infuse the forms of modernist avant-garde poetry with the content and aspirations of medieval Christian theology.

Saint Bonaventure explains that God created all things "not to increase his glory, but to show it forth and to communicate it."[48] This "showing forth" and "communication" of God's glory suggests a movement of God to and through creation, an emanating force from beyond the created universe. Samperi's poetry, radically minimalist at times, autobiographically expressionist at others, rehearses this movement or, rather, *reflects* it. And at its best, it emits its own radiance. Radiance is generated by *self-reflexivity* rather than merely mirroring God's emanating energy. What can be difficult to locate in Samperi's poetry is what the great Neoplatonic mystic Plotinus, who lived in richly cross-cultural third-century Alexandria, identifies as the *epistrophe* of contemplative life, which Stephan MacKenna rendered in his energetic translation of the *Enneads* as "Reversion-to-Source." God's energy can't only be spent into the universe; it must be reverted to the source, by action of contemplation, or, in Samperi's case, a genuinely spiritual poetry staking its claims in experimental forms. This is the poetic, mystical equivalent of the "partaking in the divine nature" that Saint Peter spoke about. In Plotinus's foundational cosmology, the primal Unity, or the One, "in its self-quest" or "in its reversion" to itself, has vision. Its act of seeing "engenders" Mind, in whose circumradiation and overflow the Soul is both its "utterance and act."[49] But this emanation is incomplete without *epistrophe*: in reversion, energy is returned to the Godhead:

> Our being is the fuller for our turning Thither; this is our prosperity; to hold aloof is loneliness and lessening. Here is the soul's peace, outside of evil, refuge taken in the place clean of wrong; here it has its Act, its true knowing; here it is immune. Here is living, the true; that of today, all living apart from Him, is but a shadow, a mimicry. Life in the Supreme is the native activity of Intellect; in virtue of that silent converse it brings forth gods, brings forth beauty, brings forth righteousness, brings forth all moral good; for of all these the soul is pregnant when it has been filled with God.[50]

"Here" in this passage is "Thither," which should be taken as the atemporal motion of the Soul reverting to its source. Put another way, here/thither is a directional intention, a volitional movement. Samperi's vision, in this light, while tightly, inwardly focused, begins to make powerful movements that are reversionary and expansive. The last two poems in "Infinitesimals," in *Lumen Gloriae*, suggest an inward, gemlike focus and an expansion enabled, as ever, by angelic vision:

each facet light accordingly
the souls responding
orienting
becoming
together
perfect
gem

~

body in grass
elliptically formed
in turn inscribed
in square
in flame
flower
center
sustained
by
four
angels[51]

Samperi's prosody in the second poem, a model of objectivist restraint in terms of its pacing and lineation but glorified in terms of what it expresses, attenuates the vision, allowing it to expand as each word takes its place, line by line, in the poem. It's as likely that the poet is seeing a cosmic vision body forth as he is looking at the flamelike colors of flowers in a garden.

By informing the melancholic actual of his observing eye with visional angelophany, Samperi in his poetry ascends a ladder he makes from it, beginning the climb to God on the long *itinerarium* that marks his work. The place where I see this happening most vividly is in one of the poems toward the end of "The Triune," the whole work of which I increasingly regard as the heart and soul of Samperi's accomplishment, this poem in particular:

> Spirit the spirit an identification
> water an image significantly subject
> the revelation the man
> resolution the projection
> the man another an extension the one below
> If point no boundary
> then point invalid
> metaphorical
> the man reference
> the universe creation
> eternity
> image
> use
> relational
> fire
> plain
> angel
> visional
> plane other
> close
> far
> approximations
> speed apperceptive
> rest background

the relation
circular
each to each
however
differential
integral
appetitive
the noetic
self
return
pilgrimage image eternity[52]

The beginning lines of the poem are incantational, building momentum through the Latinate words: *revelation*, *resolution*, *projection*, *extension*. In this poem, "man" is the reference point, generically in the usage common to Samperi's time, but also specifically in terms of himself, the poet envisioning this spirit with whom he is identifying. "[T]he man reference / the universe creation" sets up a typological comparison Samperi's verse thrives on: as man is the reference point, so the universe is the creative expansion, leading to three richly utile words in Samperi's lexicon, "eternity / image / use," all three relational to the visional angel speeding apperceptively through the lines of the poem, which directs our attention to the simultaneous differential and integral unity of the divine reality the poem invokes. It ends with a beatific reversion to source, "self / return," followed by an utterly characteristic Samperian line, "pilgrimage image eternity." The image of eternity is pilgrimage. All beings—all life in the spirit—strive toward integral, differential holiness, just as the word "pilgrimage," so Samperi makes us see, has an "image" in its heart.

2

ROBINSON JEFFERS, THE MAN FROM WHOM GOD HID EVERYTHING

What a strange poet Robinson Jeffers was. Lyrically striking if frequently obtuse, he's probably the most prolific modern poet still in print—his five-volume *Complete Poetry* contains over 2,500 pages. Popular early in his career, he died loathed by many literary readers. A glamorous loner, he lived like a reclusive movie-star/wizard in a stone tower by the sea. A wife-stealing adulterer, he was also a devoted husband, father, and family man. He was a Protestant pagan, an Abrahamic soothsayer, a human-loathing God disdainer, as theologically reckless and incisive as he was humble in the face of the natural world. Jeffers seems much better than a good poet to me, if not, by the reckoning of some, altogether great. But even in its weakest moments, a greatness runs through the whole course of his poetry. He was a poet of enormous resource, with admirable lyric and epic instincts. And his virtues, especially his attitudes toward understanding the divine, are illuminating in any assessment of what is best in twentieth-century American poetry.

Jeffers's religious vision, which William Everson characterized as an "astonishing intensity of . . . primitivistic force" that grasped "the power, the wonder, the awe of a God palpably immediate yet unalterably beyond science's continuing probe of the cosmos,"[1] suffuses all of his work, from his earliest poems, written in modernism's heyday in the early decades of the twentieth century, to his last poems, written in the 1950s and 1960s in an intimidating philosophical sobriety as he contemplated the end of his life and that of human culture more largely. Albert Gelpi describes the "erotically charged pantheism" that marks Jeffers's work, "darkened by his Calvinist temperament, Darwinian science, and Lucretian materialism."[2] Jeffers's work is challenging because the outlook it expresses is so severe. Everson reads him as a "pure example of *poetas religiosus*."[3] It is perhaps the purity and the intensity of his religious convictions—pessimistic and damning but visionary and atomic—that can make his work simultaneously so compelling and off-putting. Not incidentally, Jeffers is also one of the great nature poets of the twentieth century. In his worldview, nature and divinity are coterminous realities. All that can be known of God must be learned from the natural world.

Jeffers knew himself especially through the avian world, not as a hawk—even though he made totems of the raptors—but as a gralliform, a solitary night heron. His sense of the human world was awkward, as the early poem "People and a Heron" reveals:

> A desert of weed and water-darkened stone under my western
>   windows
> The ebb lasted all afternoon.
> And many pieces of humanity, men, women, and children,
>   gathering shellfish,
> Swarmed with voices of gulls the sea-breach.
> At twilight they went off together, the verge was left vacant, an
>   evening heron
> Bent broad wings over the black ebb,
> And left me wondering why a lone bird was dearer to me than
>   many people.
> Well: rare is dear: but also I suppose
> Well reconciled with the world but not with our own natures we
>   grudgingly see them
> Reflected on the world for a mirror.[4]

A number of the curious characteristics of Jeffers's poetry appear in this poem: the rambling, rhythmically clattering lines ("with our own natures we grudgingly see them"); the idiosyncratic punctuation ("Well: rare is dear: but . . ."); his aloof observing eye; the use of inapt but effective metaphors ("desert of weed"); the pointed placement of woozy ambiguity (does "Well reconciled" refer to us with our natures? Or to the heron and nature?); the seemingly obvious intent that yields in its retreating tide something only fleetingly certain. Does Jeffers simply dislike people and prefer the single heron? Or is it that he is glad herons are birds and not humans, that the world would be a better place without the swarms of people? The logic of the poem pulls like a tide. On the one hand, I *feel* the scene, see Jeffers in his tower looking down on the Pacific beach, writing his condescending poem. The natural world is always prettier without people. Herons have evolved precious little in the past twenty million years; they are much more stable and harmonious a species in this world than humans. The poem, written with a gloomy glee that Jeffers was to amplify as his career expanded, is a harbinger for a time when humans will no longer scramble on the rocks plucking shellfish. Someday, Jeffers knows (and even *hopes*), humans will be as rare as a solitary heron. And *rare is dear.* This is our nature reflected on the mirror of the world. Jeffers's pessimism is a perverse exultation. Does a poetry so strange ensure its own longevity?

Jeffers was famous as a poet during his life. His popularity reached its peak in 1932, when he appeared on the cover of *Time*. He was a handsome man who wrote his poetry in a monk's cell he had erected at the top of a modest turret—called Hawk Tower—on the cliffs of Carmel-by-the-Sea on the Monterrey peninsula, between San Francisco and California's spectacular Big Sur coastline. Random House's *The Selected Poetry of Robinson Jeffers* (1938) features a heavy page stock; a textural, woven cloth cover; and a beatific frontispiece portrait by Edward Weston. These details give the work a material gravity lacking in today's first editions of even our most celebrated contemporary poets. Since the heyday of his popularity—roughly between 1924, when *Tamar* was published, and 1938, when *The Selected Poetry of Robinson Jeffers* appeared—Jeffers remains in print.

Despite this enviable publication history, I wonder how well Jeffers is read today. His visibility and place in American poetry seem comparable to that of E. E. Cummings, another popular modernist who remains in print, even as his work—like that of Jeffers—has never really found its place in the academic world. Although the critical attention of university scholars and critics hasn't done much to spread the word about Louis Zukofsky or Basil Bunting beyond a small enclave of admirers of late modernism, it has allowed for the preservation of these poets' work in a context in which it can be studied and understood. To be sure, the density and hermeticism of their work encourage coteries of specialists, whereas the discursiveness and idiosyncratic stance in Jeffers's work encourage his reception as a solitary genius by readers of more general abilities. Jeffers is a poet you're more likely to find in the pocket of a backpacker in the Rockies than in the satchel of a graduate student, which strikes me as both good and bad.

It's remarkable that Jeffers is in print at all, given his fate during the Second World War and after. Consumed by a pessimistic, fatalistic sense of human self-destruction, Jeffers began increasingly to philosophize in his poetry, culminating in the articulation of his "inhumanism," not so much a philosophy as a credo, an expression of the feelings and tendencies that had been marking his poetry for decades. Jeffers included a preface on inhumanism to *The Double-Axe and Other Poems* (1948), written as an apology by someone never intending to apologize. The volume contains one of his more brutal lyrics, the I-told-you-so "Pearl Harbor," as well as one of his most autobiographically bizarre, "The Inhumanist." The second half of this poem, written in Jeffers's typical narrative style, is a series of soliloquies by an unnamed old man who agonizes over the meaning of God, determining that if God's soul is immortal, human souls are not; nor is the universe immortal. And this gap defines the human distance from the divine, leading us to folly. At one point, the old man rants:

> Down, you apes, down. Down on your knee-caps, you talking
> villains, take off your eye-glasses
> And beat your foreheads against the rubble ground and beseech
> God
> Forgive America, the brutal meddler and senseless destroyer;
> forgive the old seamed and stinking blood-quilt of England
> Forgive the deliberate torture of millions, the obscene slave-
> camps, the endless treacheries, the cold dirty-clawed cruelty
> Of the rulers of Russia.[5]

You talking villains. That sums up late Jeffers's feeling about people. Yet as a rant, there's a jeremiad intensity to admire in these lines, especially in the repetitions of "forgive," which magnify the accusatory language that follows each utterance. In the preface to *The Double Axe*, Jeffers summarized his new outlook, writing, "[inhumanism] is based on a recognition of the astonishing beauty of things and their living wholeness, and on a rational acceptance of the fact that mankind is neither central nor important to the universe; our vices and blazing crimes are as insignificant as our happiness."[6] Jeffers remained outspoken in his criticism of both the war and President Roosevelt, winning him few friends either among critics or readers. But it wasn't his politics that frosted the public; it was the implication that he hated other people.

Several years ago, my brother Michael gave me a gift of a first edition of *The Women at Point Sur* (1927). In that copy is a yellowed clipping of the Weston frontispiece portrait of Jeffers and another newspaper clipping that appears to have been part of a review of Jeffers's poetry by Dwight MacDonald, which quotes the lines:

> I honestly believe (but really an alien here: trust me not)
> Blind war, compared to this kind of life,
> Has nobility, famine has dignity.

To which MacDonald replies, "One can only hope that Mr. Jeffers some day starves to death in a dignified way." I love the archaeology of this exchange: Jeffers's book, MacDonald's harsh review, the man—Hugh Allen Wing is signed on the flyleaf—buying *The Women at Point Sur*, then clipping Jeffers's photograph and the review from a newspaper, inserting them in the book for keeping. One wonders what Mr. Wing thought of the book, whether it confirmed his own feelings about Jeffers, whatever they may have been. There's something embalmed here that articulates what I would otherwise be hard-pressed to say. It encapsulates the experience, above all, of reading Jeffers: Something as strange and harsh as it is yellowed and outdated, something weirdly worth preserving; something humane and carefully collected in the face of the poet's outlandish, misanthropic utterances.

Apologists for Jeffers operate on the assumption that Jeffers's inhumanism has been misunderstood. Krista Walter, for instance, has argued that "Jeffers was no misanthrope. . . . Rather, he rejects our self-centeredness, our need to find affirmation for being in the material world, and our tendency to transmit such a need into false beliefs in the supernatural."[7] I wouldn't deny a certain nobility in Jeffers's adoration of the natural world. I am, however, concerned that what is most bracing about his work—his conviction in the basic ignobility of humankind—is frequently white-washed in the endorsements of his supporters. Consider these lines from "Quia Absurdam," for instance, fairly typical late Jeffers:

> Guard yourself from perceiving the inherent nastiness of man
> and woman.
> (Expose your mind to it: you might learn something.)[8]

Note Jeffers's equanimity in loathing men *and* women. (In this sense, he can read like an inverse of Whitman's inclusive optimism.) The flaws and weaknesses of humans are a source of knowledge for the poet, but not in the sense of a Buddhist lovingkindness; rather, as a Gnostic inoculation against the virus of human nastiness. Thoreau seems only mildly puckish compared to Jeffers. Why don't Jeffers's admirers come clean on this count? Here is a poet who believed humans to be an indignity to creation, whose inhumanism aligns with the catastrophic wisdoms of Gnosticism, which it seems to modify for modernity. The scope of Jeffers's alienating cosmology is present *in vitro* in the following apostrophic lines from his 1924 poem "The Roan Stallion," the whole of which—recounting the atavistic attachment a character named California has to the horse of the title—is one of Jeffers's masterpieces. In these lines, Jeffers breaks from the narrative voice of the poem, which is largely descriptive, to something more like a soliloquy:

> Humanity is the start
> of the race; I say
> Humanity is the mould to break away from, the crust to break
> through, the coal to break into the fire,
> The atom to be split.
>
> Tragedy that breaks man's face and a white
> fire flies out of it; vision that fools him
> Out of his limits, desire that fools him out of his limits, unnatural
> crime, inhuman science,
> Slit eyes in the mask; wild loves that leap over the walls of nature,
> the wild fence-vaulter science,
> Useless intelligence of far stars, dim knowledge of the spinning
> demons that make an atom,
> These break, these pierce, these deify, praising their God shrilly
> with fierce voices: not in a man's shape

> He approves the praise, he that walks lightning-naked on the
> Pacific, that laces the suns with planets,
> The heart of the atom with electrons: what is humanity in this
> cosmos? For him, the last
> Least taint of a trace in the dregs of the solution; for itself, the
> mould to break away from, the coal
> To break into fire, the atom to be split.[9]

The line beginning "These break, these pierce" demonstrates what I find most compelling in Jeffers's poetry: the stilted inversion, the unpoetic verb ("deify") contrasted with two destructive verbs ("break" and "pierce"), the objectification and disdain of God (as "their God"), the grating adverb ("shrilly"), the shameless length of the line, all coming together in a way that makes the whole simultaneously philosophical, naturalistic, and ethical, even as it offers us an apocalyptic vision of what we are transforming into. The insinuation of evolution into the theology of these lines is radical stuff. The "wild fence-vaulter science" is a fugitive prophet of a new and awful God, no better than the limiting deities of the human past. The splitting of the human atom would unleash in our deaths the energy entrapped in our being. Jeffers advocates a kind of stoic physics, then, one whose theories and equations are absent any revelation but that of an abiding, necessary emptiness, to be witnessed through the dull, ignorant eyes of the creatures who invented the sciences allowing us to perceive our fates. The cool cosmic chill of the "useless intelligence of far stars" acts as a metaphor for the God he strives to know but cannot, the God he refuses to see in the "tragedy that breaks a man's face." An antagonizing Lucretius has shambled into American English in these lines, clattering with the shards of his broken Platonism. Science is a kind of shame.

That Jeffers is a nature poet—which is the primary banner under which he has been recuperated—is only because the natural world reminds him least of the people he can't abide. In his introduction to *Rock and Hawk*, Robert Hass sees in Jeffers a reclusive Spenglerian aristocrat living on the edge of the Western world, watching its civilizations tumble toward him like so many dominos:

> Jeffers seems to have been, politically and sentimentally, an old-fashioned Jeffersonian republican. He believed in the American republic as

> a commonwealth of independent and self-reliant households, and saw himself—educated at a time when small boys knew the history of Rome and had been taught the parallels between the Roman and American republics—as a defender of the spartan and honest American commonweal against the thickening of empire . . . , the inevitable and horrifying collapse of European civilization.[10]

Hass's position has more recently been reaffirmed by Charles Simic in a prominent review of a new edition of *The Selected Poems*, published in 2001. Simic's review appeared shortly after the new edition's publication. Like Hass, Simic prefers Jeffers's short poems, not quite dismissing the longer ones but certainly in no rush to advocate them.[11] The review, positive as it is, perpetuates the mistake of apologizing for Jeffers in a formula that I'd caricature as follows: He didn't really hate people, he just hated the way people behave. He was in fact a skilled craftsman, but in the shorter not the longer poems. His politics were problematic, but that's because he was like the Founding Fathers. I suppose apologies for Pound's politics and economics run a similar gamut: *The Cantos* is a failure but an important poem; ignore the politics but praise the *logopoeia*. Yet no one in her right mind would take up Pound's poetry today without taking up the problem of his politics and economics. What's wrong to me about the way Jeffers's poetry has been recently handled by these few admirers is that it ignores what I consider to be the challenge that makes Jeffers worth reading. I don't see any way around the fact that he really did dislike people profoundly; their troubled souls and catastrophic behavior are at the core of his best, most compelling work. His unsettling politics emerges out of the central conflict that dominates his thought: How to enunciate a religious, prophetic vision of land and God in a degenerating, secular, godless, witless republic.

What I find odd, in this light, is how little critically has been written on Jeffers. I'd wager this paucity results from a lack of critical ability to read him. I understand Jeffers's poetry through two of its qualities: its value and its difficulty. The value of Jeffers's poetry is its strangeness, its unreconstructed, Abrahamic sense of alienation. We get this best in the long poems, nowhere better than in *The Women at Point Sur*, a riveting poem about an itinerant minister seeking God through perversions and grotesqueries, through rape and incest, culminating in murder and sacrifice. The difficulty in Jeffers's poetry lies not so much in its content, which—owing to its focus on narrative, polemic, and meditation—is generally approachable if not totally comprehensible. Rather, its difficulty comes from the fact that Jeffers—as his one disciple and imitator, William Everson, knew and insisted—is a religious poet. We still do not know how to read him because of this. It's not an accident that Everson's two books on Jeffers are the best things yet written on the work. *Robinson Jeffers: Fragments of an Older Fury* (1968)[12] and *The Excesses of God* (1988) exert the same overriding effort: to read Jeffers as a religious poet and to see the man as a religious figure. We continue to read Jeffers incorrectly because we do not know how to read American poetry under a religious sign. What is at stake in such a reading? Why do we find it so difficult to do?

While religion has always informed American poetry, I think six poets have stood out as religious poets: Walt Whitman, Emily Dickinson, H.D., T. S. Eliot, Hart Crane, and Robert Duncan. These six, in my mind, belong in the company of other great religious poets in the Judeo-Christian lineages: Blake, Milton, Smart, Herbert, Donne, Vaughan, Hopkins, Rilke, Celan, Rumi, Ibn 'Arabi, and Dante.[13] To these I'd like to add Jeffers, who might not typically be so invoked. What we find in Jeffers's poetry is something that thrives in the work of each of these poets, something I'd formulate, somewhat simplistically, in the following terms: that there is a gulf between the world and the divine that is bridged in the poem. In Jeffers's poetry, as in the work of any religious poet, there is a vision, or a spiritual idea, that inhabits the flaw—or the rift—separating creation from the divine presence beyond it, which the poem, most compellingly in its strangeness, somehow connects. I would analogize this experience in the poem with Freud's notion of the uncanny, or *das Unheimliche*. In his famous essay on this topic, Freud hypothesizes that the German word for the opposite of the uncanny, *das Heimliche*, or "home-like," reaches a point in its definition in which it means the same thing as its opposite, *das Unheimliche*, the "unhome-like," or uncanny. This discovery allows him to revel in the notion that the uncanny "is in some way a species of the familiar."[14] What he means by this is that the more familiar something is, the stranger it becomes, to the point of unsettling us. The roboticist Masahiro Mori has suggested the existence of an "uncanny valley" in the way people perceive lifelike robots. Mori has observed that the more lifelike a robot, the more warmly and empathically people respond to it, until a certain point is arrived at in which the robot appears *too* human, so that sympathy is replaced with revulsion.[15] Out of this feeling of being unsettled or repulsed, I would argue, our sense of the sacred and the spiritual emerges. God is the least familiar thing about us but also the thing most native to us. Experiencing this separation and binding, poetically or otherwise, is at once an alienation and a spiritual attainment.

Dickinson is perhaps the poet who most powerfully generates this simultaneous attraction and repulsion from the thought of God. In the poems beginning "The Love a Life can show Below," in which she imagines the paltriness of human love as a filament of "that diviner thing" that nonetheless acts as a valve allowing Paradise to be flung into the poet's consciousness, and in "One crucifixion is recorded—only," in which she proposes that "Gethsemane— // Is but a Province—in the Being's Centre," an interiority Christ made visible in his own death. Christ's suffering affirms and amplifies her own.[16] Where Dickinson attains poetic revelation at the price of alienation, Whitman is something else entirely; perhaps we may say he is merely strange, a strange and capricious lover of men whose carnal embrace is that of God fondling his beloved. In the 1855 edition of *Leaves of Grass*, we receive a poetic vision so propulsive and strained that we must labor to integrate its cocksureness and appetite with its desolate stretches of spiritual loneliness. Thus, even as Whitman is transformed into a hub of the universe, in "Song of Myself" he recognizes his own untranslatability, requiring him to die and, at the poem's end, to leave himself to the earth.

H.D.'s contribution to American religious poetry was to notice, at last, its "occult convolutions" (Whitman's phrase) and to track their emanations on the seismograph of world war. Her esoteric modernism seems anomalous even today: "Apocryphal fire," as she has it in her masterpiece, *Trilogy*. Eliot's innovation was to envision a technique in his work for eradicating the catastrophic religious desolation of the newly emerged twentieth century. His poetry exists as a colossal shockwave in which we watch the complete demolition of culture and then, in its aftershocks, the efforts to pull things together and find meaning anew. Crane's religion is a visionary cataclysmic excess, a supersaturation of the sensorium with epical desire. Duncan, in contrast to both these poets, is predatory in his solitary pursuit of religious gnosis, resulting in a poetic career of increasingly probed depths, and greater darkness of vision, such that his late work—for instance, *Ground Work II: In the Dark*—is nearly impenetrably dense, a poetry written as much out of the lightlessness of death as it is out of the illnesses that inhabited him late in his life.[17] Jeffers experiences the gap as a piqued alienation he refuses to romanticize in the face of the natural world. He seems to say to us, bluntly: *I have never known the love of God and never will. I cannot see this life as a cipher of Divine Will; neither am I a solipsist or narcissist, in love with men. I find only the natural world consistently superior to anything else.* For Jeffers, who approaches the gulf between himself and the divine with extreme prejudice, the justice of God is the great unknowable thing. Rather than railing against this inequity, he embraces it with a saturnine acquiescence that even God can't spare humans from their fate. Only God, in Jeffers's imagination, is immortal. The human soul is just atoms.

It's this gloomy truth Jeffers spells out in his poems. He does so through a consistent and remarkable use of *strangeness*. This is his tool, his lever. It's what I like best about Jeffers, that he uses strangeness not as a device (surrealism) nor as a theme (postmodern poetries galore) but as the medium through which to engage the creator God as that God's other. Two of his better-known—and most successful—lyrics demonstrate his sense of the estranging awkwardness of God's justice, divine or otherwise. In "Hurt Hawks," a poem in two parts, published in 1928, Jeffers imagines a wounded hawk ("The broken pillar of the wing jags from the clotted shoulder") as the herald of the broken world he lives in, much nobler than the humans who have ruined it ("You do not know him, you communal people, or you have forgotten him"). Part 2 of the poem contains some of Jeffers's most memorable lines:

> I'd sooner, except the penalties, kill a man than a hawk; but the
>   great redtail
> Had nothing left but unable misery
> From the bone too shattered for mending, the wing that trailed
>   under his talons when he moved.
> We had fed him six weeks, I gave him freedom,
> He wandered over the foreland hill and returned in the evening,
>   asking for death,
> Not like a beggar, still eyed with the old

Implacable arrogance. I gave him the lead gift in the twilight.
    What fell was relaxed,
Owl-downy, soft feminine feathers; but what
Soared: the fierce rush: the night-herons by the flooded river
    cried fear at its rising
Before it was quite unsheathed from reality.[18]

Note the contrasts: a masculine hawk with feminine feathers; misery and freedom; implacable arrogance and reality. And the precise morbidity of the "lead gift." Jeffers, forced into a godlike role, or at the very least a determining one, doesn't lament it merely or relish it exactly. He tastes a certain satisfaction—maybe even a fulfillment—in being able to say such a cruel thing with such conviction. What unsettles me about the sensibility behind the announcement that introduces this episode is that it includes its crucial qualification—*except the penalties.* Put another way, the poem coaxes me to believe the same thing. The conflict Jeffers works through in this poem is the euphoria he feels slaying the mythic hawk mixing with a sense of agony in having to do it to repair the error of its injury, caused by reckless humans. This poem relates an inflation of poetic self-consciousness—infused with superego—too rapidly expanding, such that a ritual slaying exposes human, spiritual weakness refuted in the hampered creature being killed. Jeffers is neither prophet nor poet here: only a man filled with a rush of unexpected pleasure and a mean pride in knowing how to express it.

He explores a similarly morbid thought in one of the last poems he wrote, which is one of his most moving lyrics, "The Deer Lay Down Their Bones." Hiking the canyons and mountains on the Big Sur coast, Jeffers comes upon a picturesque stream putting off a bad smell. Curious, he fords it until he comes to a clearing with a pool:

. . . all about there were bones lying in the
    grass, clean bones and stinking bones,
Antlers and bones: I understood that the place was a refuge for
    wounded deer; there are so many
Hurt ones escape the hunters and limp away to lie hidden; here
    they have water for the awful thirst
And peace to die in . . .

Like the hurt hawk, these skeletal and decomposing deer are heralds for the fallen world of the wild God who doesn't care for it any more, having escaped the predators of the world only to die slowly from wounds inflicted by them. Jeffers's meditation on these bones turns poignant, much more personal somehow than the judgments he usually casts down in his poetry, when he thinks of his dead wife and how miserable he is without her:

> We have been given life and have used it—not a
> great gift perhaps—but in honesty
> Should use it all. Mine's empty since my love died—Empty?[19]

The poem culminates in a confession, a covenant:

> . . . why should I wait ten years yet, having
> lived sixty-seven, ten years more or less,
> Before I crawl out on a ledge of rock and die snapping, like a wolf
> Who has lost his mate?—I am bound by my own thirty-year-old
> decision: who drinks the wine
> Should take the dregs; even in the bitter lees and sediment
> New discovery may lie. The deer in that beautiful place lay down
> their bones; I must wear mine.[20]

Here, in a poem written thirty-six years after "Hurt Hawks," Jeffers confronts the legacy of his stoic decision to kill the hawk and to write about it. Recall the rush Jeffers felt at what *soared* from the hawk after he slew it: a "fierce rush" that startled herons "cried fear at." Seeing the deer ossuary, Jeffers imagines himself canine, loopy with grief. He will not die like an animal. He will not be slain like an animal. Instead, he will wear his death, which is his decision to write poems. Having drunk its wine, he now sips its dregs. It's a moving admission to make. The canyon separating God from man in Jeffers's mind is strewn not with dead deer but with dying poets donned in their shaman's robes of bone.

Perhaps what most interests me in Jeffers's poetry—his frightening poetic resolve in the face of God's absence from the world as he sees it—can be seen in his long poem "Cawdor," written in the same period as "Hurt Hawks," at the height of his powers, which is to say rather early in his career (it appeared in 1928; his later long poems never matched the earlier efforts). It's the length of a short novel (112 pages in *The Selected Poetry*) and reads like a perverse potboiler. The poem takes place, as does so much of Jeffers's poetry, in the hills of central California. Terrible forest fires are raging around Cawdor's farm, driving fugitives from the higher hills onto his land, including Fera and her father, blinded by the fire, and Cawdor's estranged son Hood. In his narrative poems, Jeffers employs characters to reveal basest human feelings: lust, anger, guilt, revenge, despair. Triangular relationships create the space and tension for his dramatic action: Cawdor marries Fera, Fera desires Hood, and Hood loathes his father.

"Cawdor" includes one of the most bizarre scenes I can think of in American poetry. It involves Hood, Cawdor, and his new wife, Fera. Hood, a hunter-trapper-loner, has been estranged from his father and doesn't know he's remarried. When he returns home unexpectedly, he carries with him the hide of a puma he has recently killed. Meeting Fera and learning of her marriage to his father, he offers her a gift:

> Hood unstrapped the raw stiffening
> Puma-skin from his pack. "I owe you a wedding-present," he said to Fera, "if you'll take this
> I'll get it tanned. I shot it yesterday." Fera took in both hands the eight-foot trophy, she made
> To draw it over her shoulders. "Stop. It's not dry, you'll stain your dress." "Who am I," she said impatiently,
> "Not to be stained." She assumed it like a garment, the head with the slits for eyes hung on her breast,
> The moonstone claws dangling, the glazed red fleshy under-side
> Turned at the borders, her bare forearm crossing it. "Sticky," she said and took it in-doors. "Come in."[21]

Oedipus meets Faulkner in the hills of California. Of course things get worse. Fera grows mad when her father, who lives with her and Cawdor, dies. In her grief, she desires Hood, even though she knows that by pursuing him, she will "drive a wedge / between the father and the son."[22] Meanwhile, a live puma has preyed on livestock in the area. Rejected by Hood, still crazed by the death of her father, on the evening of her father's burial, Fera pulls the puma hide over her shoulders and slinks into the nearby woods, waiting for Hood to arrive. She doesn't realize that Hood has a rifle with him; she believes his rifle is at home and that upon seeing her, he will run to fetch it, then pursue her into the woods, where he will see that the mountain lion is a woman, take pity on her, and make love to her: "Might he not even now discover a woman / In the beast's hide, pity that woman?"[23] Hood hears the crackle of twigs in the woods, spies the animal, and fires at it. Instantly he knows he has shot Fera. Tragedy doublefolded results from this act—or is it somehow preordained? In the end, a wounded Fera will recover, Hood will be slain by his father, and Cawdor will brood over his act in a mood absent of any guilt but laden with a sense of the humiliating justice he finds himself at the hands of.

I spoke before of this poem as evidence of a lever of strangeness Jeffers uses to drive himself between the natural world into which he has fallen and the unknown chasm beyond the world in which God abides in an absence. Jeffers pitches his poem "Cawdor" into this void. The emptiness is God's, an unforgivably useless intelligence peered at in the far stars. How is this God experienced, witnessed by humans on earth? Jeffers seems to propose that God abides in human hopelessness not as some beacon or light but as human disconnection, stubbornness, alienation. What is more vivifying than God's refusal to fulfill our desires? Not without compassion, but with eerie humorlessness, Jeffers peers into the body of God, reflecting what he sees in bizarre, sexually kinetic dramas, none uncannier than Fera's dress-up in the puma hide. The tension of the scene makes it feel preordained, entrapped in fate. Fera's mind is not her own but God's:

> In the pain of her mind
> Nothing appeared fantastic; she had thought of a way
> To trick death from the hands that refused life.
> From Hood's own hands. She'd not be forgotten. She drew
> The mountain-lion skin from where it crumpled away,
> And clothed herself in it . . .[24]

Similarly, when Hood fires on Fera, we sense Hood as mere instrument in the hand of God, useless:

> He knew, as she fell. He seemed to himself
> To have known even while he fired. That worm of terror

Strangled his mind so that he kept no memory
Of Cawdor and the others taking her into the house.
He was left in the dark with a bruised face, someone had struck
 him,
Oh very justly.[25]

Who is God? The punisher, the marauder. The one who strikes you in the dark. This is what the poem implies to me. It could just as easily be read as fate, but Jeffers pointedly uses the word "someone." "Cawdor," like so much else of Jeffers's poetry, is a theodicy, a treatment of the outstanding justice of God as worked through the fallen deeds of humans. Is God just? He is. Humans desire, fail, kill. And God allows them to. That's his justice. Is God holy? This is the question Jeffers's poetry most compellingly pursues, its spoor as elusive as Moses's glimpse of the backside of God or as monstrous as Oedipus's revelation that his own mother has borne his children. The hawk, wounded or aloft, is Jeffers's image for this God. Man is man, he seems to say, human, stubborn, mirthless, destroying, perversely enduring. God is an alien being, estranged even from himself, visible if not entirely identifiable to us in hawk form—no creatures in Jeffers's work are more nobly presented but so frequently wounded by human thoughtlessness as hawks. God's intelligence is a hunting bird's, as airborne as it is unknowable, as raptorial as it is heraldic.

3

SPIRITUAL OSMOSIS

Absorbing the Influence in Geoffrey Hill's Later Poetry

INTROIT

In the twentieth of the 120 sections making up Geoffrey Hill's vituperative oratory *Speech! Speech!*, published in 2000, the poet vents his proverbial spleen thus:

> THEY tell you that? Spiritual osmosis
> mystique of argot—I like the gestures
> that come with it: a kind of dumb thieves' cant.
> SPI–RI–TU–ALI–TY | I salute you.
> *Ich kann nicht anders.* It was not so much
> cultic pathology I had in mind
> as ethical satire; but you wriggle so,
> old shape-shifter. Since I am compromised
> I shall say more. Assume the earphones. Not
> music. Hebrew. Poetry aspires
> to the condition of Hebrew. Say that it ís
> a wind in the mulberry trees: who will know?[1]

This passage, on several readerly levels, is remarkable. Beyond its buoyant strangeness, I note a Calibanized hostility and anger, matched with high-pitched irony, worked into what becomes an unmediated, Prospero-like pronouncement of poetry's nature and idiom. That Hill is amending

Pound's dictum via Walter Pater—that all art should aspire to the condition of music—is important. Pound's axiom, as Mark Scroggins points out, is formal and analogical: musical form is the model for poetic form.[2] It's an aesthetizing statement, a manner of understanding one art through another. Hill's revised proverb is something different entirely: He is allying himself to an Old Testament prophetic recovery of sacred speech. His Hebrew is not that spoken by teens on the streets of Tel Aviv. It's the speech with which Abraham spoke to God; the same with which Jeremiah cursed the womb he came from; and the tongue of Ezekiel, who ate shit for over a year at God's Hebraic command (Ezek. 4:4–17). But Hill's Hebrew is not so much the language of Torah as it is the linguistic key to understanding the English he writes in. Hill's insistence that poetry aspire to the condition of Hebrew is a liturgical statement that poetry repeat the language of the creation. Ethical satire yields not to cultic pathos but to worshipful logos.

It's worth mentioning this poem's engaging typography: Here, as throughout *Speech! Speech!*, Hill employs small caps, italics, a vertical dash, and accent marks, all to add visual emphasis to an already emphatic poem. Beyond this, there's the strangeness of these lines in the context of his work. Surely, the residuum of his frequently hieratic, priestly language endures, without any of the careful formalism that made his earlier poetry such a harrowing pleasure to read. What valve, we might ask, has been opened, allowing what stuff to be spewed from it?

The change in Hill's life can be charted geographically in 1988, when the poet moved from England to Massachusetts, taking up residency in Boston, where he remained for nearly two decades, returning to England in 2006, where he remained until his death on June 30, 2016. Rather than regarding Hill's work on a continuum, I think we can read it more profitably in terms of a rift that we can locate to the time in his life when he moved from England to Boston. *Something* seems to have happened to the poet—aesthetically, culturally, perhaps even theologically—which soon after, in the middle of the 1990s, began to be visible through intimations and direct statements in his poetry. Hill's transformation at this time (there's no other word for it) is a prodigious one. How can the implications of this change be read into and through his poetry?

This question of Hill's transformation becomes even more pointed in light of the drastic increase in Hill's poetic production that began at the time of his move. Might it be accurate to describe this change as a conversion, religious or otherwise? Such a characterization is complicated by the fact that before and after Hill's change, he was unusually consumed with religious concerns. One might argue that Hill's earlier, formally driven poetry has an inward cast to it, fixed on mystical, interior realities as well as problems of social justice. But these concerns, as we shall see, prevail in the later poetry as well. So what has changed? In a word: volume. Beginning with the work produced after his move to the United States, Hill discovered a way to write poetry in an essentially unrestricted (though still often formally guided) prophetic voice. Put another way, the religious visions that agitated his earlier verse give way to religious harangues and jeremiads pouring forth almost unabated. And there really has been nothing like this change, certainly not recently. I can't think of another poet who for all intents and purposes produced an esteemed body of enduring poetic work who then, past the point of midcareer, began to produce an entirely new, equally enduring body of poetic work, while quadrupling his output. It's unheard of. And from the evidence at hand, Hill spent the years from the publication of his collected poems, *Broken Hierarchies*, in 2013 until his death in 2016 generating even more new poetry.

LITURGY OF THE WORD

First, consider in more detail his publication history from 1988 forward, since which time Hill has, as mentioned above, nearly quadrupled his poetic output: One finds 182 pages of poetry in *New and Collected Poems, 1952–1992*, including *The Mystery of the Charity of Charles Peguy*, a slim book of less than thirty pages that was published in 1983. Up to this point, the U.S. edition duplicates the content of the *Collected Poems* published in the United Kingdom in 1985, a book that claimed, impishly, "this poetry . . . has disturbed the critical consensus for three decades."[3] Beyond this point in the U.S. edition are the "New Poems," thirty pages comprising a decade of writing, nearly half of which are recycled into *Canaan*, a book published in 1996. After the appearance of that book, Hill published in quick (and surprising) succession three volumes of a major later sequence consisting of *The Triumph of Love* (1998), *Speech! Speech!* (2000), and *The Orchards of Syon* (2002). From there, seven additional volumes, one or two every year, including *Scenes from Comus* (2005), *Without Title* (2006), *A Treatise of Civil Power* (2007), and *Clavics* (2011). And the appearance of *Broken Hierarchies: Poems 1952–2012*, which includes four previously unpublished books, as well as significant expansions of three earlier books, makes for a volume of nearly one thousand pages. The poetry issued forth from Hill in the last twenty years of his life like the geysering of a geothermal force.[4]

My focus in this chapter is on the trilogy of books that accounts for the transformation of Hill's poetry: *The Triumph of Love*, *Speech! Speech!*, and *The Orchards of Syon*, along with *Canaan*, which might be regarded as a prelude to the trilogy. Some of the features of these books are worth noting as a way of generating a sense of the transformation Hill underwent until his death in 2016. Hill's metamorphosis has aesthetic and theological meanings, immediately evident in the novel visual texture of his work since 1996 and more slowly discerned in its seething content. Metamorphosis, Ovid tells us, is flux, the lord of creation. It's difficult to know whether Hill is manipulating change for creative effects or whether he, in having undergone a powerful transformation, is, like Ovid's tales, a medium through which flux thrives. Each of these books begins with a series of quotations—headpieces—that act as signposts for the poetry to follow. Invariably provocative, these snippets signify to me something of the nature of the change I would like to demonstrate in Hill's work. As a way of orienting ourselves toward these headpieces, we might consider section 18 in *The Triumph of Love*, in which Hill recognizes a kind of debt economy of faith in his fixation on the authentic moods he registers in older texts:

> It is not [possibly a lacuna—ED]
> whether we have the Psalms in Latin or Hebrew
> nor by what authority such things are committed,
> dismissed among the aeonic dense snowflurries:
> it is not in the mortgaged conversations—the synagogues,
> the cathedrals—to Caesar and the great Pharaoh.
> Distinctions are as nothing, but identity
> is pulled apart. Try definition—is this a dead
> march or a death march? It is a dead march.[5]

Two things to note in these lines: Hill's own coercive rhetoric transforms the mortgaged conversations he imagines—ones that have allowed

Judaism and Christianity to survive their oppression by Empire—into the aeonic dense snowflurries of language in which it is impossible either to commit or dismiss the meaning of such exchanges, and that same rhetoric drives him to conclude these lines with the oratorical trick of a question, which is not so surprising. What's strange is that he answers his own question: it is a dead march. (March of the dead? Or is dead being used here as in "dead heat," to signify that it's impossible to say who's going to win this march—unto death?)

Let us consider, then, the orienting quotations of these four books of Hill's, as well as some of their contents. After an apocalyptic headpiece gathered from quotations of three books from the 1560 Geneva translation (the so-called Bible of the people, a product of the Reformation) of the Old Testament into English (*ô Canáan, the land of the Philistims, I wil euen destroy thee without an inhabitant*, from Zephaniah 2:5), *Canaan* opens with the poem/address "To the High Court of Parliament," initiating a sequence that, along with "Mysticism and Democracy," runs like Duncan's "Passages" throughout the volume. As in nearly each of his earlier books, all of the poems in *Canaan* have titles or, in the case of the sequences, dates to orient them. This is a polemical book, inasmuch as it is a transitional book: a prelude, for great stylistic surprises are in store in the books to come. While most of the poems are unrhymed—still unusual at this point for Hill—some of the poems retain the recognizable tightness of so much of his earlier poetry, as in the opening of "To the High Court of Parliament, November 1994":

> Keep what in repair?
> Or place what further
> toll on the cyclic
> agony of empire?
>
> Judgement and mourning
> come round yet again
> like a festival
> of scratched heroic film.[6]

There is the off-rhyming of *repair*, *further*, and *empire*, a familiar feature of a Hill quatrain, positioned against the almost objectivist quarrel of the second quatrain, which struggles into a kind of dactylic stagger (JUDGEment and MOURNing come ROUND yet aGAIN like a FESTival . . .). And there is the nearly consistent five-syllable count per line. Compare this to the opening of one of Hill's best-known poems, also one of his earliest, "Genesis":

> Against the burly air I strode
> Crying the miracles of God.
>
> And first I brought the sea to bear
> Upon the dead weight of the land;
> And the waves flourished at my prayer,
> The rivers spawned their sand.
>
> And where the streams were salt and full
> The tough pig-headed salmon strove,
> Ramming the ebb, in the tide's pull,
> To reach the steady hills above.[7]

Hill's iambic tetrameter in these lines, perfectly stated in the poem's opening, nearly as sing-songy as the opening of Frost's "Stopping by Woods on a Snowy Evening," yields to a variety of metrical and rhymed expressions in these ten lines, from the trochee in the second half of the fourth line to the rough, syncopated rhythms of the eighth line (which I'd scan "the TOUGH PIG-headed SALmon STROVE," still four feet, but clubbed, spondaic ones, let's say). These variations, however, he resolves in the once-again perfectly expressed iambs of the tenth line. In spite of these differences, and even including the skilled off-rhyming of strode/God and strove/above, the verse from *Canaan* feels somehow freer, looser than what gets spoken in this earlier voice. What feels consistent, however, is the morbidity—the hostility and anger—that marks Hill's most vivid pronouncements. Hill's opening question in "To the High Court of Parliament"—*Keep what in repair?*—is best read as a viciously cynical sneer, in kind with the image of pig-headed salmon ramming the ebb of water they swim dumbly into.

With *The Triumph of Love*, Hill abandons the shapes of most of his earlier poetic forms.[8] In hopes of replicating the experience of entering into Hill's later work, either as a familiar reader or as one newly introduced to it, I want now to describe some of the seemingly superficial elements of the later trilogy and then to contextualize and analyze these elements toward making claims about the kinds of meaning—specifically religio-historical meaning—Hill is expressing in these works. It may seem a little odd to fixate on the look of these books and the style of work in them, but the appearance of these books in rapid sequence (for poetry at least)—1998, then 2000, then 2002—is the main signal by which readers recognize Hill's seemingly sudden change. *The Triumph of Love*, which is composed of 150 sections, whose lengths vary from one line (including the first, "Sun-blazed, over Romsley, a livid rain-scarp," Romsley referring to the place of his boyhood) to fifty-eight (section 125, the most theologically dense in the book), opens, similarly to *Canaan*, with scriptural quotation. This time, Hill begins with Nehemiah 6:3, shown first in Hebrew and then translated into Latin, Lutheran German, and King James English.[9] In his native tongue, the verse runs: "And I sent messengers unto them, saying, I am doing a great worke, so that I can not come down: why should the worke cease, whilest I leave it, and come downe to you?" As much as the quotation anticipates the great work ahead, alluding to Hill's (possibly ironic) pride toward his project, perhaps even to his foreknowledge of the great volume of work that is to come, the repetition of the text four times in four different languages urges readers to puzzle out the meaning of this message, descended from its original prophetic language into three of its most powerful evangelizing tongues. Entering into the book, *The Triumph of Love* introduces us to a sense of an overriding compositional system (one section for each of the psalms) as well as to the frequent appearance of intrusive, chorusing voices, including, occasionally, that of the poem's snide editor, who interjects his comments in brackets, whether as Hill's superego or as a kind of outside voice, it's somewhat hard to say.[10]

These novel features in *The Triumph of Love* explode in *Speech! Speech!*. Systems dominate this book: The poems are each twelve lines long, each numbered one through 120 (one for each of the days of Sodom), and each is peppered liberally with the typographic features described above. These Hill explains (and visually demonstrates) in section 117, as a "Poetics of self-rule," an autonomy:

> CAPITALS | stage directions and other
> FORMS OF SUBPOENA. *Italics* | words
> with which Í—*sometimes*—surprise *myself*.[11]

In a poetics piece published in the *Guardian* on September 21, 2002, Hill explained, "At one point in *The Orchards of Syon* (XXIII), I say, 'I write / to astonish myself.' This self-astonishment is achieved when, by some process I can't fathom, common words are moved, or move themselves, into clusters of meaning so intense that they seem to stand up from the page, three-dimensional almost." The passage above is a legend for that surprise: Hill seems as charged writing about it as we ought to be experiencing it as readers. It was the strange way *Speech! Speech!* opened to me when I first read it that has attached me so much to it: Even as I felt I didn't understand most of the references (of which the poem is a thicket), I was captivated by the heedless confidence of so many of the poem's pronouncements. What I take to be this "heedless confidence" deserves a bit of elaboration. The poems in *Speech! Speech!* proceed with the force of oratory, a kind of gathering insinuation of rhetoric, improvisation, and range of reference, projected with a speed and urgency whose momentum promises delivery and deliverance. I think the morbid comedy of so much of this book arises from Hill's astonishment at the things issuing forth from his mouth. Not quite logorrhea, Hill does seem to be channeling great energies and feelings here. As a reader, it's hard for me not to be thrilled by the effects of Hill trying to master such tension and power.

With *The Orchards of Syon*, Hill brings his newly gotten poetic voice into its "valedictory" register, one that is less vitriolic and more plangent, more reflective, offered as a kind of conclusion or coming to peace. As with the previous two books, *The Orchards of Syon* opens with a headpiece that invites a perspective into the project at hand. This time it comes from Thomas Bradwardine's *De causa dei*. Thomas of Bradwardine, so-called Doctor *profundus*, once confessor to Edward III, later named archbishop of Canterbury, appears throughout all three of these books as a grounding theological presence. Bradwardine's repeated appearances suggest not so much a role he plays in Hill's imagination as it signifies Hill's reliance on this figure to articulate some sense to us of how he relates to the material he is producing in his poetry. Take, for instance, Bradwardine's notable intrusion into section 125 of *The Triumph of Love*, in which Hill confesses:

The intellectual
beauty of Bradwardine's thesis rests

> in what it springs from: the Creator's grace
> *praecedentem tempore et natura* ['Strewth!!!
> 'already present in time as in nature'?—ED]
> and in what it returns to—our arrival
> at a necessary salvation.[12]

Hill concludes this section of *The Triumph of Love* with an equally perplexing pronouncement in which he rephrases the Latin from Bradwardine into an antiprogressive, antimodern medieval theological imperative that we would do best to take with all seriousness as we make our way through these books:

> I have been working up to this. The Scholastics
> mean more to me than the New Science. All
> things are eternally present in time and nature.[13]

In the first quote, Hill appears to be paraphrasing Bradwardine's Latin: *to yield before time and nature*, or, as the cantankerous "ED" has it, "already present in time as in nature." In the second quote, compounding this thought, Hill advocates Thomism and its project of dialectical reading over Vico and his progressive/cyclic sense of history (the so-called New Science), arguing for simultaneity that is an argumentative clarity. Perhaps. Hill's advocacy of Bradwardine's scholasticism is an oddly personal touch because in it Bradwardine speaks of having been struck by the truth, which "struck me like a radiant light of grace." Bradwardine is perhaps channeling Hill through these words. Likewise, the two other headpieces to *The Orchards of Syon*, one from D. H. Lawrence's *The Rainbow*, the other from Thomas Traherne's *Centuries of Meditation*, strike placid notes to orient us to this final poem. ("Everything was at rest, free, and immortal," announces Traherne; Lawrence speaks of how his character's "mood of inspiration began to pass away.") Hill's third book-as-poem consists of seventy-two twenty-four-lined sections, one for each of the Alexandrian sages who assembled in the third century BCE to compile the Septuagint, the Greek translation of the Hebrew scriptures, the first such complete collection of what Christians commonly regard as the Old Testament. Hill preserves some of the typography from *Speech! Speech!*, though softened here, used less frequently, less emphatically: the vertical dashes persist, as do the accents. Full capital letters are used to invoke the names of poets present in the text, including CELAN, WAT, HOPKINS, COLERIDGE, MONTALE, BACHMANN, along with phrases in other languages, a function italics similarly perform throughout the text. The tone of this sequence of the poem is more meditative, more discursive than the previous two books, but nevertheless as painstakingly instructive as well.

The book's title refers, quite complexly, to several things: First and foremost, to Syon House on the Thames, an Abbey founded by Henry V in 1415. The Brigettine nuns of Syon undertook the translation of what has come to be known as the *Dialogue* of Saint Catherine of Siena, a fourteenth-century Dominican lay sister, canonized in 1451 and made Doctor of the Church in 1970.[14] They called their version *The Orcherd of Syon*, after their abbey, playing on the mystical sevenfold and fivefold divisions in Catherine's text reflected in the planted rows of their orchards. This text is considered crucial not only as a propagation of the sainthood of Catherine but as a specimen of Middle English language and translation.[15] Its layers of authenticity cannot have been lost on Hill when he began imagining his own new poetic language. He saw it as nothing less than redemptive:

> The nether way to salvation, if
> I so undertake it: *the nether*
> *way of the flood* claimed sainted CATHERINE
> speaking of perdition. Life against life
> in her scale of plenitude; the flood's
> foulness like smashed Warsaw sewers,
> with more long-buried rites. Mere violence
> now of denial; trees to windward
> snow-ghosted; the light
> enters upon its own darkness and falls
> mute . . .
>   Redemption
> is self-redemption and entails crawling
> to the next angle of vision.
> Press the right word, the scenes change. Who can
> not be affected: Spring releasing, shire-
> wide, the nature of waters, a world
> that flows and rises for us just as you see it?[16]

The spring released in this poem is not just a torrent of historical association or derivation: In Hill's imagination, there's a convergence of poetic knowledge and history. Saint Catherine's redemptive flood brings up the modern image of the sewers of Warsaw, "with more long-buried rites." Even redemption has its costs.

These superficial changes in Hill's work that yield to depths of poetic transformation hint at other changes: personal, temperamental, spiritual. It's always tempting to read snippets of biography into a poet's work, if only because life story so often gives context to the work. But Hill's changes suggest a huge renewal, rebuilt from an upheaval or catastrophe in his life. As it turns out, one need not look very hard to find out what happened to Hill—which is strange, given the privacy and austerity of the first half of his life and work. If one label can be applied to Hill's newer work, it is *opened.*

THE LITURGY OF THE EUCHARIST

So what happened to Hill when he moved to America in 1988? Simple answer: He began to take antidepressants. Much has been made of this "revelation," one Hill announced in his interview with Carl Phillips, published in the *Paris Review,* but beyond Hill's own remarks, little of help has been said. Hill first admitted this change in section 109 of *The Triumph of Love,* initiating his confession with a curious, esoteric assertion:

> Salt, sulphur,
> mercury: more potent by far
> than metaphysics whose demoted angels
> have been caught dancing
> with impropriety . . .
>
> Since when has our ultimate reprobation
> turned (*oculos tuos nos con-*
> *verte*) on the conversion or
> reconversion of brain chemicals—
> the taking up of serotonin? I
> must confess to receiving the latest

elements, *Virgine bella*, as a signal
mystery, mercy, of these latter days.[17]

Regarding the "taking up of serotonin," Hill told Phillips:

> I don't know how I survived almost sixty years without the medication I now have. From late childhood, I suffered from chronic depression, which was accompanied by various exhausting obsessive-compulsive phobias. *Totally undiagnosed, of course. . . . And it wasn't until I came over here that this began to be treated.* . . . It's completely transformed my life. . . . I am now, so to speak, positioned squarely inside myself. This has freed me in some way as a functioning human being.[18]

Beyond this, Hill alludes to the history of medicated poets, most obviously Robert Lowell, in the third section of *Speech! Speech!*, which begins:

How is it tuned, how can it be un-
tuned, with lithium, this harp of nerves? Fare well
my daimon, inconstant
measure, mood- and mind-stress, heart's rhythm
suspensive . . .[19]

Note the persistent inclination to regard this psychopharmacology in alchemical language: Salt, sulfur, and mercury (transformative agents in alchemy) in the first poem; a daimon in the second. Two additional things strike me in these admissions, the first medical, the second therapeutic. Lithium, a naturally occurring salt, is normally prescribed for a bipolar disorder, from which Hill evidently does not suffer. When he initially sought treatment for his problems, he was prescribed lithium, to little effect. Nor is he taking Prozac, as has been sometimes misreported.[20] Nonetheless, he appears to be taking some combination of SSRIs, or selective serotonin reuptake inhibitors. Serotonin, as one of the body's endocrines, delivers information from nerve ending to nerve ending. It's a messenger/catapult. Propelled from its nerve's ending by a blast of electricity, serotonin hurls its message across the synaptic cleft, where it is caught by its serotonergic receptor-partner, who hurls it onward to and from the brain. SSRIs function not by inhibiting this process but by encouraging serotonin to linger in the synapse; this, it has been discovered, it makes us feel "better," something Zoloft advertisements, ubiquitous it seemed for a time, visualized for us as a glum-looking cartoon blob perking up to twittering birds and butterflies after taking the efficacious drug. (Interestingly, Ecstasy, or MDMA, functions similarly to create more enhanced, euphoric feelings. Indeed, it is on the basis of experiments with prescribing Ecstasy that SSRIs have been administered to treat depression.) So, messages aren't necessarily slowed down in the person; rather, the body/mind feels alleviated in delivering these messages. The nerve-harp, we might say following Hill's expression, is tuned to its harmonics. When Hill in his interview admits to Phillips that in "the few years since I finished *Canaan* . . . the phrases are coming faster, and my discovery of where they seem to be leading takes place much more speedily,"[21] we ought not to attribute this to his medication but to the fact that his obsessive-compulsive tendencies are no longer inhibiting him from tracking a thought, a line, a phrase as it occurs to him. He need no longer "perfect" a line to allow it into being and to spur others into being too. The drugs seem to have made Hill feel that things in him had opened up, especially as far as language is concerned.

Much more interesting to me is Hill's implicit denunciation of British mental healthcare—and perhaps more broadly British culture—in his insistence that his condition went "totally undiagnosed, of course," followed by the information that he only began to be treated upon taking up residency in the United States. In an interesting portrait of Hill from the *Guardian* in August 2002, Robert Potts revives a description of Hill from his college days, that he was "walking around Cambridge as if he'd been raped by God," along with reports that Hill was generally miserable for most of his professional life in England.[22] It's worth asking: why did his problem go totally undiagnosed? Having taken so thoroughly to his American therapy, one supposes Hill himself was not averse to mental healthcare. Was it something in his British working-class background that prevented him from seeking help? Or some problematic mode of being endemic to British culture? It is notable that in terms of therapies, U.S. psychology and psychiatry are overwhelmingly characterized by psychopharmaceutical treatments. Prescriptions of antidepressants are so prevalent that "therapy" is more likely to be a piece of paper with a doctor's signature than it is any sort of communication between therapist and patient. Not knowing of what Hill's therapy has consisted, I don't want to speculate. But I do want to suggest that at the heart of Hill's poetic and personal transformation lurks *America*. There's no question that in the "land of the free" Hill discovered something of the "large looseness" Henry James in *The Ambassadors* attributes to Lambert Strether's fellow American Waymarsh, who would appear in their Paris hotel's lobby every morning sprawled out on its couches. What do we make of Hill's new large looseness?

POUND

Though frequently seen as a poet in the image of Eliot, called thus to carry on an Eliotic legacy (for instance, in his review of *Speech! Speech!*, William Logan berates Hill for not managing his poem as well as Eliot managed "The Waste Land"),[23] Hill has exhibited what seems to be a serious, long-standing investment in the work of Ezra Pound. "Our Word Is Our Bond," from *The Lords of Limit*, is a painstaking analysis of Pound's misguided sense of poetic justice via Coleridge, Dryden, and Butler, among others. Hill's essay "Envoi (1919)," a treatment of "Hugh Selwyn Mauberley," given as a talk in 1986 but revised in 1987 and published in *The Enemy's Country*, bears more directly on my argument here. Put simply (and simplistically), in this essay, composed right before he moved to America and then started getting "better," Hill seems to *convert* from an Eliotic to a Poundian position in poetry. This is to say, from a position of a poetic, atemporal vision of the absconded sacred to a prophetic vision of history, which in Hill's case, we can see is an inward vision, as when, above, Hill speaks of being "squarely inside myself." And it is through this vision that Hill allows himself to "see" language and to experience it as a creative flow.

Toward setting up this shift from an Eliotic to a Poundian position, I want to consider that Eliot's poetic position, which Hill seems complexly to have attended to, if not to have tried to imitate, became untenable to Hill as he began to undergo this significant life transformation. Denis Donoghue, describing the effects of "The Waste Land," asserts that "the words acquire the kind of aura, or the kind of reverberation, which we feel in proverbs; with this difference: proverbs appeal to our sense of life, and inherited wisdom in our sense of things; Eliot's words appeal to primordial images and rhythms that can be felt, though they cannot well be called in evidence." Donoghue usefully locates the power of Eliot's poetic power in his position toward words, how he endows them with extralogical qualities that cannot easily be summoned as proof. Donoghue continues, "Nearly everything in Eliot's language arises from the pressure he exerts, upon himself in the first instance and thereafter upon the reader, to register the force not of oneself that makes for truth."[24] Hill, writing on Eliot's Clark Lectures (which were published as *The Varieties of Metaphysical Poetry*), describes the "centre of gravity" in Eliot's argument, observing how his "anxious shifts and reservations complicate rather than clarify" that center.[25] Although his concern is a different aspect of Eliot's work, I think we can make an equation between Donoghue's sense in Eliot of the reverberations arising from truth pressures and Hill's sense of centers of gravity marked by anxious shifts and reservations. In another place in this same essay, Hill, in characterizing Eliot's poem "Marina," argues: "The voice of the poem is acutely conscious of attempting to explain, to itself and to others, matters more properly explained in other ways."[26] Hill, who published this essay, called "Dividing Legacies," in 1996, had made the determination that it was more valuable in his own poetry to clarify rather than complicate, in spite of his own anxious shifts and because of his newfound freedom from reservations, not the center of his gravity but what he elsewhere calls the "extraordinary pitch of signification" to which ordinary language can be raised in things such as poetry.[27] He discovers this pitch by cultivating a more prophetic vision of history in his poetry, a move that opens him to Poundian vistas and what might be described as Poundian error in the poem.

Hill's essay "Envoi (1919)" is a piece of high, serious praise for Pound. A crucial quotation from this essay grounds us in Hill's understanding of Pound and in his sense of the way Pound exemplifies a larger poetic project into which Hill would involve himself in the years following its initial presentation in the Clark Lectures he gave in 1986:

> Pound was clearly moved, and considered himself instructed (as who would not?), by the luminous implications of those lines in the thirty-third canto of the *Paradiso* in which "substance and accidents and their customs" are bound together by love "in such wise that that which I speak is a simple light." It seems to have been Pound's lifelong endeav-

> our to find the means whereby that Dantean conception could be registered in the demonstrable technicalities of English verse.[28]

Pair this with a similarly helpful quotation from Pound, from his essay "Dante," in *The Spirit of Romance* (1910), in which Pound appears to invent modern epic poetry in English and certainly provides the matrix out of which Hill's later work can be seen to emerge: "The *Divina Commedia* must not be considered as an epic; to compare it with epic poems is usually unprofitable. It is in a sense lyric, the tremendous lyric of the subjective Dante."[29] *Luminous implications* suits Hill's current understanding of poetry more than *acute consciousness* in explanation of a belief or a position, lyrically or in life. Hill's own subjectivity has become his subject, but even this turn is marked by lingering self-consciousness, by a manner in which history keeps plunging into his words. Consider section 89 from *The Triumph of Love*:

> Stunned words of victory less memorable
> than those urged from defeat; not that the vanquished
> are more to be believed. In effect
> it cries out for silence: whose
> silence would you say? I say endure
> by way of enduring: the secular
> masques, *Laus et vituperatio*. What
> is [ambulance] you may ask; has it come
> down to us from the dead language of Canaan?[30]

[In line 8 above, "ambulance" is mirrored in Hill's text, so that it reads from right to left, as if seen on the hood of an ambulance.] The praise and blame (which is what *laus et vituperatio* means) that Hill feels come down from the dead language of Canaan—presumably Christ's Aramaic but possibly also the Latin of Canaan's subjugators. Hill's expression of history—or historical truths—binds him to silence, even as he froths to speak. Interestingly, Hill opts not for silence, nor for rants, but, somewhat in the model of Pound, for a kind of willful error, expressed in monological self-questioning and self-correction.

That Hill is speaking of himself, or of his own position to some degree, is my understanding of "Envoi (1919)." Like Pound in "Hugh Selwyn Mauberley," Hill uses the occasion of his essay on Pound's poem to say farewell to England. Likewise, Hill embraces a Poundian labor, in that from this point forward his work is thoroughly engaged with the tremendous lyric of the subjective Hill and, furthermore, its value, as perceived through its distant origins in the formations of English speech, then through various religious, oratorical, and poetic epochs and modes, and into his own latter-day imagination. In his Tanner Lecture on Human Values, entitled "Intrinsic Value: Marginal Observations on a Central Question," Hill locates the worth of poetry in its evocative powers arising from mechanical, technical masteries. Using a musical analogy, he speaks of how "Syntax . . . establishes the *Grundbass* (as we would speak of the ground-bass in a Bach *continuo*) in the midst of the *Abgrund*: the abyss, the deep, in the psalms of penitence and lamentation," such that language—arising out of the manipulation of the pedal of grammar—becomes a "faculty of reflective integration."[31] Lines from *The Triumph of Love* articulate this point:

> Mysticism is not
> affects but grammar. There is nothing
> mysterious in grammar; it constitutes
> its own mystery, its *practicum*.[32]

Hill concludes his remarks on value with a romantic, not-quite-Eliotic pronouncement: "A poem issues from reflection, particularly but not exclusively from the common bonding of reflection and language; it is not in itself the passing of reflective sentiment through the medium of language."[33] Here reflection isn't Wordsworthian; it's an active contemplative power of intellection, of the mind aspiring toward what is ultimately religious expression of an "inner voice."

How can I say this? I don't have to. Hill himself has said as much. In describing how he has abandoned the view of poetry that dominated his early work, namely, from Allen Tate via Eliot, that "the poem is achieved by the fullest possible objectification of individual subjectivity," Hill asserts, in his newfound understanding of "self-knowledge," that "The instrument of expression and the instrument of self-knowledge and self-correction is the same. There is a kind of poetry—I think that the seventeenth-century English metaphysicals are the greatest example of this, Donne, Herbert, Vaughan—in which the language seems able to hover above itself in a kind of brooding, contemplative, self-rectifying way."

Citing examples of other such writers—Dante, Milton, Wordsworth—Hill concludes, "I cannot conceive poetry of any enduring significance being brought into being without some sense of this double quality that language has when it is taken into the sensuous intelligence."[34] That expression and self-knowledge coincide is the nexus through which Hill's gnostic apperceptions of language seek a transcendent knowledge of the divine.[35] In "A Pharisee to Pharisees," Hill's remarkable essay from 1989 on Henry Vaughan's poem "The Night," Hill asserts: "Language is a vital factor of experience, and, as 'sensory material,' may be religiously apprehended."[36] Hill's own transformation is one directly involved in the effort to regard language as a kind of religious experience, not merely as its vehicle or its recorder. In these late poems, Hill has given himself over to a simultaneity of history, speculation, poetry and poetics, and liturgy to generate an experience, for himself and reader alike, that activates *religiosity*. In making this formulation, I am thinking specifically of Hill's previous remark on language value as being informed in its reflective quality. Here, reflection should not be taken to mean a mirroring; rather, I take Hill to mean by reflection this ability to "hover above itself in a kind of brooding, contemplative, self-rectifying way."

Hill's thoughts on Vaughan in "A Pharisee to Pharisees" are useful toward understanding his idea of contemplation. Vaughan's poem turns on a recreation of the moment recorded in John 3:2 when Nicodemus, a Pharisee, confesses to Christ his belief in Christ's divinity. The poem is a series of meditations on that scene in which Vaughan addresses with intimacy his audience, confessing his own doubts, sewn as they are with the negative theology characterized by Dionysius the Areopagite, who insisted God could only be approached through active negations of both contemplative experience and the language that recorded that experience. Vaughan's poem culminates in a stanza characteristic of the "magnetic originality" Hill finds throughout this poem:

> There is in God (some say)
> A deep, but dazling darkness; As men here
> Say it is late and dusky, because they
> See not all clear;
> O for that night! where I in him
> Might live invisible and dim.[37]

The value of this poem to Hill is that even as it performs an act of metaphoric conversion ("Poetic metaphor is a means of converting the actual to the real"),[38] it resists any analytic description of its meaning, such that it acquires something like sentience: "The poem is acutely aware of immanence, as it is of imminence; there are serene celebrations of indwelling; even so, something remains within and withdrawn when all has been quantified and qualified."[39] This remainder is the reflective quality of language Hill at last finds in a "brooding, contemplative, self-rectifying" transparence over his poetry and the poetry he admires. A description of the virtues of Vaughan's poem serves, then, as a model for the work ahead of Hill at the time he wrote this essay:[40]

> If we regard "The Night" and its several darknesses . . . we discover how the sympathetic attraction of otherwise disparate images and echoes from Old and New Testaments, from a variety of non-scriptural sources and from Vaughan's own writings creates a positive embracing of abnegation, a transferring of potentiality from the darkness of a stricken soul, a stricken cause and a stricken church into visionary intensity.[41]

Visionary intensity stands for the state Hill has transformed into, one in which his brooding, contemplative, self-rectifying obsessions have been channeled into luminous implications marked by the extraordinary pitch of signification he counts as most valuable in writing, his own and others.

It wouldn't be right to hallow this transformative work of Hill's too highly. The luminous implications of this change filled the poet just as readily with agitation and morbidity as with a light of understanding. What looked new to the work at the time and continues to amplify in it is an expansive sense of humor. Beyond this, as perplexing as it is refreshing, Hill in the poetry in this trilogy of books is concerned with metaphysics, theology, law, ethics, sacred history, and the general worldview; in short, it is a prophetic vision. In his irascible essay "Of Diligence and Jeopardy," in which he berates the editor of Yale's edition of Tyndale's New Testament for not abiding by the original spelling, Hill admits "a sense of jarring, of discomfort, as things naturally inherent in the common processes of endurance and endeavor, belongs to a different, outmoded, order of understanding," one he finds echoed in Tyndale's own warning to his readers: "Count it as a thynge not havynge his full shape / but as it were borne afore hys tyme / even as a thi[n]g begunne rather then fynnesshed."[42] To this outmoded order of understanding, with its jarring language and its eruptions of vile humor, Hill directs his energies, even as he believes the self-knowledge it will yield him is a thing begun rather than finished. What impresses, then, in the poetry Hill began to create at this time is the way he transforms his self-knowledge into a visionary knowledge through an act of poetic confession, a move that allows him to sponsor personal information in his poems through a kind of openness—the openness of making mistakes, or errors.

Confession is a too, too sullied word in poetry. One little-used understanding of the act of confession is not that of tell-all but rather as sacrament. In confession, we admit to the sacred reality in which we dwell. Philip Sherrard, in his essay "Presuppositions of the Sacred," insists: "We cannot talk about the sacred without presupposing God, just as we cannot talk about sunlight without presupposing the sun, however many mirrors it may be reflected in. Moreover, God is not the principle—the original cause—of all making sacred. He alone is sacred."[43] In Hill's poetry, confession is similarly an act in the arcanum of language, conducted in the confessional that is language, affording him direct speech to God. The word *confession* comes from the Latin root *fatum*, an utterance, to which the intensive prefix *con-* is added. In this sense, to confess is closer to how we understand *testify*, as in to bear witness. As a way of demonstrating what I mean by confession and its relation to the transformation of self-knowledge into iconic knowledge, I want to take a look at some lines from one of the later inclusions in *The Orchards of Syon*, section 45.

Much of the questioning and self-reflection that concerns Hill in *The Orchards of Syon* is addressed in this twenty-four-line poem. I don't take the sequence of this book to be progressive in the same manner that both *The Triumph of Love* and *Speech! Speech!* are. Rather, *The Orchards of Syon* follows more of a spiral pattern, such that its themes repeat (somewhat obsessively) but also deepen as the poem proceeds. Forty-five begins with emceeing that quickly turns into a series of surprising pronouncements:

> Listen, Meister Eckhart is here, ready
> and eager to tell us his great news:
> that we caught aright the revelatory
> scream from the carrousel; that there's a divine
> presence in destitution; that yes, we loved

> bright Harry Heine and Frank O'Hara
> as more than passing attractions when
> *I pass* was the catch-phrase and they unheard of;
> that the heavy residues from easy loving
> render us breathless.

Meister Eckhart, Heinrich Heine, Frank O'Hara. Even James Merrill's dreams of the afterworld don't include these three. Meister Eckhart, spokesman for this section of the poem, is above all the confessor of the *via negativa*, on which an aspirant employs *apophasis*, or unsaying, which Michael A. Sells defines as what happens when the effort to affirm transcendence leads to "a propositionally unstable and dynamic discourse in which no single statement can rest on its own as true or false, or even as meaningful."[44] As such, Eckhart denies transcendence even while achieving it in the intuitive suspension of his language in regressive acts of unsaying. While Eckhart is no poster boy for the Negative Way in Hill's poem, he is its figure of utterance, or confession. This leads Hill to assert, "The topos / of the whole is gratitude," which he follows by alluding to Rilke's own visitation by the spirit (of language): "Duino's / cliff-hanger we witnessed, and its consummation." Yet here, rather than flying off into a rhetorical exchange with the better (or worse) angels of his nature, Hill transforms the ironizing voice of the beginning of this section into plangent waves of lulling truths:

> Wait, I've not finished. A radical
> otherness, as it's called, answers
> to its own voices: that there should be
> language, rituals, weddings, and wedding-nights,
> and tapes which spin fast forward, stop, reverse;
> that there is even now hawthorn, this bush
> pregnant with the wild scent and taint of sex;
> that there áre men and women, destinies
> interlocked; and dying, and resurrection.[45]

Less rhapsodes, Heine and O'Hara stand as poetic realists, or at least as poets unafraid to explore the world on the carousel of their poetry, rather than the metaphysical realities (or the wars and conflicts over which we brood) that have so preoccupied Hill's earlier poetry. Even Meister

Eckhart is meant to speak not as angelic messenger but as a pointer to the Negative Way, which, in Hill's case, is back to the world. In section 47, Hill elaborates:

> Come down from your high
> thrones of question, good doctors of wisdom.
> Now Í am at ground level and must grope,
> whereas the blinded archangel stands clear
> on his chance tottering ledge.[46]

Hill requires high ideas to enable his rhetoric, but he wants them down in the gutter of his thought. Even the Orchards of Syon are manured: "In the skeletal / Orchard of Syon are flowers / long vanished; I will consult their names."[47] When he does so, he discovers deciduous hawthorn bushes, whose spring flowers bear the musk of sex. And in the funk of the wilting hawthorn petals, Hill senses fecundation, in his dying and resurrection. The confession here is this: in poetry as I die so am I risen. My destiny in it is interlocked. It's also, not incidentally, an admission that confessional poetry can be humorous; optimally, morbidly funny.

ITE, MISSA EST

To repeat: All religious poetry addresses religious language, even as it arises out of such speech. Ideology, faith, discernment, revelation: if turned to verse, these become adornments of religious language. English should be reckoned as one of the greatest proselytizing languages in human history. English was calcified, ensinewed, and muscularized in the Wycliffe-sponsored New Testament, then a century and a half later in Tyndale's majestic one-man show, for which he was burned. Even today, the most beautiful, most majestic writing in English, into which Tyndale's versions are almost wholly absorbed, is the Authorized Version, or the King James Bible, as we commonly call it. The muscle of our tongue is rooted in dewy, disobedient Genesis, shaped by covenant and Law, flexed in prophetic utterance, and then is pressed against the teeth of crucifixion to clap against the roof of apocalypse.

Hill's embedding of his recent verse projects in scriptural language, dangled as they are with epithets taken from scripture, is not accidental. Nor is the fruition of this project in a book entitled *The Orchard of Syon* happenstance: *The Orcherd* of the Brigettines, as mentioned above, paved the way for Wycliffe and then Tyndale. And while it might be overstepping the bounds of argument to suggest that English—like, say, Hebrew or Sanskrit—is in fact a religious language, it isn't to suggest its most compelling momentums and idioms arise from a religious gravity. When Hill began, putting to paper the lines of his poem "Genesis," he set out to be a religious poet. That, at last, and not even ironically, he became, through a process of shedding his formerly brooding British self-knowledge for a more eagerly embraced iconic knowledge, arrived at through an American therapy, still brooding, but now in the sense of gestating. Just so, contemplative and self-rectifying, to himself while he was alive and now to his readers as we marvel at the great stack of work he has left behind for us to consider.

4

PROPHETIC FRUSTRATIONS

Robert Duncan's *Tribunals*

I CAN'T UNDO THE GRIEVOUS HUMAN SITUATION

As a poet, Robert Duncan could be ferocious. His commitment to poetry was so complete and his ideas about poetry were so high-minded, he demonstrated a habit during his life of lashing out against those who he believed in their own work and thought endangered his ideal of what poetry is and thus diminished the value of the art. As often as not, the objects of his attacks were friends, most notably the poet Robin Blaser, a key figure in the formation of the legendary Berkeley Renaissance and with whose translations of the French symbolist Gérard de Nerval Duncan took serious issue, and the poet Denise Levertov, with whom Duncan had an avid correspondence but whose political views, which practically aligned with his own, he disagreed with nevertheless. Onto both poets Duncan spilled his vitriol. Vitriol refers to sulfates of metals used in alchemy. Vitriol is caustic; its purpose is to degrade another compound. Duncan's vitriol was belittling. What would compel him to destroy important friendships? One answer is that for Duncan poetry is a cosmic act, as much a vocation as an art. In the first chapter of *The H.D. Book*, Duncan wrote:

> The authority of the poet was a voice of the spirit. To be a poet meant an even fanatic allegiance to a vision or dream, in order that there be Poetry. Men commonly spoke a vision or dream with mistrust. . . . A

> poet must follow his own ideas or feelings wherever they led. In a way, instead of having ideas or feelings, the poet lets ideas or feelings "have" *him*. Seized by an idea.[1]

The capitalization of "Poetry" in the second sentence is characteristic of Duncan's attitude.

For Duncan, the poet is a kind of prophet, seized into service like the oracle at Delphi or Isaiah before the command of God. This role he connects both to myth, which is a cosmic, holy plot, and *dromenon*, which is a form of ritual play. The poet attends principally to the compulsions of both these powers; when the poet strays, he commits something like heresy. In "Rites of Participation," one of the core chapters in *The H.D. Book*, which is Duncan's compendious reading of literary modernism in English through the lenses of myth, esoteric truth, and psychoanalysis, Duncan insists:

> The power of the poet is to translate experience from daily time where the world and ourselves pass away as we go on into the future, from the journalistic record, into a melodic coherence in which words—sounds, meanings, images, voices—do not pass away or exist by themselves but are kept by rime to exist everywhere in the consciousness of the poem. The art of the poem, like the mechanism of the dream or the intent of the tribal myth and dromena, is a cathexis: to keep present and immediate a variety of times and places, persons and events. In the melody we make, the possibility of eternal life is hidden, and experience we thought lost returns to us.[2]

Later in this essay, first published in 1967 but written earlier in the 1960s, Duncan alludes to the predestined election that endows poets with powers of a Freudian hermeneutic to allow them "in their vision—to keep the dream of 'everyone, everywhere.'" "The very heightened sense of the relatedness of everything," continues Duncan, "sets poets apart. The very secret of the impulse in poetry is the troubled awareness the poet has of meanings in the common language everywhere that those about him do not see or do not consider so important."[3] These statements from "Rites of Participation" are characteristic of Duncan's prophetic, cathectic vision of poetry—which generates attachments of ideas and language to meanings both hidden and revealed. At the core of his poetry is a prophetic understanding of language and vision whose authority he holds sacrosanct, even as it risked destroying crucial friendships.

His vision of poetry came to its fullest expression in the late 1960s, when he composed the "Passages" that belong to the series of poems he named *Tribunals*. Of the *Tribunals*, the broadest, most complete expression of his prophetic powers is the poem "Before the Judgment, Passages 35." *Tribunals* was first published in a deluxe edition by John Martin's Black Sparrow Press in 1970. This was a book object that famously infuriated Duncan, contributing to the vow of publication silence he took—not publishing another book of new poetry until 1984, when *Ground Work: Before the War* was issued by New Directions.[4] That these events are sequential is worth attending to. But are they consequential? Did Duncan enter into his silence because he was so frustrated with the way his work was being published, or was this in a sense an inevitable decision on his part, arising from deeper poetic concerns his publication problems merely alluded to?

Three statements by Duncan in letters to Denise Levertov from the late 1960s and early 1970s suggest the tensions at work in Duncan's thought during this period of intense political and creative anxiety for him, tensions that reinforced his consternation about his poetry publications. On August 30, 1966, speaking of the way he perceived U.S. policy in Southeast Asia—a point of significant concern for both him and Levertov, whose son Nik was of draft age—Duncan wrote:

> It struck me this morning that what has been impending in "Passages" and I don't know when or how it will emerge at the level of the poem's content is—that the Vietnam war is a stripping away of pretense and hypocrisy from the social order in which we live and a showing forth of the true face. As, in the Bible the joy in the catastrophic rings true because a wish is made evident.[5]

The "Passages" Duncan is imagining in this letter are the core, prophetic inclusions in the sequence of *Bending the Bow*: "The Fire, Passages 13," "The Multiversity, Passages 21," "Up Rising, Passages 25," and "The Soldiers, Passages 26." All four of these poems are directly concerned with the war in Vietnam and its consequences in the United States. In intuiting the content of these poems to Levertov, he is beginning to articulate the sense that "Strife"—in a Heraclitean sense—plays in his work, a notion that War is as revelatory a state in the imagination as peace or well-being. "'War is both King of all and Father of all,' Heraclitus says. Among poets throughout the world or within any nation, men are at war, even deadly war, with each other concerning the nature and responsibility of poetry."[6] This is how Duncan begins his essay "Man's Fulfillment in Order and Strife," which he wrote in 1968. In another statement, written to Levertov on February 26, 1970, Duncan apologizes to her for the way he attacked Hayden Carruth—a friend of Levertov's whom she deemed too psychically fragile to withstand Duncan's vehemence—stating, "I can't undo the grievous human situation," a paraphrase of sorts for "what's done is done," even as he expresses regret for the way he treated Carruth. (Duncan wrote an essay severely criticizing Carruth's understanding of William Carlos Williams's poetry as expressed in a review Carruth had published in *Poetry* in 1964.)[7] But he follows his apology with the draft of a statement he imagined might justify his vitriol, writing: "There are times when my own views regarding the nature and meaning of poetic form flash forth with an intolerance that betokens remnants of the Puritan bigot in me, whipping the poor would-be heretic anthologist or critic publicly in the stock or driving him forth from the covenant of the righteous into the wilderness."[8] In this statement to Levertov, Duncan is alluding to an act of protest, which he regarded as a form of witness, which he undertook during the stressful time of the war in Vietnam. He had taken to wearing a peace button on a reading tour, so that people would ask him what it meant, giving him the opportunity to profess his antiwar views. But even this kind of protest was inadequate to the poetic tasks he felt were at hand. Explaining himself, he wrote: "Even 'Up Rising' is not this kind of witness; for ultimately it belongs to the reality of that poem and a vision of Man. And I do not answer for myself in my work but for Poetry."[9]

All of these statements, which are utterly characteristic of Duncan, suggest a triangular tension that is articulated—sometimes strenuously—in Duncan's poetic work from this period. This is especially true of *Tribunals*, which can be regarded as a culmination of the forces manifesting themselves in these statements. In one corner of the triangle, there is war, or War, as he frequently writes it, which shows to us a true face of our social order. On October 4, 1971, Duncan wrote to Levertov: "THERE HAS BEEN NO TIME IN HUMAN HISTORY THAT WAS NOT A TIME OF WAR."[10] There is the sense, then, that the Vietnam War was revelatory to

Duncan, showing him an irrefutable truth of the nature of reality, not aside from but consonant with the suffering and agony that war wrought on its combatants as well as those, like Duncan and Levertov, who protested the war at home. In the second corner of the triangle, there is Duncan's anger—the flashing forth of intolerance—that is connected directly to the publication of poetry or ideas about that poetry. Duncan's anger toward Carruth is a smaller instance of a larger tendency to respond to what he perceives as poets' betrayals of poetry by attacking them publicly. The two most catastrophic such confrontations Duncan staged, as already mentioned, were against Robin Blaser, for his translations of Gérard de Nerval's "Chimères," and against Levertov, over her use of the Vietnam War in her poetry, which resulted in the dissolution of their friendship.[11] We also witness this flashing forth of intolerance by Duncan in his response to John Martin's publication of *Tribunals* with Black Sparrow, a minor squabble that seems a tremor to a more catastrophic quaking of Duncan's poetic self.

The third corner of the triangle, which is related intrinsically to the other two, is the notion that poetry—as an equivalently prophetic mode of discourse—is inviolate and inviolable, such that he can say to Levertov that he does not answer for himself in his work but for Poetry. He is a messenger, a transmitter of Poetry's true face, which is revealed in Order and Strife just as it ought to be transparent in its published form. Duncan's attitude reminds me of an analogy from Islam, in which the place of the Quran is similarly inviolate and inviolable. Muslims hold that the principal miracle of Islam is the revelation of the Quran to Muhammad over the course of twenty-one years in the seventh century CE. Furthermore, when making analogies to the salvific nature of Christianity, Muslim scholars have proposed that while Muhammad and Christ both represent exemplary types as the foundational figures of their religions, the truer analogy is that as Christ is to Christians, so the Quran is to Muslims—that the Quran is the way through which salvation is attained. In Islam, the Quran's salvation is only available in its Arabic form; translations are invariably understood as interpretations. The inviolability of the Quran extends to its transmission and publication: in order for a new edition of the Quran to be published, it must be checked meticulously by a scribe whose sole purpose is to ensure that none of the Arabic is misplaced, distorted, or misread. Each edition of the Quran in Arabic bears a seal attesting to its lack of blemishes, amounting to a book-by-book imprimatur.[12] Duncan's position toward poetry—or Poetry—is surprisingly consonant with this Muslim view toward the Quran. That he felt violations against poetry as a blasphemy is not, therefore, surprising. The question worth asking is how personally he took these violations. Was Duncan pursuing a grander vision of poetry in his flashings forth against Blaser, Levertov, or John Martin, the publisher of *Tribunals* with Black Sparrow Press? Or were these evidences of a more deeply entrenched personal anxiety—one that would be expressed (as in "squeezed out under pressure") in his anger over the way his publications were handled?

The publication of *Tribunals* in 1970 serves as a heuristic viewpoint from which to understand this triangular tension—of War, Anger, and Poetry—in Duncan's work. Duncan found himself furious with the way his poems were laid out in this edition. Was it typesetting and orthography that really provoked such ire in Duncan? He felt his burgeoning prophetic powers betrayed by the misrepresentative laying out of his poems in this edition of *Tribunals*. The transparent content of his prophecy is a broadly issued condemnation of the American government and culture in its pursuit of war in Vietnam, treated—as it ever is in Duncan—in the light of a highly allusive mythopoetic reading of the present. George Butterick, in one of the earliest reviews of *Ground Work: Before the War*, wrote, "I am of an age that I cannot read 'Before the Judgment,' for example, and not feel the old surge of righteousness in my veins, my body alive in an all-stage alert, morally armed. . . . [*Tribunals*] were poems that gave focus and legitimacy to our feelings, that gave leadership—when poets could still command audiences of thousands, by authority of their words."[13] I think we can take such a contemporaneous reaction to this poetry as in kind with Duncan's intentions. Butterick is feeling the force of Duncan's prophecy, responding to its vigilance, and even allowing himself to imagine a blessèd time when poets gathered vast audiences over whom they felt their influence radiate and project. A powerful poetry this was, to say the least. What, then, is the content of this prophecy, and why was its manhandling by a printer so upsetting to the poet?

BAD FAITH: COMPOSING AND PRINTING *TRIBUNALS*

Readers of Duncan's poetry, both fans and detractors, have confronted the difficulties of Duncan's typographic imperative in the New Directions edition of *Ground Work: Before the War*, from 1984, "typeset" almost entirely in the Courier font of his IBM Selectric. On his blog and elsewhere, Ron Silliman, for instance, has argued that the physical ugliness of this edition has prevented many a reader from entering the poetry.[14] Duncan's dictates on the typesetting of this book can act as a visual fortress, as barbed wire the reader needs to crawl under to get to the poetry. For a book with many of my very favorite Duncan poems, it's certainly my least-favorite-looking of his books. On October 4, 1971, a year or so after the publication of *Tribunals*, Duncan declared to Levertov:

> I've been typing the first volume of the H.D. Book for publication, having decided to issue it at this stage in typescript edition. I have come to dread printed publications—I've had such bad luck with proof-reading and with faulty printers. And now I have it to issue all first editions from my typewriter straight off. Where any errors will be my own. Coercion has always seemed to me the only true evil; and it's a form of coercion to rage against what somebody else does to one's copy when right at hand is the means to do said copy for oneself.[15]

Duncan's determination here suggests to me less that he had a command or grasp of what's involved in typesetting than that he understood his raging against his printers and typesetters was misplaced, leading him to coercive arguments that themselves were disobedient to Poetry.[16] By appropriating the means of his poetry's (and prose's) production for himself, he intended to circumvent his tendency to "rage against what somebody else does," a persuasion that defies the prophetic permission he obtains from Poetry in the first place. Typing his poetry and then distributing it allowed Duncan to reassert his priorities.

The decision to mutiny against typesetters and to take over this work himself follows directly from the controversy of the publication of *Tribunals: Passages 31–35* by Black Sparrow Press in 1970; these poems are among the first in the chronologically arranged *Ground Work: Before the War*. Those who acquired one of the 250 hardcover editions of *Tribunals* were given a first public glimpse at the trouble brewing in Duncan's imagination. Included in this edition, in a pocket glued onto the back cover, was a stapled booklet entitled "Robert Duncan, *The Feast: Passages 34*" and subtitled "Facsimile of the holograph notebook and of final typescript." An introductory note to this pamphlet, dated November 1970, asserts: "The printer's work, where the poet himself is not the printer, is an extension of the author's intention; the typed copy, where the poet works in typing, is the realized statement of those intensions."[17] That Duncan was an adherent to the School of Typing is no surprise, beholden as he was to Charles Olson's notions of projective page space, illuminated in "Projective Verse." That Duncan worked for a period as a typist only reaffirms his vocational involvement with the typewriter. In the booklet's introduction, Duncan describes how the typewriter allows him to surpass the handwritten drafts of his poems in his notebooks, such that the machine virtually collaborates in the composition of the new draft, creating new developments in the poems, thanks to the special "spacings and relationships" generated on the page. The typescript, then, per Olson's idea, becomes the "score" of the poem, as close as a reader can get to its essence, barring a performance of the score by a skilled reader. One of the interesting revelations in his letters to Levertov is the way both poets shared their work with each other, almost always in typed manuscript. They traded them back and forth, creating copies with carbons (much of their sharing occurred before the advent of the photocopier), frequently typing out the work of others they received (especially Creeley's work). They both seem frequently disaffected by seeing each others' poems in book form, preferring to read the work in typescript.

The development from typescript to typography in Duncan's mind represents not an advance but a regression through refinement, thus a problem. In the pamphlet included with *Tribunals*, he writes, "the printed version . . . subject to close-space conventions of modern printing, in striving for a homogenized density of type on the page against open spaces, rides over decisions that appear in the typed version as notations of the music of the poem, minute silences in the space after a comma or a period."[18] A serious, if idiosyncratic, concern, but one that betrays Duncan's problematic understanding of the relationship between analphabetic characters (periods, commas, and dashes, for instance) and text. Similarly confusing is Duncan's dismissal of the development of typography over several hundreds of years in the West, a tradition, owing to its origins in Western religious and Renaissance culture, toward which you would imagine Duncan would be very sympathetic. The subtlest, most nuanced evolutions in type are among the analphabetic characters, which give print and aesthetic eras so much of their character. As the poet and typesetter Robert Bringhurst, in *The Elements of Typographic Style*, asserts: "Punctuation is cold notation; it is not frustrated speech; it is typographic code."[19] Duncan's critique of the printed version of his poems in Black Sparrow's *Tribunals* voices above all his frustration at not seeing his prophetic "speech" reproduced in the typesetting of his book.

In the printed text of the introductory note for the inserted booklet to *Tribunals*, its publisher, John Martin, had the parenthetic phrase "(though not this printed version)" inserted in Duncan's phrase "the printed version . . . subject to close-space conventions of modern printing," further infuriating the poet, who called it an "unauthorized amendment of my text."[20] The booklet itself is a holograph of Duncan's notebook, in which his poem "The Feast" arises out of his handwritten improvising of phrases and sentences, followed by a carefully typewritten version of the poem that translates the notebook into typescript before our eyes.[21] As an artifact, this booklet is as astonishing as it is pleasing: a chance for the reader to track a poem from handwritten origin to typeset fruition. The dissonance the booklet emits, however, is something belatedly attended to: Only upon the publication of *Ground Work: Before the War*, with its own typewritten version of "The Feast," do we have the chance to compare the version typeset by Saul Marks for Black Sparrow—and then to realize that not only is Marks's typesetting fastidious to the intentions of Duncan's poem, but that it attains the ideal goal of all typesetting; namely, in Bringhurst's words, that "typography . . . is idealized writing" and that the satisfactions of its craft come from "elucidating, and perhaps even ennobling, the text."[22] In his typesetting not only of "The Feast" but of the rest of *Tribunals*, Marks honors Duncan's lines with generously wide pages, good margins, and an abiding sense of the pace of Duncan's poetry, visible in the use of leading between lines and stanzas as well as the ample caesurae found throughout the volume.

Duncan nonetheless railed against this act, focusing his rage on what he believed to be the too-small spacing between letters and the commas or periods following them. (In typesetting, this spacing falls in the category of proportional letterspacing and kerning, which is the taking into account of letters' slopes to generate a harmonious-looking page.) In his preface to *MAPS 6*, the journal John Taggart edited in the 1970s, beginning an issue devoted entirely to his work, Duncan inveighs against both Martin and Marks:

> Nor was I wrong in my sense of [their] bad faith. When all was done, as the reader turning to *TRIBUNALS* can verify, on the first page we find the copy unchanged from that earliest galley proof sent in August, some four months before. Correction, and pointed out especially, and corrected and argued again, there, unrepentant, are the printer's stubborn settings of the lines:
>
> a severd *distinct* thing;and the stars also
>
> and
>
> in the influences of the stars,as it pleaseth.
>
> The all-important articulations between movements of *Passages 33* are to the last sacrificed to Saul Mark's [*sic*] dislike of the look of blank spaces marring his page and to the publisher's contempt for what he takes to be the author's fussy discriminations.[23]

Duncan then proceeds to vent his spleen in this preface against the issue of *MAPS* that Taggart was preparing for the poet. Taggart, owing to budget constraints, was unable to provide Duncan with proofs for correction; nor for the same reason could he agree to allow Duncan to provide typescripts that would be reproduced in the magazine. Duncan only reluctantly agreed to allow his poems and notes to be typeset in the issue after Taggart phoned to assure him that everything would be as carefully proofread as humanly possible. Even so, Duncan was dissatisfied enough to devote his entire preface to the justification of the use of his typewriter.

Duncan's profusion of frustration with typesetting, in his "Preface, prepared for *MAPS #6*," published in 1974, authorized his new-book silence. A decade later, he published *Ground Work: Before the War* with New Directions. Moreover, the physical appearance of that volume is visual evidence of Duncan's frustration. The history of self-published or self-designed poetry in English is long and complicated; Duncan's contribution to this lineage offers nothing surprising (even at the level of using the typewriter), at least not in comparison to, say, Blake's illuminated prophetic books or to Whitman's 1855 *Leaves of Grass*. What it does indicate, however—in visual relation to the rest of Duncan's printed poetry—is that something about the content and the materiality of the poems in this volume is so important that Duncan felt only his own publication of the work would satisfy its message. The material force of this prophecy is felt first and fullest in this volume in the soaring, difficult lines of its most ambitious poem, "Before the Judgment, *Passages* 35."

LURKING IN THE HEART: DUNCAN'S PROPHETIC MANTLE

In "The Concert," *Passages* 31, Duncan uses a definition of prophecy as a point of departure:

> "Prophecy,
>
> which uncovers the mystery of future events
> but which also reveals what lurks in the heart
> —prayers . . . song and especially ecstatic
> speaking in tongues"
>
> They shout, leaping upon the tables,
> outpouring vitalities, stammering—[24]

Prophecy in poetry is not a telling of the future; rather, it is an expression of present necessities free of mediation. As Duncan indicates, historically and culturally, prophecy has been perceived as a kind of ecstasy, uttered by prophets from altered states of consciousness. To speak of Duncan as a prophet is to try to understand what is prophetic in poetry as well as to determine the nature of prophecy itself. For Duncan, prophecy is what arises from a conscientious, vigilant answering for Poetry. He takes this in part to be a visionary state, but more importantly it is an incantational rising up through the levels of poetic insight into an aural and lexical Platonic realm, one that is ever present but invisible and inaudible to most of us because we lack in our consciousness the melodic coherence in which words do not pass away. The prophet in poetry is one who keeps the poem present.

This is as difficult to fathom as it is grand in scope. There's an enclaved, hieratic sense to Duncan's understanding of poetry as prophecy, an understanding that a skeptical reader might well dismiss as esoteric cultishness. How do we place a prophetic sense of poetry in the context of Duncan's aggravations, making his position clearer to us? The poet Lew Daly, in conceiving of a belated prophetic tradition in American poetry, proposes the necessity of "a combative poetics of decision before the tribunal of spiritual force."[25] Daly speaks of the recovery, through a prophetic poetry, of "news of a power beyond the reach of mediators, and, unlike politics, unmanipulatable at the level of language, like dictation in the Prophets is."[26] Daly regards the unmediated, untampered quality of such poetry as proof of its covenantal, consecrated nature—not that it defies published speech or politics but that in its catastrophic austerity, it rectifies these things:

> With the incursion, in public, of a specifically auditory character of revelation and therefore of divinity, as manifested among the classical prophets of the Bible, coincided a kind of dehiscence in the meeting-point of history and the infinite, which is the point at which the very principle of public prophecy indeed re-covenanted, as historicity itself, the word of God in absolutizing ethics and the sacrifice of self.[27]

In other words, the biblical prophets, in bursting open the word of God, transformed the act of listening into one of covenant, binding the eternal promise of God to the time in which this truth is first heard (perpetuating it eternally). Thus, a bursting-forth of prophetic speech has the power of commanding subservience. It is into such a sense of time and word that Duncan utters his poems.

To Daly's sense of a prophetic poetry, I am inclined to add a hermeneutical sense of prophecy as imagined by Moshe Idel in *Absorbing Perfections*, his vast analysis of language and its arcanization in Kabbalah. In that work, Idel makes a telling distinction between prophetic experience and the prophetic intellect, suggesting that while experience must necessarily always have authority in matters of spiritual authenticity, it is the imagination (which he calls the "emanated intellect") that allows for the insights that permit experience to thrive:

> Knowledge of the inner aspects of the Torah is conditioned on the attainment of the highest intellectual faculty, the prophetic intellect,

> which is seen as tantamount to prophetic experience. Understanding the secrets is a function of blurring the gap between God as intellect and the human intellect; the latter acquires a divine, holy intellect, which is the sine qua non for fathoming the secrets of the Torah. The Pentateuch, a text thought to have been written under divine inspiration, can only be properly understood by re-creating an appropriate state of consciousness.[28]

In this light, I suggest Duncan's poems of this period of the late 1960s are best understood as vehicles for re-creating an appropriate state of consciousness, one in which the truth of Poetry is made clear (I believe it is the poetry's regeneration of this state in the reader to which Butterick was responding in his review of *Ground Work: Before the War*). For Duncan, the poem at its core is both inviolable and unmanipulable. The ambiguity that this position inspires in the poet, however, is one of utmost anxiety. Indeed, for Duncan, poetry is the vocalization of Poetry's sacral, prophetic truth and his simultaneous anxiety that his truth is being compromised in the poetry itself, or even by poets (as with Blaser and Levertov). And into this snare, Duncan's publishers regularly stumbled.

That the prophetic frustration driving Duncan's poetry is fixated on the *made* quality of poetry, its very wroughtness, is perhaps Duncan's novel contribution to a definition of prophecy, one apprehended even as he was beginning to envision the project of *Passages*. "Before the Judgment" marks out a deliberately juridical setting, but one not fixated on condemnation so much as asserting our belatedness, in standing, always as we do, both *after* and *behind* the Judgment we witness. Duncan's poem constructs its vision of the present out of four distinct literary references meshed into the backdrop of the Vietnam War. Passages from Dante's Malebolge cantos of the *Inferno*, in both Italian and English, mark our progress through the Hell of war. Similarly, Pound's "Hell" Cantos (XIV and XV) provide invective vocabulary, allowing Duncan to invoke as well the Hydra of Usura, a hybrid figure of the apocalyptic Book of Revelation and Pound's rage. But perhaps the most striking, because most mythologically strange, inclusion in the poem is Duncan's frequent references to passages from Hesiod's *Works and Days* that describe the beings who lived during a Golden Age now lost to us, referred to throughout "Before the Judgment, Passages 35" as "Golden Ones." In one of the most vivid moments in the poem, Duncan writes:

For they go about everywhere over the earth,

attendant, daimons not only of men but of earth's plenitudes,
ancestral spirits of whatever good we know,

wherever judgment is made they gather round watching,
what the heart secretly knows they know,

clothed in mist, golden, ever existing, the host that comes in to conscience,

deathless they swarm in Memory and feed at the honeycomb.[29]

Duncan proceeds to refer to these daimonic beings by their Hesiodic epithet: *epichthonoi*, or "spirits of the earth," later in the poem calling them "the Golden Ones," hearkening to the "Age of Gold" in which they emerged and the "Ancestral Design" that forged them. Duncan's "Golden Ones" serve as emblems of the lost covenant, of the speech vanished with their assumption into a ghostlier existence. They exist, on the one hand, as proof of the certainty of his prophecy but, on the other, as reproof of its inherent failure because they are mute to the world that cannot hear them or understand their wisdom. Their swarming in the honeycomb of memory is as vital as it is entombed, only faint buzzings in our unconscious.

Hesiod's reference to the "Age of Gold" as well as to the Heroic Age, the Age of Silver, and down through a line of metallic degenerations results in part from his desire to situate himself and the divinities populating his imagination properly, especially in relation to the Homeric epics. The idea of an idyllic past corrupted is as central to the biblical tradition as it is the Greek mythological tradition. The difference is that in the biblical tradition we are given two stories of failure: the disobedience of Eve and Adam, followed by the miscegenation of angels and human women, resulting in the propagation of the *nephilim*, the grasshopper-legged race of giants whom God felt the need to eradicate from creation.[30] In the Hesiodic tradition, these *epichthonoi* are indeed golden, a brief shining moment in divine-human relations. But gold is a color of loss in this poetry. Hesiod, in *Works and Days*, describes:

> First of all the deathless gods who dwell on Olympus made a golden race of mortal men who lived in the time of Cronos when he was reigning in heaven. And they lived like gods without sorrow of heart, remote and free from toil and grief: miserable age rested not on them; but with legs and arms never failing they made merry with feasting beyond the reach of all evils. When they died, it was as though they were overcome with sleep, and they had all good things. . . . But after earth had covered this generation—they are called pure spirits dwelling on the earth, and are kindly, delivering from harm, and guardians of mortal men; for they roam everywhere over the earth, clothed in mist and keep watch on judgements and cruel deeds, givers of wealth . . .[31]

Following the Golden Ones come the people of the Silver Age. Hesiod's poem is, then, not so much a chronicle of generations and creative mistakes, as in Genesis, but rather a record of degeneration, of the fall from Olympian communion and perfection to the war and strife of the Iron Age in which Hesiod found himself. Like Hesiod, Duncan looks from war and strife back to a golden time, not to persuade himself of an Edenic past but to assert his conviction that only through war and strife is the revelation of a Golden Age visible, that "the catastrophic rings true because a wish is made evident," as he wrote to Levertov in 1966.

Duncan surrounds this mythos of the Golden Ones in his poem with pointed references to Dante's progress through Malebolge, quoting passages in both Italian and English, to register his profound discomfort with the evil he feels encroaching into him through Vietnam and the political actions and protests in the Bay Area in the late 1960s. "Before the Judgment" begins, memorably:

> Discontent with that first draft.   Where one's own
>   hatred enters   Hell   gets out of hand.
>
> Again and again   Virgil   ever standing by Dante
>   must caution him.   In Malebolge

where the deep violation begins,

Mentr' io laggiu fissamente mirava,
lo duca mio, dicendo "Guarda, guarda"[32]

The first lines are crucial toward understanding the anxiety and chaos this poem generates for Duncan. "Discontent" is malcontent, thus an informing evil (and a nod to Dis, who reigns in the underworld). His sense of failure in the first draft (with its pun on military conscription) is an admission to or an intuition of an evil, a chaos—through whose opening his own hatred has entered—a mean-spirited coerciveness. It has gotten out of hand because the writing hand, the instrument of a prophetic consciousness, has let it—was obliged to let it—slip through. Thus Virgil's warning to Dante in the "evil pockets" (*Malebolge*) reverberates in Duncan's ear: *Guarda, guarda.* These last lines translate: "The while below there fixedly I gazed, / My Leader, crying out: 'Beware, beware!'"[33] This caution leads Duncan into a visionary catalogue of the horrors of the deep violation: the immolation of fields, forests, and villages with Agent Orange in Vietnam and the greed of oil barons whose "smoking tankers crawl toward Asia," leading him to quote again from Dante:

men with fossil minds, with oily tongues
"to lick the mirror of Narkissos"[34]

In *Inferno* 30, Master Adam, the counterfeiter suffering from dropsy, chides Sinon the fevered perjurer, who is so thirsty he desires to lick the mirror of Narcissus, which Robert Hollander informs us "would thus reflect Sinon's true hideous self, one he would destroy in the thirst of his fever."[35]

Similarly, Duncan punctures his prophecy with harangues and insults against figures in the Bay Area political scrums of the Vietnam protest movements, including San Francisco's mayor Joseph Alioto, who oversaw the city during the student strikes of 1968 and who officially nominated Hubert Humphrey for president at the infamous 1968 Democratic National Convention in Chicago; Samuel I. Hayakawa, a professor of education who was brought in as president to manage the rapidly deteriorating student strike at San Francisco State in 1968 after its president,

John Summerskill, was forced to resign in the wake of the strike and the creation of a Black Student Union; the Yippies' cofounder Jerry Rubin; as well as Nixon and Reagan. Much as in "Up Rising," these figures are represented as archons, emblematic of a "deep violation," the evil from which we need protection in the care of the Golden Ones. Duncan says of these figures, "as we go upwards the stupidity thickens, / reflections in the oil slick multiplied."[36] One can understand Duncan's loathing of Nixon and Reagan, as well perhaps of Alioto or even Hayakawa. But Jerry Rubin's presence deserves some analysis. Rubin and his fellow prankster Abbie Hoffman belong less to a political action group than to an artistic tradition of the absurd. The stunts of Rubin and the Yippies—like running a pig for office—had much more in common with Dada, surrealism, and actionism than with Sacco and Vanzetti or the Haymarket. Their quest was the exposure of meaninglessness in public settings. To this type of "art"—let alone demagogic politics—Duncan was extremely antipathetic, as his letters to Levertov make clear. He frequently chides Allen Ginsberg and his fellow Beats for the poetic stunts they regularly pulled. And there's a sense that his disappointment in Levertov stemmed from his perception that she too was pulling a stunt in an effort to avoid inspecting her feelings toward the war. Thus he has Kali—the Hindu goddess of war and chaos—stand for Levertov in his "Santa Cruz Propositions."[37]

Speaking of Thoreau, Lewis Hyde suggests that the purpose of prophecy is to "induce in us that second sight by which we see the workings of an invisible world."[38] This accords with Duncan's argument that through prophetic poetry, "in the melody we make, the possibility of eternal life is hidden, and experience we thought lost returns to us."[39] Duncan's hostility is increased by what he perceives to be the blindness of the participants in the world affairs that so anger him, events he strives to reconceive through a vast project of interiorizing his vision. Duncan's process of understanding such events, then, is analogous to what happens to a person in mourning, in terms of Freud's formulation, who desperately tries to connect to the memories—or "golden" ghosts—of lost "objects": people, places, ideas. The failure of our vision infuriates him, inspiring his affection for the hidden, Golden Ones mournfully watching over him and the world. To these Golden Ones he commends both our care and his prophecy, for only they have eyes to see truly what Duncan witnesses. Like the Hidden Imam of Shi'i Islam, Duncan's Golden Ones slumber in a spiritual reality simultaneous with our own, into which they emit pulsations of knowledge, frequencies of judgment, which we might only dimly perceive in our unattuned reception. The reality of his time—the late 1960s—is so thoroughly saturated with evil, even dreams seep with visions of horror, whether for president, soldier, poet, or *epichthonoi*:

> The president turns in his sleep and into his stupidity seep the
> images of burning peoples.
> The poet turns in his sleep,   the cries of the tortured and of
> those whose pain survives after the burning   survive with
> him,   for continually
> he returns to early dreams of just retributions and reprisals
> inflicted for his injuries.
> The soldier gloating over and blighted by the burning bodies of
> children, women and old men, turns in his sleep of Viet
> Nam   or,
> dreamless, inert, having done only his duty, hangs at the edge of
> such a conscience to sleep.
> The protestant turns in his sleep, setting fire to hated images,
> entering a deeper war against the war.   A deeper stupidity
> gathers.
>
> The Golden Ones, ancestors of the Good, cloak themselves in
> Sleep's depth,
>
> eternally watching.[40]

Duncan includes one curious dreamer in his list: the protestant. Presumably, because the word isn't capitalized, Duncan is referring here to war protestors, not Protestant Christians; such protestors increasingly earned his scorn through the years of the war. Yet it's this "deeper war against the war" that Duncan feels he is seeing in his wakeful, prophetic state, transmitted to him from the sleep of the Golden Ones. He initiates this catalogue of sleepers with an oracle from the Golden messenger: "*In this mirror . . . our Councils darken.*"[41] These darkening deliberations are as inevitable as sleep but as difficult to interpret as dreams. The art of the poem, as we have seen, is like the mechanism of the dream: to keep present a variety of times and places. "Keeping present" is the work of the prophetic intellect—a re-creation of an imaginative state that the inviolable truth of the poem can thrive in. By invoking a dream state, however, Duncan brings us into his most personal-prophetic sanctum of poetic force, the apocalyptic dream at the center of his work.

"Before the Judgment" concludes with a sweeping apocalypse, intriguing—in this light—for its near lack of any kind of Judgment:

> As if from the depths of Hell, the sleepers seek rest in what they
>   are,
> so that again   the Wish of Death lifts them
>   and passes over them.
>   This
>   pain you take
>   is the pain in which Truth turns like a key.
>
> . . . .
>   the Golden Ones meet in the Solar Councils
> and their alphabet is hidden in the evolution of chemical codes.
>
>   In this place the airy spirit
>   catching fire in its fall from flight
>   has started a burning of conscience
>   in the depths of earth and the primal waters,
>   and all of Creation rises to meet him,
>
> as if to answer a call,   as if to call   into Being,
> forth from a raging Absence, even among men,
> the Body of "Man" cries out   toward Him.
>
> Children of Kronos,   of the Dream beyond death,
>
>   secret of a Life   beyond our lives,
>
>   having their perfection   as we have,
>
>   their bodies a like grace, a music,   their minds   a joy,
>   abundant,

foliate,   fanciful in its flowering,

come into these orders as they have ever come,   stand,

as ever,   where they are acknowledged,

against the works of unworthy men, unfeeling judgments, and
cruel deeds.[42]

Two striking elements stand out for me in these passages. The first is the metaphor of truth turning in the poet like a key in a lock—this movement he analogizes to pain, which I take to be an internal, prophetic pain of coming to terms with Poetry's difficult verity. He is speaking of the mute Golden Ones, who find themselves as if in the depths of Hell, wishing for death but passed over, preserved in preternatural half-life, condemned to their Aeonic, Gnostic Solar Councils, from which their disembodied knowledge radiates into the slumbering world. The other element is the subtle but unmistakable evocation of what I take to be the myth central to Duncan's creative enterprise, his so-called Atlantis dream, a recurring dream from Duncan's childhood spelled out obsessively in his mature poetic work. In this dream, Duncan finds himself in a meadow where children dance in a ring. The grasses sway, then bend toward him in deference, as do the children, because he is clearly "It." The dream shifts, and Duncan finds himself in an underground cavern, which is a throne room. The throne is empty. He recognizes that he is King, and with this understanding comes the panicking revelation that he has failed, at which point the dream darkens and the cavern bursts with flood. Duncan's theosophist family interpreted this dream for him as an oneiric memory of Atlantis, where his soul had last been incarnated. Duncan feeds off this dream incessantly in his poetry, from direct expressions of it in master poems such as "Often I Am Permitted to Return to a Meadow" and "Poem Beginning from a Line by Pindar" to more embedded interpretations of the dream in poems such as "Apprehensions," "My Mother Would Be a Falconress" and "Achilles' Song."

That Duncan's apocalyptic conclusion to "Before the Judgment" revisits the themes of this dream—the depths of the earth and the primal waters, the willowy bodies of the Golden Ones like a grace, dancing with an abundant joy—is not surprising. What strikes me here, however, is the inversion of the narrative Duncan envisions: First comes the catastrophe, the catching fire and the burning of conscience, which bears Christ into life (whom I take to be the Body of "Man")—a figure of redemption. Then comes the vision of the Golden Ones fanciful in their flowering, coming into their orders, intuitively making for me a motion like the children in the grasses of Duncan's dream. Before the judgment, then, there is a holy order of life, one Duncan absorbs through the overlayered destruction of the world of strife he lives in and perceives through his own catastrophic dreams.

Duncan's Atlantis dream is the inexhaustibly interpretable, prophetic source of his poetry. As such, it is as unmanipulable as it is mysterious and foreboding of a doom of meaning. Toward this source Duncan is unwaveringly curious and protective. The dream authorizes and confounds his poetry, in its insistence that the teleology of meaning is catastrophe. I take this dream to be as generative an individual creative myth as Blake's childhood conversations with Ezekiel or Dante's adolescent enchantment with Beatrice. It seems to inform the whole of his art. What is difficult and troubling about "Before the Judgment," then, is not that it rearticulates the myth central to Duncan's creative life but that he concludes a poem about Vietnam with a vision of his Atlantis dream, such that one not so much anticipates the other but that Vietnam verifies for him the sacral, inviolable prophecy out of which his poetic effort springs. His prophetic frustration, in this light, is an admission of coercion, on the one hand—the sense that he has been lured into an obsession with the Vietnam War—and a fearsome protectiveness, on the other, the feeling that his dream is Poetry itself and that his work as a poet is to speak for this dream.

And so Duncan's prophetic frustrations come fully into the light. The Golden Ones—compassionate, Platonic beings—are powerless, except as witnesses and transmitters of a truth turning in him painfully, like a key in a lock. Unlocking is opening, thus seeing. Duncan seeks to transform the witness of the Golden Ones into an active, articulate vision, one of a feeling judgment he finds absent in unworthy men and their cruel deeds. Only Duncan himself—as a poet turning in his prophetic sleep—can sufficiently act as intermediary to this insight. His pen and his typewriter are extensions of his own being. Typography, however, represents a reversion to blindness, to an inability to "see" the poem as he sees it, written in a golden alphabet hidden in the chemical codes of his vivid dreaming. For Duncan, politics—a kind of derogated prophecy—is only redeemed in poetry. In this light, his own war protest was not a physical marching in the streets but a publishing silence. Here, following Duncan's own lead, we misread him because his protest of silence was never a mutedness (he was too outspoken for that) but instead a blindness, or a blinding to any publication of his prophecy but his own.

5

WHAT LIES BENEATH MY COPY OF ETERNITY?

Religious Language in the Poetry of Lissa Wolsak

RELIGIOUS LANGUAGE, RELIGIOUS READING

North American poetry of the past thirty years, especially experimental work, has been characterized by a preoccupation with legibility, such that the work seems to be a response to the question, "Can this be read?" In this respect, poetry has begun to mimic a kind of academic discourse, one in which *meaning* is questioned, usually suspiciously, as a way of generating theories about knowledge (or art, or political philosophy, for instance). Ben Friedlander has suggested a spectrum on which poetry might be understood, with "intelligibility" standing on one end of a continuum and the "registration and production of sense impressions" on the other.[1] I find this span useful for thinking about poetry and meaning: Whether merely "intelligible" or the abstract, allusive, or surreal product of sense impressions (among which is the associative play of language itself), poetry means something, if only that it seeks to communicate something intelligible, or to record sense impressions. Readers ask, "What is this I am reading? What is this supposed to mean? How best to read this poem?" Because of our familiarity with writing built on disrupted syntax or interruptions in grammar, for instance, most readers, I wager, when confronted with work that is difficult to understand—work whose legibility or intelligibility is called into question—feel comfortable enough to register the sense impressions of such work that they can allow its difficulties to slide over them, normalizing them as a stylistic feature rather than as a challenge to sense making. This sliding over disengages the reader from recognizing either intelligibility or legibility in a poem. The work becomes understood, somewhat simplistically but acceptably, as "difficult." In a further simplification, such difficult work becomes "Language poetry" or "avant-garde," both labels once pejoratives marking the scorn of so-called mainstream critics. Nowadays, stripped of most of their value, these labels typically signify a familiar mode available to a creative writer, a mode neither better nor worse than, say, "love poetry" or "confessional poetry."

My academic training is in religious studies. This field, like that of literature, is many-plotted and subdivided, marked by various surveying techniques as well as time-tested or novel excavation strategies (not to mention their requisite conflicts). Difficulties occupy a different space in religious studies than they do in contemporary poetry. Difficulty in contemporary poetry, as I've described, seems frequently to be used as a technique; in religious thought, it is more likely to be used as a tool or to be seen as the product of necessary conceptions. How to understand this difference between technique and tool? In music, for instance, the use of a vibrato in singing is a technique, one that affects the way the voice sounds. A song can be sung with vibrato or without. The performance of the song will be affected, but the song itself will not. In the same example, the voice itself is the tool used to produce the notes that make the song. A song can't be sung without a voice. In this sense, then, I think when difficulty is used by a poet as a tool rather than as a technique, the poet is getting to something more fundamental, what voice is to vibrato.

Let me give two examples of what I mean. We know from works of medieval Christian theology that it was never expected that a work—of scripture, of commentary, or of poetry—be comprehended in order for it to be useful. Indeed, difficulty was regularly built into medieval religious writings to work as keys, which, once discovered and turned, would act to open more intimate realms of meaning. Furthermore, a work—a psalm, for instance—would never be taken "literally," in our conventional use of this term. Its meaning would be understood to exist on several simultaneous levels, of which only the lowest might be commonly perceived. Perhaps the most helpful example of this notion is Dante's sense of the "polysemous" by which literature can be elucidated, whose fourfold meanings are literal, allegorical, moral, and anagogical (or mystical).

In his *Letter to Can Grande*, Dante offers an example of these readings applied to a verse from the Book of Exodus:

> And for the better illustration of this method of exposition we may apply it to the following verses: "When Israel went out of Egypt, the house of Jacob from a people of strange language; Judah was his sanctuary, and Israel his dominion." For if we consider the letter alone, the thing signified to us is the going out of the children of Israel from Egypt in the time of Moses; if the allegory, our redemption through Christ is signified; if the moral sense, the conversion of the soul from the sorrow and misery of sin to a state of grace is signified; if the anagogical, the passing of the sanctified soul from the bondage of the corruption of this world to the liberty of everlasting glory is signified.[2]

In Dante's cosmos, one strove through literal, symbolic, and moral readings of text to peer at the anagogical meanings underlying them. But this is knowledge arrived at only through great difficulty—and only ever partially in this life. The liberty of everlasting glory is a gift of death.

Nowadays (to give my other example), the work of scholars of early Christianity has demonstrated for us, by way of the massive discoveries of scrolls at Qumran and at Nag Hammadi, that the Christian narrative that was accepted as a monolith, arriving for us out of the Gospels and the New Testament, is in fact a kind of creative fiction—not in its contents (or not necessarily) but in its arrangement. Rather, we know now that what appears to be the continuous narrative of Christianity is more meaningfully a series of broken strands, which, over the centuries, are picked up, rewoven, twisted, snapped, lost, and then retrieved. The complexity of this new vision of early Christianity has done nothing to diminish interest in this narrative, in understanding it. Indeed, Christ—the figure about whom more has been written than anyone else in Western culture—remains as confusing and as compelling as ever when approached within this richer, more complex historical context. As the work of scholars as diverse as Elaine Pagels, Karen King, Robert Eisenman, and Marvin Meyer has demonstrated, Christ's legacy in worship was twofold: there was Jesus the wisdom figure, who spoke in quasi-riddles of an interior knowledge of the Kingdom of God, and there was Jesus the resurrection figure, who defied death. The absorption of the former figure into the latter is one of the most complex stories of early Christian thought and history, as is the survival of the wisdom figure in the caches of scrolls discovered in the last sixty-five years.[3]

In both of these examples, we encounter the value of religious language—in terms of its complexities and its power. By power I mean something similar to what Northrop Frye calls the *kerygmatic*. In his second study of the "Bible and Literature," *Words with Power*, Frye indicates four categories of language: factual/descriptive, conceptual/dialectic, persuasive, and mythic/literary. Frye contends—and this is behind his reasoning that the Bible, in spite of scholarly evidence, is best understood as a totally unified book—that in myth and literature, the dividing line between emotional reality and mental reality, between the subjectivity of the mind and the objective reality of the world, is obliterated. Furthermore, within mythic/literary language, Frye posits a kind of language unique to religious expression, which he labels kerygmatic language, which is to say prophetic and proclamatory. He means, in essence, inspired language, either that spoken by God or through a prophet. Kerygmatic language represents God's immaterial essence, pointing to "the universe next door."[4] Religious language, in the way I'm imagining it, is powerful because it begins in intelligibility but then begins to, or seeks to, move beyond it. Medieval Christian writers sought an excess of human meaning in their expressions; the languages of the scriptures of Christ sought to record his dangerous meanings in verifiable expressions, available for immediate adoptions. My point is that the languages and tools of religious studies, theology especially, are of refreshing use when confronting the difficulty of contemporary poetry. Rather than shifting the blame of difficulty to the increasingly bloviated categories of Language writing or the avant-garde, why not, when it seems appropriate, try to perceive the meaning of such difficulty in explicitly religious terms, recognizing that from their inception certain kinds of expression are loaded with power such that they require special strategies for comprehension?

A MEANS BY WHICH SOMETHING IS DISCOVERED

Lissa's Wolsak's poetry occupies a mysterious, asynchronous realm conjured from broken bits of observation; scattered neologisms; scientific, psychological, and hermeneutical jargon; and a lettristic quasi-shamanism (best captured in the subtitle to one of her books: *12 spirit-like impermanences*). A jeweler and metalsmith by training and trade, Wolsak entered into a life of poetry much later than most: her first book, *The Garcia Family Co-Mercy*, was published in 1994, when she was forty-six. Since then, she has published another book of poetry, *Pen Chants, or nth or 12 spirit-like impermanences* (2000), and has issued lengthy installments (called *anas*) of a work in progress, *A Defence of Being*. Recently, all of this work, along with additional new poems, has been assembled in *Squeezed Light: Collected Poems, 1994–2005*. Her work demonstrates a simultaneous care and meticulousness—something one is (perhaps misleadingly) tempted to attribute to her work as a jeweler—and an excitement of passionate engagement.

In *An Heuristic Prolusion*, an unusual poetic testimony, Wolsak identifies through the terminology of quantum physics the spiritual compulsions that generate her creative viewpoint: "~Quantum physics engages the term 'qualia,' defined as those temporary states flagging our 'immediate' reality . . . no more than dispositions . . . things can float free." The "redness of red, the painfulness of pain. The whatness . . . that which gives things qualities. Qualia are the essential features of consciousness."[5]

Her work elucidates these transient but luminous states of frequently intense feeling that underlie the normal flow of our attentions, the experience of which shapes our perception of reality. "Heuristic" is the hinge on which such an observation as this one swings. When in 1916 Einstein published what the historian of religion Ioan P. Couliano calls "one of those very few books that matter in human history," namely, *The Special and General Theory of Relativity*, he worried over the title before allowing it to be printed. "Theory" struck Einstein as an inapt word for what he was offering. He toyed up to the very end with calling it "An Heuristic Viewpoint of Relativity," wanting to stress the *viewpoint* he was offering in his tract. Wolsak's *Prolusion*, like Einstein's *Theory*, strikes me equally as both a viewpoint onto and a test of reality, in her case a redolently poetic one, as in *Pen Chants*, when Wolsak writes:

> these arches   are but rooves
>
> of earlier churches
>
> cold spots where galaxies

would eventually form

I brought my sacred body

and caused it to sit..[6]

As Einstein regarded relativity, so we should regard her heuristic as above all a theory, a provisional testing of reality. Both words, *heuristic* and *theory*, allow us to understand the hypotaxis and neologism by way of which she constructs her lyrical mosaics, as above when "rooves" (bridging a sonic image of *roofs* and *grooves*) opens to a cosmic perception of a primordial corpus Dei in the act of beginning its *indwelling*, a term I draw from Christian mysticism, meaning the abiding of God in the heart and the soul. (Traherne wrote in his *Christian Ethics*, "By the indwelling of God all objects are infused, and contained within.")[7]

As a "heuristic," Wolsak's work is very much an experiential probing, rife with play and invention in words (among those to be found in the first ten pages of *Pen Chants*, for instance, are *diaphane*, *luo*, *ingled*, *tungusic*, *gnos*, *devastatrix*, *sauvis*, *rhus*, *oospecie*), punctuation (most notably her characteristic "double point" [..] which frequently begins or ends lyric installments in her poetry, acting as a visual stutter, a lyric hiccough), and page layout/prosody. Among *theory*'s meanings, buried in its earliest usages—ca. 1600, according to the *OED*—is the act of looking at something or contemplating it. In Christian history, *theoria* has frequently been understood as a synonym for contemplation, which in Catholicism and Orthodox Christianity means the same thing as the Buddhist understanding of *meditation*. (The range of spiritual reference in Wolsak's work stretches over Christian notions of negative theology; to Jewish mysticism and ethics, especially those of Maimonides; to the Buddhist mystical philosophy of Nagarjuna and Madhyamyka Buddhist doctrines.) Contemplative, *theoretical* prayer is prayer that loosens itself from reason to focus on the Divine in a reflective, ruminative way. Which is to say that if I call Wolsak's poetry "theoretical," I mean that it is mystical in Dante's anagogical sense or, perhaps more accurately, *pneumatic*, which is to say "breathed out" from the *pneumatikos* or *spiritus*, the breath-source, which is the indwelling soul.

AN ICONIC BEYONDSENSE

The "somatics of openness" that drives Wolsak's work, to use a phrase from *Pen Chants*, is the source of the disorientation that makes her poetry—in its searching and its grasping—both possible and ecstatic:

> eustasy, erosis, predicta, illusionism . . . ,
>
> lustral, tribulated, august . . .
>
> misnomers all[8]

These misnomers lead into the negative but sensuous light in which to perceive her poems, a kind of "divine darkness" perceived through apophatic devotions, understood through a simultaneous derangement and arrangement or conscientious organizing of the disordered states out of which her poetry arises. Apophaticism, or negative theology, consists, according to Bernard McGinn, of both subjective and objective negative descriptions of God "according to which God is said to be unknowable and ineffable to our mode of perception and expression."[9] Despite being hard to put into words, "the consciousness of God as negation . . . is the core of the mystic's journey," which includes the uncovering of an unusually expressive language to do so.[10] "Apophaticism," warns the Orthodox theologian Vladimir Lossky, "is, above all, an attitude of mind which refuses to form concepts about God."[11] To this Lossky adds a sense of the contemplative imperative such refusal inspires: negative theology "forbids us to follow natural ways of thought and to form concepts which would usurp the place of spiritual realities."[12] Poetry, for Wolsak, is the sense by which unusurped spiritual realities are perceived, in a "beyondsense" she cultivates through active, Olsonian apprehensions and language:

> ~ I delimit my world through interoceptive (a receptor of the viscera responding to stimuli originating within the body), proprioceptive techniques, assembling, phrasing multiplicities where the containment of all possible meanings moves beyond its own oscillation, toward a relation to some or all of those juxtaposed but shifting magnitudes. Atomic reflection, in beyondsense.[13]

I want to think, then, of Lissa Wolsak as a theological poet not in order to bolster an orthodoxy or to suggest her work represents any explicit faith. Rather, theology permits us to consider her work's mode of giving pleasure through experiment; furthermore, it allows us to regard her work as an intuitive functioning of the creative imagination, one shaped by a desire to articulate the deep space of beyondsense into which her poetry sends exploratory probes.

So how do we understand Wolsak as a theological poet? What are the terms of her theology? In an important essay, "The Icon and the Idol," from his book *God Without Being*, the Catholic theologian Jean-Luc Marion proposes of theology, first of all, that besides being the writing that gives its writer the most pleasure, it is also that for which its writer must obtain forgiveness in every instant, in that such speech can never satisfy its Author, who is, in this case, Christ, the ultimate *theo-logos*, or Word of God. Marion speaks of the idol as a dazzling spectacle that captures the gaze, such that "the gaze ceases to overshoot and transpierce itself, hence it ceases to transpierce visible things, in order to pause in the splendor of one of them."[14] "The idol," he asserts, "thus acts as a mirror, not as a portrait."[15] Beyond the dazzle of the idol, which blinds us, is the *icon*, emerging in the invisible. The icon is never seen, but *appears* or, better, *seems*. It is energy and not essence (which belongs only to God), such that its semblance "never reduces the invisible to the slackened wave of the visible."[16] In the invisible, we stand "face to face" with ourselves, "our face as the visible mirror of the invisible." This is a semantic reorientation of *reflection*: not looking or gazing but being seen, *seeming*. Marion asserts:

> Thus, as opposed to the idol which delimited the low-water mark of our aim, the icon displaces the limits of our visibility to the measure of its own—its glory. It transforms us in its glory by allowing this glory to shine on our face as its mirror—but a mirror consumed by that very glory, transfigured with invisibility, and, by dint of being saturated beyond itself from that glory, becoming strictly though imperfectly, the icon of it: visibility of the invisible as such.[17]

Wolsak's poetry, according to these terms, is iconic in its restless, relentless transfiguration of self-knowledge—a kind of mirroring of the self—into an *iconic* knowledge: a revelation of things invisible in the visible through an intuitive cohesion of language. This cohesion, which might also be called *epinoia*, which in Christian Gnosticism means creative or inventive consciousness, prompts the qualia, or temporary states flagging immediate reality, that form the essential features of consciousness.[18] Marion's sense of the divine *icon* is synonymous in my mind with Wolsak's understanding of *beyondsense*, which is, for her, poetic knowledge—*gnosis*—never grasped, only received, epiphanically.

How does one—how does Wolsak—articulate this consciousness? In contemplative terms, only by backing into an expression of it. Sometimes this is accomplished through negation, as in these disorienting lines, where the accent marks represent the blindfolded embodiment of silence: "I am mostly silence . . . distaff // but it is not so // as I have heard from ```` // that blindfolding eliminates stress."[19] At other times Wolsak presents a fragmentary, mosaic set of perceptions, so that broken bits of language contribute to a holographic vision of the consciousness expressed in the poem:

.. go with me,

disquisit hour of terse

touch and sight,

transhumance,
fever them selves[20]

In these lines (the conclusion of *The Garcia Family Co-Mercy*), the reader fills in the remainder of the words implied by the symbol of the dot, leaving us with "disquisition" and "terseness," but the same dot severs/fevers "themselves" with an aporia neither touch nor sight can completely fill. Wolsak's poem alights on consciousness through an excited quasi-silence, ordained through a linguistic geophagy:

arouse then
my tungusic.. my gnos..
I am full of rammed earth[21]

The call to "arouse" here serves as a kind of invocation of the spirit (proxy for the muses, perhaps?). It is preceded by a statement about the "speech-blows" of the "many-bodied // suspensi spiritus" who is "not our own" and who is "waking, just as I sleep"[22]—a hypnotic juggernaut who delivers potent messages. The poet's arousal, then—her coming into wakefulness or contemplative attention—is stymied by two interferences. First is "tungusic," which blends the English *tongue* with the Swedish *tung* (for "heavy") in a neologism drawn from *Tungus*, the name for the eastern Siberian people thought by ethnographers and scholars of religion to be the group from which shamanism originated.[23] This she follows with *gnos*, the root of knowledge, clipped by a characteristic ellipsis. Rather than ascend into some trance realm of higher gnosis, the poet-shaman at this moment devours earth, or recognizes the humus packed deep inside her. This moment reveals to her an abiding, necessary "via immanencia," a way into the present.

TRANSHUMANCE AND CO-MERCY

I don't want to take Wolsak's work as entirely oblique in its references nor made up exclusively of a reality revealed to her fragmentarily. The iconic beyondsense her poetry emerges from is perhaps best thought of as made up of quantum particles, surrounded by the qualia of perception that make a nimbus around the actual. Her theology, such as it is, feels experiential; its expressions are necessitated by epiphanies and insights culled from her everyday life. Take this lyric from *Pen Chants*, for instance:

. . . . in bussing silence.

then it is *we*

allow the cello to wander

open among

aestheocratic

gift economies,   grok

therapeutic America, expire my

omni-range, my mordant jealousy of space, my

permanently blowing curtain,   my

breastlessness[24]

Let's try to reconstruct the scene in which this lyric took shape: she's on a bus, experiencing a kind of communion with the other—her own otherness?—inviting a kind of perception or potency of language and understanding, signaled by the wandering away of the cellos. Is she listening to music on headphones? Or is this an aural hallucination, an imagined accompaniment to her vagarious thoughts? She's trying to connect—to her fellow passengers, or to the world visible outside the windows of the bus? "Bussing" also carries the archaic sense of "kissing," which adds to this scene a level of intimacy. In any case, this feeling is opening her to the "aestheocratic / gift economies" of "therapeutic America," which she wants to "grok," a coinage of Robert A. Heinlein in *Stranger in a Strange Land*, meaning "to understand intuitively."[25] Her desire to grok what she is seeing/imagining leads her into a purgative, plaintive mode in which she asks to be "breathed out" (*ex-* + *spirare*), or that these lingering qualia of hers be breathed out of her body: "omni-range," "jealously" for "space" (which can be taken as a desire for possession, for a house, for land, for acquisitions), a "blowing curtain" (representing transience, perhaps), and, at last, her breastlessness, the most startling word in this lyric. Does this indicate an actual condition—a mastectomy—or is this in reference to a kind of spiritual state? Likely, it's a reference to the lack of such a spiritual state, or the difficulty of attaining a kind of communion in the current American world, supersaturated as it is with commerce and greed, driven by aesthetic and religious misconceptions that justify economies and hegemonies that render even a healthy woman feeling "breastless," in a state of surgical incompletion. I move through this set of readerly questions not to demonstrate explicit meanings in Wolsak's poetry but, rather, to suggest that her work feels based in the realities and materials of life, her life or an imagined other's life, one whose otherness is distinctly feminine.

Wolsak's poetry can usefully be construed as consciousness mirrors—reflections of an eternal state gleaned in the motion of words and thoughts through the imagination. We might perceive, then, some of her stylistic quirks—the frequent neologisms and her punctuation oddities—not as poetic fanciness but as survival techniques: a means of recording the transpiercing transience otherwise lost in the fleetingness of thought. In an interview from 2000 with Pete Smith, responding partially to his question of her "late" appearance on the poetry scene, she addresses the silence out of which her art arises:

> For me, to speak at all, is suspect, just as it is almost always suspect to speak under the constraints of linearity, where the main question is: which surface must I appear on? In my work I presume to move through that silence which linear language admits, its lack of fullness, its utter necessity, placing a slight emphasis on the grace/civilizade/intuition of one who interprets its urgency. From silence of early and late dogmas, of duplicity, of closed human circuits, of refuge and resistance to cultural engulfment, of fixed and encrypted ideas, and obliteration that also naturally inheres in the language, then of all that had gone before, and that which holds love in fear. Very much from the silence of reflection, strong wishes, autonomy, a vulnerable defense of being.[26]

By her own admission, "co-mercy" and "transhumance" are the terms through which she composes her poetry. Transhumance she amplifies as "acts of symmetry, reciprocity and redistribution of generosity, forgiveness, love per se, and in doing so, ceasing or suspending the revenge cycle."[27] Co-mercy we can understand as a kind of compassion via alienation—the merciful feeling that ensues from recognizing one's otherness as something shared by each person you encounter. In *The Garcia Family Co-Mercy*, Wolsak puts it this way:

Compassion

is largely exile

.. contradict

the ways in which

the world

says no[28]

But perhaps the strongest statement Wolsak makes about these terms is in the opening of *An Heuristic Prolusion*, where she connects *co-mercy* and *transhumance* explicitly to silence, which we can understand—through a synesthesia of Marion's terms for understanding the icon—as a mode of listening to the invisible, to the reflection of the divine infinite. She writes,

> ~ I speak as one silenced. *Transhumance*, as understood and utilized in late 12th c., early 13th c. France, was an agricultural motion or migration, a seasonal moving of livestock and the people who tend them . . . but transhumance also was a possible personal~social act of symmetry, reciprocity and redistribution. Co-mercy, the art of harmlessness, equivocating sexual/theological, fiat, fiat lux . . . to lay the supremely ambiguous, phantomatic faces .. to let, to kneel, along the place of the abyss, to linger as long as possible .. where the same relation may be observed throughout the whole universe, where significance "bleeds into an unconstrainable chain."
>
> What lies beneath my copy of eternity?
> What coils-up .. in spoken space?[29]

Even though the words come from different sources, I can't help but hear in Wolsak's *transhumance* Dante's assertion in the first canto of *Paradiso*, "Transumanar significar *per verba* / non si poria; però l'essemplo basti / a cui esperïenza grazia serba."[30] *Transumanar* = passing beyond humanity. There's something of this in Wolsak's migratory *transhumance*, a motion beyond the human, pulled into the spiritual by an unearthly signal, an inward migration. Note how during the main paragraph in the quotation from *An Heuristic Prolusion* her sequence of observations breaks down, as signaled by ellipses and then double stops, a kind of hesitation as she imagines the lip of the abyss (which she feminizes in *Pen Chants* as the "upflung abysse"). This leads her to two questions that serve as Virgilian guides to her work: The Dickinsonian "What lies beneath my copy of eternity?" And the more distinctly idiomatic "What coils-up .. in spoken space?" Beneath her copy of eternity is *beyondsense*, an iconic thrumming of silence, source of spoken space. "Coils-up," hyphenated as it is, feels adjectival, descriptive, rather than verbal. The double stop seems to indicate a missing participle: an announcing source of spoken space. In either case, it is absent. Wolsak's disruptive grammar leads us here into that space, peeling back the copy of reality she reads from to see what reveals itself underneath.

MORTISCIENCE

Underneath her thoughts, in the blackness of creative origins, there is also, strangely, a morbidity: death, in fact. Much like the Tibetan Buddhist understanding of the *bardos* the departed soul passes through—thronged with fantastic figures of death—Wolsak's conception of "Being" is one rife with dead bodies. A recent work, *A Defence of Being* (2005), proceeds more apocalyptically than her earlier books. It is presented in a series of lyrics divided into sets of *anas*, by which she means a collection or book of memorable or odd sayings, though one can hear as well the Greek prefix "ana-," which denotes *up, upon, back, again, new, throughout.*[31] Wolsak appears in *A Defence of Being* to be compiling the elements of a revelation but also to be looking into the moment of a vast catastrophe, one in which death and destruction are, as ever, sources of knowledge. Wolsak's poem occurs under the sign of another orienting term of hers, *fencelessness*, which we should add to *transhumance* and *co-mercy.* Fencelessness is a state of being "defenced," which she describes as meaning "that there must be a turning point from revenge, a completely new mode of *commerce*, so that rather than the capitalistic taking advantage of a person, place or thing, one . . . is inspired by compassion, and acts accordingly, and this is an initiatory opening process which must be begun by each of us."[32] The imperative of defencing one's self, which is a challenge toward personal/social insight, is nonetheless fraught with ardor. She characterizes this imperative in the poem by imagining the underworld—both a Hades and a Hell-on-earth. The following two passages from *A Defence of Being*, for instance, are less Dantescan tours through Hell than Vajrayana imaginings from a new Book of the Dead:

Perhaps..I say,
love's whipscorpian cadaver
omnivorously wavers *be*
'tween feeding and lidless

vigilance, yet.. free to reply to
human prayers
***

Awing us
in the open place
which inflects
being . . . as in union or rapture,
aside not yet all that would be
fatherhooded
will of nations, how much
iconic depravity in play,
on paths unknown to any vulture,
the algebraically intractable corpse-vine
bore on us
matchless
monuments to ascending vanity
in superposition just
enough death-rouge
holographically at hand how
then . . . ought each of
the said things intrude upon us now?
being scient is of
minute moment
loom-shuttles still[33]

In the first lyric above, Wolsak connects Eros and Thanatos in the image of a poisonous scorpion that acts as predatory muse for Being itself: consumptive and watchful. Implicitly horrible. Nonetheless, to this god-thing humans pray—even as it preys on us. The second lyric gives an awful but appealing form to death, which "Aw[es] us / in the open place / which inflects / being" but is also figured as a patriarchal monster, "fatherhooded" and clothed in depravity and constricting vines. The question nestled in this poem—*How then ought the said things intrude upon us now?*—is asked of the thanatoptic oracle that is the poem. The oracle answers: knowledge is only ever glimmering, a momentary still point in the shuttling of the loom. ("Scient" is an obscure adjective for "learned." Thus, to paraphrase Wolsak above: being learned—having knowledge—is of the fleetingest instant; death is always at hand.) "[M]inute moment" also refers to "enterprises of great pith and moment," in Hamlet's soliloquy (III.i.86), by which Wolsak intends to suggest moving power, importance, and consequence. Like Hamlet, Wolsak is meditating here on death in the face of being, the "dread of something after death" that makes life momentous.[34] I'm compelled to coin words to describe the knowledge of death Wolsak is working toward/out in these poems: *thanatognosis*, an intuitive knowledge of the meaning that death shadows underneath our copies of eternity; or *mortiscience*, a prescience of death, a learnedness of the "unthought known" in which our true body abides.[35] It's important to recognize that Wolsak's sense of this prescience of death is not liberating, at least not here. What is represented here is very much a hellish oppression. Part of the awareness of death—the knowledge that you will die and the knowledge that the world is made of death—is the repulsion of that knowledge.

One further passage from this second *ana* of *A Defence of Being* elaborates the Dantescan scene by way of Gustav Doré's renowned illustrations of the *Inferno*:

Perhaps..
Dore's throngs *fff* tremolando with

covered heads in

their origins from mercy, tell

what birth-throes and pan-

ic-stricken volleys, which

of its sacral self, in

suppurating shirts of blood shout-

ing intimacies that

they should ever feel wonder,

Ex ante

according to what lies ahead

it is enough that

sapience before

all else piing and a-

loof under mocking fire, we,

disclosively welling up, shall

cling to nothing, tidal-

tugging on our ex-

cruciating wet rock, wrap-

ed in willow-splints[36]

The possibilities of this scene—introduced to us through that "Perhaps" followed by the double point—come into focus in the following lines. "*Ex ante*" is a curious inclusion in the poem, since it is a term derived from economics, meaning based on forecasted, predicted results. (Its literal meaning is "what lies ahead, beforehand, as before," which would trigger Wolsak's attraction to the term, in that it ciphers *beyondsense*, but it's interesting to inject a sense of economics in her critique: fencelessness requires new, more generous, less murderous bartering among poets and the rest of the world.) The economies of the dead in this lyric work on punishment—a torturous clinging to a "wet rock" wrapped in "willow-splints." Our knowledge of this impending state determines our punishment in it. Knowledge is the coin of this realm. Being is something "piing and a- / loof under mocking fire," so that pi, the calculation of which is infinite, is a numerical equivalency for our self-knowledge or awareness. I think Wolsak is also saying here that foreknowledge is infinite (that is, "sapience before / all else piing"), and even as we may be punished for casting our thoughts endlessly ahead into the unknown, in this life or the next, we shall remain "aloof" under the mocking fires of eternal punishment because knowledge informs the "sacral self" toward which we feel abiding wonder and awe. The flesh is refigured as a garment of our suffering: "suppurating shirts of blood" in which we "shout" (or are the shirts somehow vocalizing?) our "intimacies"—a bleakly ironic portrait of our condition in this life. Despite the horrors of this scene, Wolsak presents it as co-merciful, a picture of the sacral self originated in mercy. The lyric is a redemptive song.

HORIZONTAL READING

In passing beyond humanity, in rising into the imagined infinite in her poetry, where death and transfiguring knowledge await, Wolsak requires a different strategy of reading, one that deliberately sidesteps her obscurities and seeming difficulties of legibility and meaning. I propose we read Wolsak, as I have been attempting, horizontally rather than vertically. I take this notion from the arguments of John Dominic Crossan, a scholar of early Christianity who has suggested that the four canonical Gospels yield a vastly different—implicitly more interesting—story when read horizontally rather than vertically. Crossan suggests that because the four Gospels were chosen for deliberate theological reasons to represent the "true" story of Christ, they each offer consistently different versions of his life and teachings, which, through the centuries and through negligent reading habits, we have synthesized into a whole, "true" story of the life. So, for instance, we might speak of Christ's sufferings in the Garden at Gethsemane, without realizing that Mark's Gospel speaks only of a garden where Christ went to suffer on the night before his crucifixion, begging mercy from the Father, while John's Gospel speaks of Gethsemane, where Christ triumphantly confronted the Roman centurions, willingly giving himself over to his captors.[37] Over the centuries, Crossan claims, we have moved from understanding the Gospels as *interpretations* to perceiving them as immovable, literal fact. He implies, then, that a horizontal reading of Gospel texts—a method reopening them to interpretation and heuristics—reveals meaning, whereas reliance on vertical, consecutive readings tends to obscure meanings and the theologies that drive the sequencing in the first place. By invoking Crossan's understanding here, I don't mean to suggest we take Wolsak's poetry as gospel. Rather, I want to appropriate Crossan's notion of reading toward understanding Wolsak's writing. Reading *Pen Chants*, for instance, as a consecutive sequence might distort its meaning, misleading one to a progressive reading of its lyrics. Reading it mosaically—or horizontally—allows for its images and ideas to settle into a holographic image.

I am not entirely certain what a horizontal reading of Wolsak's poetry would look like. I take my own reading of her work as a provisional beginning. The real difficulties of her work—a kind of (en)tranced grasping after gnosis—are too easily sold short by a fixation on the veneer of lexical, syntactical difficulty, which can flatten the effect of the work. In bringing some of the tools or ideas of religious studies to looking at poetry, I want to suggest a different—let's call it *horizontal*—approach to difficulty. Rather than excusing difficulty as a byproduct of a manipulation of language, let's use it as a door into another room or universe of thought.

Wolsak's composition practices bear out this notion of a horizontality at work in her writing. The production of a poem for Wolsak is a layered, cumulative process, one in which she immerses her senses into the act of writing. She begins by noting words, fragments, soundbites, and neologisms in a notebook she carries with her everywhere. She then highlights what seems important from these notebook fragments, writing them out longhand onto "great big drawing sheets. I pour over these spread out on the floor so I can see everything at once." At this point, she begins to "listen" to her writings, letting them begin to "speak to each other, forming affinities." This part of the process she likens to a kind of chemistry, one in which word molecules join together intuitively or thematically. From here, she begins another set of longhand drafts, one in which she brings the poem together in a manner that allows for maximum saturation of her creative senses, most especially the ear, "with particular attention to meaning." She describes this process as a "froth of confusion, so much going on at that point I can't see anymore, but in some way I think it is all about not seeing at first and 'going' blind until meaning springs forth." At this point, then, she begins to compose drafts on a word processor, whose function is to allow her to see the work again, to work on it further.[38] In this sense, Wolsak brings a normative, vertical conception of poetry into her work only in the last act of composition. Prior to this, in listening to the pleromatic invisible of her beyondsense, she is compelled into apophatic, horizontal acts of reading and writing.

Not all difficult poetry is religious poetry; nor are the languages of religion and theology necessarily helpful toward understanding even such transparently spiritualized writing as Wolsak's. We need to tread carefully when insisting on religiously inflected readings of contemporary poetry, for fear mainly of losing sight of the composition. I don't want to suggest that Wolsak's poetry be treated exclusively in light of religious discourse and language. Hers is vigorous work as likely responsive to contemporary literary strategies as to religious thinking and consideration. But I do want to suggest that an academically inflected culture of reading contemporary poetry imposes constraints on literary thinking that are ultimately as transient as their dogmas are inviolable.[39] Work such as Wolsak's suffers from the constraints of an academic perception, in that in its terms it seems to welcome reading strategies that are looser, more intuitive. I don't think of religious studies as a great liberator for thinking about poetry, but I do find its premises and tools helpful, because more open, in considering work like Wolsak's. Rather than glossing over her difficulties, a horizontal reading of her poetry cultivates an environment in which to perceive its strangeness and to accept its prospective possibilities toward meaning. What lies beneath Wolsak's copy of eternity? Poetry. Let it be so, then, for each of us who read her.

6

CATHOLICS

Reading Fanny Howe

Whether Fanny Howe proves to be the most important American Catholic poet of the twenty-first century, there is little doubt that Catholicism is at the heart of her creativity and that her Catholic identity gives force to and creates tension in her poetry. Since the deaths of Thomas Merton in 1968 and William Everson in 1994, Howe is one of the most visible Catholic poets in the United States and the best-known Catholic poet affiliated with experimentation.[1] Yet there has not been much critical discussion of Howe's religion, in spite of the frequency with which she discusses it in her prose and even considering that this aspect of her work has been recognized by the organizations that bestow prizes on American poets.[2]

In my mind, Howe's Catholicism is the most interesting thing about her writing, which is to say that the vexed, bewildered (to use her preferred term) expressions of her faith in the context of an experimental poetry lend her work an unmistakable aura of conviction and surprise and give to it a rare value in relation to much of the rest of recent American poetry. It makes sense, then, to try to locate her faith as a way to begin to understand her unusual body of work, which extends from lyrically charged and often lengthy sequences of poetry to speculative essays, short fiction, and novels, as well as verse plays. Howe's two most important writings about her Catholicism are the poem-essay "Catholic," collected in *The Wedding Dress*, her "meditations on word and life," published in 2003, and the introduction to that volume. Howe's faith infuses and defines her writing so that evidence can be gathered throughout her work toward making an argument about what makes her writing Catholic.

MISFORTUNE

Howe's Catholicism presents a problem both to the reader and to the poet. As a convert to the faith, she wrestles with and contextualizes this conversion in her work: what brought her to this moment, why it happened, and what its consequences are. "What my conversion was meant to do," she has written, "was to keep me safe from irony, to keep my childhood hope intact, to allow me to live with a certain schedule that occurred outside human time. Even if my faith was on a low burn, I still went to mass."[3] Likewise, her readers—a good number of whom have been affiliated with so-called experimental writing, though her work has recently been reaching a larger audience—feel compelled either to aestheticize or to politicize her religious beliefs in an effort to make her work conform to the often narrow (and typically secular) interests of innovative writing.

Howe is a prolific poet. Since 1997, when *One Crossed Out* was published by Graywolf Press, she has published eight additional books of poetry: *Selected Poems* (2000), which received the Lenore Marshall Prize; *Tis of Thee* (2003), a verse play; *Gone* (2003), which includes within it a book-length poem entitled "The Passion"; *On the Ground* (2004), which includes a number of sequences, many of them related to recent political events, including those of September 11, 2001, and the military responses by the U.S. government, which Howe abhors; *The Lyrics* (2008); *Come and See* (2011); *Second Childhood* (2014); and *The Needle's Eye* (2016). In addition to these volumes of poetry, Howe has recently published three books of fiction—*Indivisible*, *Economics*, and *What Did I Do Wrong*—as well as *The Wedding Dress* and *The Winter Sun*, a series of autobiographical essays. I think her prolixity results from elements of the work itself. Speaking only of the poetry, there is a sharpness of response, even an invective trait, that feeds on current events or, perhaps more accurately, the sometimes desperate cloud of unknowing in which most of life is lived, particularly as individual life is involved with the political, economic, and social uncertainties that loom and gather force at the hands of ruling powers. One has the sense that Howe writes her poetry fairly quickly—

one reviewer, discussed below, has suggested, disparagingly, that she writes it "automatically"—and that the work of poetry does not involve a great deal of revision for her. There is a resonant immediacy to the work that feels as though it would be damaged by overwrought circumspection. In an interview, Howe has described her writing process as an "echo chamber" in which "the sentence passes through me and around in a circle and hits something out there and then comes back in again . . . I suppose that it's like an ear, and I'm inside of the ear and outside of it at the same time."[4] What Howe is getting at in her poetry is not defined by issues of craft, per se. However, she avails an unusual, even exceptional sense of what poetry is to make these poems happen. Poetry is not the subject but is the medium of her poems; nonetheless, she requires poetry to express herself.[5]

To explain more carefully: I take misfortune to be Howe's main theme. Misfortune should be understood to be simultaneously a material and metaphysical condition. It has no author. Which is to say, God typically has nothing to do with this misfortune. Nonetheless, if you accept that you have access to an experience of God's being, it can be argued that the condition of misfortune might allow you greater access to an experience of God. For me, perhaps the best description of misfortune is found in Simone Weil's essay "*The Iliad*, or the Poem of Force." Weil's work is unusually important to Howe—there is an overlayering of biography, a shared set of political and philosophical convictions, and Howe's intense admiration for Weil. In her essay "Love and Work," which chronicles the effort to make a video about Weil, Howe writes, "I have read SW for so long, and so intensely, I often don't remember what she believed, stated, or knew. In a sense my stupidity is a sign that I have incorporated her work into myself."[6] In Weil's essay about *The Iliad*, written in 1939 just as war was about to engulf Europe, she states, "Moreover, nothing is so rare as to see misfortune fairly portrayed; the tendency is either to treat the unfortunate person as though catastrophe were his natural vocation, or to ignore the effects of misfortune on the soul, to assume, that is, that the soul can suffer and remain unmarked by it, can fail, in fact, to be recast in fortune's image."[7] I think Howe takes as the task of her poetry the effort to recast the soul—her soul—in misfortune's image. In Weil's own terms, such a project must necessarily be related to the Gospels. In the same essay, Weil proposes that what she calls the Greek genius had its "last marvelous expression" in the Gospels just as it had its first in

The Iliad. She writes: "The accounts of the Passion show that a divine spirit, incarnate, is changed by misfortune, trembles before suffering and death, feels itself, in the depths of its agony, to be cut off from man and God." This existential condition marks the Gospels with "the accent of simplicity" she admires in Greek thought. "This accent," she asserts, "cannot be separated from the idea that inspired the Gospels, for the sense of human misery is a precondition of justice and love."[8] Howe's poetry resounds with plaints of human misery but is overarched by a vivid and often viciously critical sense of justice, inspired throughout by transcendental love, which comes mysteriously and unconditionally from God. Her expression of this justice, which arrives in Howe's work with urgency, is what speeds the poems along. It's also what directs Howe's poetic expressions toward aphoristic, axiomatic statements, ones that have a typically judgmental ring to them.

God in Howe's poetry is often enough actually clothed in misfortune. *One Crossed Out*, for instance, is a book-length sequence of poems about a homeless woman, May, whose piercing intelligence is magnified by the misery of her condition. In a lengthy serial poem entitled "Plutocracy," May suggests,

> When you eat alone you don't exist
> for anyone but the dish.
> Like the spaniel (the dog of invincible obsession)
> you might stare fixedly into a water glass for hours.[9]

Later, she is prompted to ask unanswerable questions: "*What if the rosary is a heresy? / What if the world is divine? / What if hell is a permanent state of mind?*"[10] Similarly, the main character of "The Passion" is a homeless, neglected man with Christlike qualities who may in fact be Christ:

> He managed his agony
> but lost his looks and all his currency
>
> For him time was a vacuum
> filled with his visions
>
> They held him above history
> like valium

> or something flat in heaven
>
> He was always gone or leaving
>
> claw-lines—white across a brick building—[11]

I think these two passages serve to illustrate the unusual tenor of Howe's work, thematically speaking. She's preoccupied in her work, as in the first example, with the conditions of existence, with what happens to the self—what it thinks—while it is struggling through its life. Likewise, she's concerned with representations of the effects that capital—the struggle for money—has on human life, as in the selection above from "The Passion" or, again, in "Plutocracy," which contains near its beginning the lines, "It's as if money's eyes are located inside a pyramid. / Unfit for the rest of human habitation."[12] The conditional in these lines is important to Howe's poetic vision: the poetry is constantly trying to make sense of this misfortune, either by analogy, by metaphor or simile ("They held him above history / like valium"), or by transcendental, if somewhat unaffected language ("something flat in heaven").

These selections provide a glimpse of the dominant technical features of Howe's poetry. There is a flatness of affect in her writing that, rather than erupting into metaphorical or lyrical flourishes, coalesces into aphoristic or even gnomic statements or questions. For instance, "When you eat alone you don't exist / for anyone but the dish" has a tutelary, experientially lonely tone to it, whereas "They held him above history / like valium" moves into the mysterious, but complexly, because it's unclear what value, besides its somatic effects, valium has in this axiom. Is it forgetfulness? Is it a negative value, an indication of the absurdity of his homelessness? Both of these features, the tutelary and the experiential, abound in Howe's poetry. In "The Passion," we find, "When the camel's knees fold / it's the end of poetry."[13] And later, making use again of the question:

> So what is the relationship
> between time and the soul?
>
> Time has no temperature either.[14]

This aphoristic flatness is, for me, encapsulated in the title of one of her earlier sequences, "In the Spirit There Are No Accidents," reprinted in *Selected Poems*.[15] That sequence contains an especially instructive section that orients the axiomatic nature of the work to its axiology, which is to say the implicit judgment in much of Howe's work, and its cry for justice:

> Sister Poverty, welcome to my cloister
> All that lowers must draw close
>
> In the world of wretches & the exploited
> Of the accidentally destroyed
>
> The strike of each heart
> In the distant body
> Ups the odds that there's a why but, why[16]

That concluding "why" isolates the Furies-like justice the poet would seek in the world. In the spirit there are no accidents, but the wretched and the exploited die accidentally nonetheless. There must be meaning to such fate, but even so, she desperately questions it. That second *why* in the line above is what transforms these lines into poetry.

Note as well in the sheen of Howe's language the way she generates tension in her poems. Flatness as often as it yields an aphorism just as often rushes into a question, a judgment, or a predicament. There is a specificity to her language, particularly when she evokes the urban scene in which so many of her poems take place, as in the "claw lines—white across a brick building" above. Likewise, there is rarely anything fancy about the language she uses, or, when there is, the fanciness is invoked to serve the poem, not to draw attention to her language, as in these lines from "The Passion":

> At the transverberation
> your heart is pierced
>
> with such a piercing
> you leave the sphere of doubt
>
> Take heart
> Lose heart![17]

And these lines illustrate another feature of Howe's use of language in her poems. She often fixates on common words typically loaded with meanings, such as "heart." "My heart was pierced" would be something clichéd to say in a poem or anyplace else. By using this phrase unflinchingly, and by introducing it with "transverberation," resonant of "vibration," "transpiercing," and the introit to the Gospel of John, she allows the poem to descend into a considerable bewilderment in its final two lines. Which is it, we might ask. Take heart, or lose heart? Or is it always both? Note, as well, that in this selection and in the others quoted before, there is a relative absence of many of the features of free-verse prosody. Howe's lines are nearly always unenjambed. She frequently completes phrases on a line-by-line basis or, as often as not, splits the phrase into a couplet. Much as her poems are made up of lines, their lyric properties do not rely on rhyme (internal or end rhyme), the expression of audible meter, or prosodic tactics such as enjambment or pointed line breaking. Nonetheless, the poems feel entirely to be poems. These sequences couldn't be written out as stories, something Howe would know as an accomplished fiction writer.

CRITICAL ANXIETIES

So, where does Howe's Catholicism fit into her work? Critics think it is either connected to her vision of social justice or that it is a mask to hide the "quasi-religious, quasi-intellectual"[18] poverty of her poetry. For instance, the critic Steve Evans wrote the following: "[Fanny Howe's] excellent collection *Gone* joins two other recent books, *The Wedding Dress* and *On the Ground*, in a rapidly expanding oeuvre the driving force behind which is *a ferociously oppositional Catholic faith*."[19] This statement, which, to be fair, appeared in a lengthy, journalistic review of the state of poetry over the course of the ten months surveyed and which was obviously not intended as a critical assessment of Howe's work (in fact, it's the only mention of Howe in the entire piece), nonetheless betrays an anxiety typical of a reader of so-called innovative poetry faced with evidence of Catholicism, or Christian content and context, in a book of poetry. Evans here expresses a desire to recognize the overriding religiosity of Howe's writing while qualifying it in such a way as to make it suitable to secularized, postmodern reading tastes. Howe is Catholic, which connects her to a vast, rather conservative religious organization, but her faith is "ferociously oppositional," which points to its social features and to Howe's political stances, which are acceptably leftist, "oppositional." Her concerns as a Catholic resonate with the social-justice concerns of many Catholics, including Pope Francis, who has made attention to poverty and the environment hallmarks of his pontificate. But she's also a fervent Catholic, one who attends Mass regularly and whose work is suffused with the images and mysteries of her Catholic faith. What kind of Catholic she is remains the question to be asked.

In his review of *On the Ground* in *Poetry* magazine, Brian Phillips accuses Howe of willfully obfuscating the meaninglessness of her poems by clothing them in a religious aura. His mean-spirited appraisal of the book begins, "Fanny Howe's poems fail intellectually, they fail as ideas about poems, before they fail as poems; but the intellectual failure can be harder to notice, as the reader is so seldom in jeopardy of discovering what the poems are about."[20] Phillips describes his distaste for Howe's poetry in terms of his consternation at reading "pages at a stretch" of "garbled half-lyrics slung in neutral white space."[21] He suspects that Howe is merely throwing off "soft clouds of profundity" and that the philosophical and existential "bewilderment" she advocates is merely a ruse "to justify what must be very close to automatic writing."[22] He contends that Howe's poems "surround an aggressively self-assertive and quite deliberately constructed tone of visionary conviction with a numinous, indeterminate haze that deflects criticism on both sides."[23] In describing the "sides," Phillips notes what he perceives to be the way that Howe is manifestly preventing readers from criticizing her poetry. Here his true argument reveals itself. Were Phillips concerned with offering a critique of Howe's poetry, he would likely concentrate on the poetry, evaluating its worth. Instead, he conjures an absurd fantasy in which Fanny Howe is somehow manufacturing rhetoric in order to prevent readers from noticing the emptiness of her poetry. Does Phillips really think Howe would go to so much trouble? Evidently he does, because instead of looking at her poetry, he spends the bulk of his review attacking the nature and expression of her religious views as found in her critical prose. I think Phillips has some valid criticisms, especially that Howe's language is often deliberately plain or vague and that the aphoristic tone is frequently as befuddling as it is clarifying. But Phillips's real argument is that Howe is religious in her poetry and that her religiosity amounts to a solipsistic "romance" that permits an "essential vacuousness."[24] In essence, he is accusing Howe of being a fraud. But what kind of fraud? His opening makes clear that he's less concerned with her fraudulency as a poet than he is with her evidently fraudulent religious convictions.

Since the time this review initially appeared, Howe has become a regular presence in *Poetry*, including her prose. Three selections from *The Winter Sun*, a book that can be described as a spiritual autobiography, appeared in the magazine and on the Poetry Foundation's website. As already mentioned, in 2009, Howe received the Poetry Foundation's most prestigious prize, the Ruth Lilly Poetry Prize. In bestowing the award on Howe, Christian Wiman, the editor of the magazine and a professed Christian himself, praised her work as belonging to no specific doctrine. Rather, it

> lives by the senses and waits for the world to disclose itself, rather than banging away at it with the ice pick of the intellect. Its deepest fidelity is to life, not art. It is feminine, almost always, and it is everywhere in the work of Fanny Howe. . . . The loneliness of poetry, of existence, of consciousness is also everywhere in Fanny Howe's work. It is for me part of what makes it so authentic and moving.[25]

Wiman's downplaying of Howe's faith even while extolling her virtues as a religious poet of an existentialist sort bespeaks a continuing discomfort with discussing Howe as a Catholic poet. In awarding her this prize, why avoid mention of the Catholicism that has motivated so much of her creativity?

CONVERSION AND CATHOLIC POETRY IN AMERICA

It's time, at last, to look at Howe's Catholicism and to witness how it informs her work. Howe's faith has an interwoven narrative and content, which depict her conversion to the church under strained circumstances in her life and the ideas she carries from that conversion into her creative work. Understanding Howe's Catholicism is not an easy task. I think the opinions of Evans, Phillips, and Wiman bear this out: it can be frustrating trying to track her beliefs because they don't neatly fit into the prototypes for the American Catholic poet that we have at hand (let alone spiritual or religiously inflected poetry more broadly); or, it can make readers uncomfortable that being a Catholic is one of the things that makes Howe's work interesting.

Catholic poetry in America has tended to have a fairly low profile, with a few notable exceptions. Thomas Merton, for a period, was probably the most famous convert to Catholicism in the world and certainly the best-known monk, whether in America or abroad. Even as he turned in the later part of his life toward political activism (including protesting U.S. involvement in Vietnam), Merton is still best known for his spiritual and autobiographical writings, especially among Catholics. Merton's *The Seven Storey Mountain* is among the most widely read spiritual autobiography written by a Catholic next to Saint Augustine's *Confessions*. In contrast, I think his poetry goes largely unread. As such, Merton was a Catholic who wrote poetry, at least in the imaginations of his readers, rather than a poet who became a Catholic. Undoubtedly a complex figure, Merton, in his life and work, nonetheless follows a legible track for most readers. Indeed, most of his work these days is published by presses oriented around religious interests; while he was living, New Directions, a poetry press devoted to experimental and international writing, was his principal publisher.[26]

The other American Catholic poet of note in the twentieth century was William Everson, who, like Merton, converted to Catholicism and entered a religious order, in his case, the Dominican priory of St. Albert's in Oakland, California, albeit as a lay brother.[27] Renaming himself Brother Antoninus, Everson devoted himself almost entirely to religious themes in his work, issuing several collections under his new name, which were well received (most notably *The Crooked Lines of God*, an excellent book published in 1959 and nominated that year for a Pulitzer Prize), and he gained popularity and notoriety for his impassioned, audience-excoriating poetry readings on the West Coast, where he was dubbed the "Beat Friar." Everson, again like Merton, was politically active, in his case, before his conversion: he was imprisoned in a work camp in Oregon during World War II for his conscientious objection. (This is the place where he learned, not incidentally, how to operate a printing press, a vocation that would occupy him for the rest of his life, and especially during his years at St. Albert's.) He converted to Catholicism in 1948 while he was in the throes of a passionate love affair with the poet and artist Mary Fabilli, whom he would marry but soon after separate from. Nevertheless, Everson quickly became involved with Dorothy Day's Catholic Worker movement in Oakland, eventually settling in to living and working at St. Albert's. Everson never gained the popularity that Merton had. In 1969, he left the Dominican brotherhood to resume life as a layperson, readopting his earlier name and marrying a woman he had been counseling at the priory. He never renounced his religious beliefs—his later work resounds with Catholic symbol and myth—but he entered at this time into a life less visible. Everson is largely read today from the angle of his poetry, where his Catholicism is understood in terms of the narrative of changes in his life. He was a better poet than Merton, so it makes sense to read him through his poetry. But his conversion and the poetry he wrote as a result of it tend, just as Merton's writings do, to follow a recognizable track. Everson fits comfortably into our sense of religious conversion, just as his work is readily associated with that of the California poets whose company he imitated or sought, such as Robinson Jeffers, Kenneth Rexroth, and Robert Duncan, to name a few.[28]

Howe's conversion, as described in the introduction to *The Wedding Dress*, is every bit as spectacular and interesting as Merton's and Everson's. Even so, her Catholicism is difficult to make sense of. In an interview, she confessed, "I always say that I am (instead of a Roman Catholic) an atheist Catholic. I am half an atheist; I am at home, so to speak, in a secular intellectual environment."[29] I understand this statement as an expression of the existentialism that served as an orienting ideology when Howe was coming of age and beginning to engage the world politically. Nonetheless, I can imagine this label—atheist Catholic—being problematic to another Catholic. Catholicism can espouse existential properties, but atheism cannot be attributed to any of its ideologies, beliefs, or practices. In *The Winter Sun*, Howe writes, "I had been raised and continued to live among skeptics, scholars, atheists, and artists. . . . I knew that God has been proved a failure at intervening on people's behalf within my lifetime."[30] Howe's profession of atheism arises out of a milieu of practical despair. In her interview with Eve Grubin, Howe contends, "One thing I really believe is that God doesn't care who believes in God or not." This makes a good gloss to her atheism: it's not that she doesn't believe in God, it's that she doesn't believe God responds to our plaints or faith in familiar ways. "I think it's our choice to seek God or not," she continues. "It's been called a non-reciprocal relationship. All of the laws have nothing to do with what happens when you get folded away in that wave."[31] This last sentence alludes, I think, to her conversion, the great pivotal event in her inner and outer lives.

HOWE'S CONVERSION

Howe's identity as a Catholic vexes her in the same way her belief in God does. After describing how she does not ever think of herself as a "Christian," quipping, "but you would have to be Catholic to know why this is the case," and after describing the word "Christian" as associated with nationalism and as being ideologically antipathetic to the Gospels, she observes, "On the other hand, Catholicism is queer. It is malleable and reaches extents of thought that really can't rest anywhere, in terms of nation or specific culture. When people call themselves Christians, I get scared."[32] Howe typically textures her faith with qualifications and consternations. It doesn't sit easy with her, but it also feels native to her, idiomatic. In a symposium on Christianity and poetry in which she participated, Howe admitted, "For me the word 'Christian' is fraught with ugly connotations, many of them historical, prissy, close-minded and self-promoting." She added, "It is a 'white' word."[33] This impression speaks directly to her conversion.

It might seem strange for me to declare the introduction to *The Wedding Dress* as one of Howe's most important statements about her Catholicism to anyone who has given it a cursory reading. This essay is largely a description of the tribulations and misfortune Howe experienced as she tried to raise her mixed-race children in the racially divisive Boston of the 1960s and 1970s. Howe's Catholicism, as I read it, has three components: a mystically configured theology; a belief in and reverence toward the sacrament of the Mass, especially the Eucharist; and a commitment to political and cultural justice that Catholic communities, at their best, enact. Howe's introduction speaks directly to this third component, which was the one that helped her raise her children in a time of need and ultimately inspired her to convert. Howe describes how she met Carl Senna, whose father was Mexican and whose mother was African American. They were drawn together because of shared creative, political, and philosophical interests. They married, and in quick succession Howe gave birth to three children by him. Senna was Catholic; his mother was devout. She attended daily Mass on her way to her job at the courthouse in downtown Boston. "We had the children baptized," Howe writes, "and I began attending Mass with my mother-in-law hovering at the back of the church, and feeling myself excluded and estranged from the rituals."[34] Nonetheless, Howe continued to attend Mass and eventually "grew increasingly comfortable sitting at Mass and participating in everything but the Eucharist, for many years."[35] But even as she became more comfortable in the Mass, her life in Boston was fraught by racism toward her children and by the poverty that afflicted her, in part because of the kind of activist life she and her husband were committed to but also because she felt herself denied any opportunities by white-dominated Boston. "Boston," she tells us,

> recalcitrant and class-divided, was a poor choice to live as a mixed couple. Even the most enlightened white academics had no black friends, or tokens only, and fled quickly to the suburbs for the schools. . . . There is very little cross-cultural exchange even at the most privileged level in Boston. From that point down, the divisions have enlarged and darkened and continue to enlarge and darken. [36]

Howe's conversion is directly keyed to her experience of racism during this time. In spite of the poverty in which her family lived, Howe felt it to be a "fertile but lonely time."[37] When Senna's mother died just before the birth of her third child, Howe felt a grief that connected to a feeling of something inside her changing. "Some worldview," she admits, "was inexorably shifting in me, and I felt side-lined by conversations and remarks that would have slid by unnoticed before."[38] She adds, "I quickly learned that white people are obsessed with race, and the subject comes up at least once in any three- or four-hour gathering."[39] She describes an event at which she listened to a group of whites discuss the racial tensions in Boston at the time, indicating quite clearly that if lines were to be drawn, they knew which side they would be on. Howe took these statements of fear and paranoia as ciphers for their faith, which was ultimately as exclusive as their politics. "I feel that my skin is white but my soul is not, and that I am in camouflage."[40] She felt no company in this world; unfortunately, the world of her family was dissolving around her. She and

Senna split up, leaving her to fend for her children and herself, which "was all that drove me."[41]

Her devotion to her children led her from one precarious, impoverished situation to another, always with their well-being as her guiding desire. In the midst of this struggle, she found allies: other poets and writers, other souls disenfranchised from positions of safety in society, particularly other single white mothers with mixed-race children. She squatted with them, communed with them, formed food and babysitting co-ops with them, and continued to write. Through cunning and subtle manipulation of the Boston school system, Howe's daughters graduated from public high schools, and her son was provided with a private education through the generosity of the "many now-despised liberals during this period" that sought to open up alternative schools to nonwhite kids in order to help them escape the public school system. In the end, Howe's commitment to her children compelled her to convert. She confesses:

> It wasn't until five years after my divorce, when I joined those ranks of single white mothers, that I converted to Catholicism. I would have to say that my children led me to that place because I learned everything I ever hoped to learn about consequence from giving birth to them, from raising them, and from saying goodbye to them as they entered their generation's world.[42]

It's impossible not to understand Howe's conversion to Catholicism as an expression of solidarity with her children's racial identities and then, metaphorically, with an institution that provides welcome, ideally, for all kinds of difference. In her poem "Shadows," she writes:

> There is something between them
>
> It climbs colorlike
> The shades of pain
> Describing their skins
> Like a map's edge of ocean
> It laps from her to him
>
> They do feel that third person![43]

It should be pointed out that Howe's sense that "Christian" is somehow a white word while "Catholic" is somehow not is in actuality untenable. By "Christian," she seems clearly to mean "Protestant," but even that's not tenable either. According to a recent survey, 78 percent of African Americans who identify themselves as Christian further identify as Protestant. Only 5 percent identify as Catholic.[44] Howe's description of Christian as a white word refers more meaningfully, then, to herself. It seems clear that Howe devoted a lot of energy as a young woman to putting some distance between herself and her patrician upbringing. To make matters more complicated, one of Howe's daughters, Danzy Senna, has published a memoir about her father, which involves some investigation into his mother's somewhat murky past. This is the woman who inspired Howe's conversion. Senna, prompted largely by family lore, believes that her father's father was not a Mexican boxer named Francisco Senna but, instead, a white Irish Catholic priest named Francis Ryan, with whom Senna's grandmother had a prolonged affair—long enough to have three children by Ryan. While this complicates matters about Howe's declaration that her soul is somehow not white, it doesn't change the fact that Carl Senna was indeed mixed-race and that Howe's marriage to him was fraught with the social challenges that ensued from their mixed-race marriage.[45] Nor does it change the fact that Howe entered her Catholic faith through a door marked with color and race.

"CATHOLIC"

If Howe's introduction to *The Wedding Dress* is her *Confessions*, her poem-essay "Catholic" is her *City of God*, the most complete expression of her theology. It's an immediately impressive piece of writing, made up of thirty-seven sections that present an elaborated Stations of the Cross whose initial notes are depression and despair but whose finale is a fraught but compelling redemption in the Eucharist. Yet there is something vexed about this piece, noted immediately in the ambiguity of the form of writing it represents. Its first publication was in *Chicago Review*'s spring 2003 issue (49:1), in which it was listed as a poem. And "Catholic" frequently conforms to a conventional sense of poetry: several of the sections are made up of lines of verse, and all of them are suffused with Howe's lyric intensity. "Catholic," strangely then, is included in *The Wedding Dress*, where it fits under the label "meditations" appearing in the book's subtitle but where it stands out as the least essayistic, most aphoristic piece in this book of Howe's prose. Subsequently, because it was initially published as a poem in *Chicago Review*, it appeared in *The Best American Poetry* anthology for 2004, edited by Lyn Hejinian.

"Catholic" is strung on the tensions in Howe's poetry described above: an existential flatness of affect that coalesces into aphoristic, lyrical statements often clothed in mystery. Yet the piece involves essayistic elements as well, in a way suggestively more confessional than her poetry ever really seems. The opening two sections are illustrative of these features, the aphoristic lyricism and the confessional quality:

1.

What can you do after Easter?
Every turn of the tire is a still point on the freeway.
If you stand in one, and notice what is all around you, it is a
 pile-up of the permanent.
The churn of creation is a constant upward and downward
 action; simultaneous, eternal. If you keep thinking there is
 only an ahead and a behind, you are missing the side-to-side
 which give evidence to the lie that you are moving
 progressively.
If everything is moving at the same time, nothing is moving
 at all.
Time is more like a failed resurrection than a measure of
 passage.

2.

The drive from the I-5 along Melrose to Sycamore.
The drive up La Brea to Franklin and right then left up to
 Mulholland.
The drive along Santa Monica to the rise up to the right and
 Sunset.
The drive along Sunset east past the billboard of the man on a
 saddle.

> The drive from the 405 up onto La Cienega and the view of hills.
> The difference between nirvana and nihil.[46]

Two thoughts might occur to the reader of these opening sections of "Catholic," particularly in light of Howe's somewhat unusual title. (Is it meant to describe the contents of the piece? Or is it a label for the author herself?) First, there is an immediate sense of the existential drudgery of commuting long distances for work. Howe, we learn from the biographical notes on her books, taught for many years at the University of California–San Diego but lived for a time in Los Angeles, from which she commuted down to La Jolla to teach. One senses, particularly in the references to nirvana and nihil, that she was miserable doing this. The first section conjures an existential endlessness familiar to anyone who has killed time doing something she doesn't really want to do, usually for the purpose of making money.

In this work, Howe is also engaging in apologetics, the part of theology seeking to explain faith and practice to those who don't necessarily share either the faith or the practice. One of the most famous examples of apologetics appears at the beginning of Saint Thomas Aquinas's *Summa Theologiae*, in which he offers five ways of the existence of God. He presents these not as proofs of God's existence but rather to show how it is intelligible to believe that God exists.[47] In the following passage from "Catholic," Howe traces her relationship to Aquinas's thought:

> He was concerned with being, not doing. And his love for the world was so intense, it infused his thought with compassion for all things. He has been compared to Confucius, Sankara, phenomenology. He makes it possible for some people now to remain Catholic despite enormous misgivings and a consciousness of the Church's bad acts. He's not the only one who makes it possible, but he is an important one because he is still considered an Angelic Doctor of the Church, one whose thought remains foundational in Catholicism. You can find his mind there, waiting, permitting, guiding right into modern day life. He saw each person as an important piece of a magnificent puzzle made by and for God.[48]

To whom is Howe apologizing in "Catholic"? In part, she's providing a means for her readers, many of whom are baffled by her Catholicism, to understand her faith. Yes, she admits, the church is presently responsible for unpleasant, even grievously wrong acts. And it's impossible not to be conscious of these acts, even while "remaining" Catholic. Yet even as it's possible to believe that the apologetics is offered to unbelieving readers of contemporary poetry, it is just as likely, and perhaps more important creatively, that she is directing this apology to herself. In another essay in *The Wedding Dress*, Howe wonders: "But what will happen to language now that the word 'God' has fizzled into the existential absurd, so that past and present are buried in instant parries and thrusts from the emptiness ahead?"[49] In "Catholic," Howe seeks an answer to the emptiness of the absurd, to the existential absence she finds abiding in the word "God."

As in her other work, "Catholic" makes metaphysical and ethical commentary on misfortune, telling us "to die prematurely without having found any consolation for disappointment is an injustice." "A person wants," she continues, "to be known, to add up, to be necessary."[50] Her meditations unfold and vary according to the flow and blockage of her commute from Los Angeles down to La Jolla. She's thinking about politics, of course—"Asshole or jerk? Which gets to be President"[51]—but she's also sensing in the tension of her situation a prophetic register, strengthening her axiomatic statements with kerygmatic intensity: "As I get older I don't remember what things are, only what they look like and are named. The way Los Angeles becomes hell at night after being purgatorial all day. When allegory enters time, it is the sign of profound danger."[52]

The allegory is Dante's, of course, the poet who most completely absorbed the teachings of Aquinas, whose own invented cosmology provides the architecture by which, even today, most people in the Christian world imagine the afterlife. The profundity of the danger is not merely that Dante's Hell has come to life—everyone has likely seen something like this, driving through Gary or downriver Detroit or any number of other cities at night. The danger is the supersaturation of reality with the spiritual trials necessitated by faith in that reality. "Why did I end up living in unhappiness for so many years? Unhappiness was the desert, literally and figuratively. / Trees that don't move. Sun on dry dog turds. Black immobile shadows. Temporary infinity."[53] Her spiritual crisis—coming to terms with the emptiness residing in the word God—was transforming into a crisis of reality, imprisoning her in an immobile, temporary infinity. "But something worse, generally, was occurring in the world around me, as it also occurred to me. The restlessness, the consciousness of a disappearing base and goal, the lack of home and civic engagement. I loved no city that I recognized."[54] Dante, famously and mythically, begins his spiral into Hell in the same state of mind: "So bitter it is, death is little more," in Longfellow's translation.[55] Like Dante, Howe expresses her condition in terms that are at once particular—Fanny Howe driving miserably on the freeways of southern California—and universal—a suffering soul in the cities of the latter days of the capitalist, alienated empire issuing existential plaints.

Howe's response to this condition, this state of lovelessness and disengagement, is to reengage the world, but not merely through selfless love, which she endorses unequivocally: "If something you do is good for more people than yourself, you can be pretty sure it is the right thing. (That is, it will make you happy.)"[56] Rather, she regenerates her connection with her life and the larger life of the world through uncertainty. "I pretend that I can take a step," she writes, "with D–th directing traffic and earthquake and heartbeat and hate, is all I know of faith." "Doubt," she adds, "allows God to live."[57] How?

Two possibilities are suggested in "Catholic." The first makes a mysticism of doubt, transforming it into a mode of critical perception. Howe proposes, "Sometimes you are privileged with a glimpse of the other world, when the light shines up from the west as the sun sets and dazzles something wet. The world is just water and light, a slide show through which your spirit glides."[58] This transient perception is underwritten by Aquinas's nature—inasmuch as Howe senses it—as well as his thought: "Aquinas knew that thought was contaminated, but he took circumstances into account and was not a judgmental kind of man, but he didn't have much truck with morose delectation, that kind of morbid indulgence in painful thoughts. Why, because they really undermine hope."[59] Howe's Catholic faith serves, above all, to sanctify her thought.

The complement to the mystical vision of doubt is the Eucharistic vision with which she concludes "Catholic." As she struggles with the daily process of soul erasure as she makes her way in the world, buying material and selling her time, existing in the temporary infinity of her dreadful commute, Howe summons a virtue in paying attention to suffering and its redemption in communal recognition, something the mass ritualizes in the sacrament of the Eucharist. Everybody is invited to the table, or so she believes. I take this concluding passage to be the flaming, sacred heart of Howe's faith, a genuinely moving and sincere glimpse of paradise: "This is why I keep moving and only stop for the Eucharist in a church where there are sick, vomiting, maimed, screaming, destroyed, violent, useless, happy, pious, fraudulent, hypocritical, lying, thieving, hating, drunk, rich, poverty-stricken people."[60]

In one of her interviews, Howe confessed that she felt the taking of the Eucharist was like "eating beauty."[61] Just prior to this Eucharistic vision, Howe describes in an intensely self-lacerating passage the time she was coerced by a "tramp" (I can't think of another poet who could use that word without irony) to spend the night with her in a place where the tramp—whom Howe describes as having "medical problems"—had a couch but wanted Howe to sleep upstairs on a "thin bed." She feels ashamed about capitulating to this woman's needs, especially so when she recognizes the tramp didn't care about Howe, admitting, "Now I realize that I did it because I wanted to know where the ground of being weakens."[62]

Both of these passages are required to complete Howe's Eucharistic vision. The Eucharist, of course, completes Catholic initiation by ritually renewing and thus perpetuating Christ's sacrifice on the cross, making of love a sacrament, making of unity a sign, and making of charity a bond. Each time the host is taken, the believer renews her commitment to this ongoing initiation, to bringing its meaning into a world of doubt, desolation, and confusion. The *Catechism* speaks of the Eucharist in the economy of salvation. Howe's economics, as we've seen, is revisionary and critical of the capitalism that dominates the world we live in. Sacrifice is the currency of salvation. Praise and thanks are the outcomes of the Eucharistic vision. What is Howe praising and giving thanks to? Doubt. Doubt and its vivifying mystery. The divine element it brings into consciousness.

CATHOLICS: A NEW SCIENCE OF THE DEIFUGE

In the roundtable interview in which Howe participated with four other poets to discuss the nature of a Christian poetry, Howe at one point somewhat impatiently insists, "Catholicism is for me a necessity more than a conviction."[63] Conviction would contradict the fulsome doubt and bewilderment that inform her work and her life. "Religion in so far as it is a source of consolation is a hindrance to true faith," writes Simone Weil.

"In this sense atheism is a purification. I have to be atheistic with the part of myself which is not made for God. Among these men in whom the supernatural part has not been awakened, the atheists are right and the believers are wrong."[64] Howe's is a poetry of necessities and purification rather than one of convictions and placations. I think she is more melancholy than redemptive but in no way that detracts her or keeps her away from her soul.

The title of this chapter is meant to ring with two possible meanings. The first is one of communion. I think of myself and Howe as Catholics, both poets, both Americans, both engaged in making creative sense of the world we are thrown into. I sometimes have the thought, "If Teilhard de Chardin could be a Catholic, if Fanny Howe can be a Catholic, so can I." But I also mean for the title to suggest a new creative science I would call Catholics, such that it would belong in a taxonomy alongside Ethics, Economics, Physics, and Metaphysics. "There exists," urges Weil, "a 'deifugal' force. Otherwise all would be God."[65] Let Catholics, then, be the science that tracks the force of the deifuge. And let Howe's poetry serve as one of its core teachings.

7

ROBERT DUNCAN'S CELESTIAL HIERARCHY

ANGELIC POWERS

Chapter 4 looked at Robert Duncan's religious convictions and vexations through the lens of prophecy, in particular his prophetic outlook on poetry itself, which he tended to regard as a genre of inviolable truth. In this chapter, Duncan's religiosity is explored less in terms of his often adamant convictions and more in terms of the dynamic structural elements that constellated his beliefs and richly informed his late poetry, in particular his interest and involvement with angelic powers, a fascination he derived in part from his dedication to H.D.'s *Trilogy*, in particular, "Tribute to the Angels." Writing about H.D.'s poem in *The H.D. Book*, Duncan contends,

> [The] angel is an attribute of God. The old gods and the new, the Greek world and the Christian-Judaic world, have been found in the synthesis of a poetic-theurgy. As in the Cabbalistic system, the source of the voice, the self, is hidden. These angels-gods-guardians are attendants of the poetry itself, the voice in its manifestation. Patrons of the hour of writing, of naming the patron of the hour.[1]

Duncan invariably regards these angelic powers as participants in the great cosmic ritual that poetry in its privileged literary mode uniquely articulates.

To many, *Ground Work*, the first part of which was published in 1984, the second part of which was published shortly before Duncan's death in 1988, appears as the most Sphinx-like of all Duncan's poetry, a monumental riddle erected at life's end. Yet the pleasure of these poems doesn't come from solving them or answering them but from reading them. For all that can be said about Duncan's writing, too little has emerged about what a dedicated, inventive reader he was. *Ground Work* is replete with the evidence of his far-flung, elaborate, and creative reading, from Greek myth to newspapers. He discovered as much in Thom Gunn's *Moly* as he did in the metaphysical poetry of the seventeenth century, and among poets who lived in the twentieth century, perhaps only Osip Mandelstam, Ezra Pound, and T. S. Eliot were as great as readers of Dante. By the time he was writing the work included in the second volume of *Ground Work: In the Dark*, Duncan appears to have absorbed Baudelaire so completely that he begins channeling the poet in his native language. (And, as Clément Oudart has demonstrated, in "Et (*Passages*)" he begins to channel Pound's "Canto I" into French.)[2]

Among Duncan's poems, some of the strongest evidence of the inventiveness of his reading can be found in one of the most perplexing and least attended to sequences in *Ground Work*, "Regulators," which appears as an unnumbered "Set of Passages" in *In the Dark*. Characterized by capacious, sprawling, heavily caesura'd lines that occupy the entirety of the wide trim the book is given, "Regulators" seethes with daunting allusions, a mythos of catastrophic disintegrations, and bizarre angelic messengers clad in disease who constellate the poetic heavens of the sequence. The opening of the first poem of the sequence, "The Dignities," sets the excessive tone for the rest of the "Regulators":

> Bonitas . Magnitudo . Eternitas . Potestas .
> Sapientia . Voluntas . Virtus . Veritas . Gloria
>
> Blesst the black Night that hides the elemental germ,
> the Day that brings the matter to light and its full term.
> For goodness' sake we'll snuff the candle out and turn again to
> dark,
> for there the spark occluded rests most firm bright flower
> of what we know, *bonny fleur*,
> your seed returns to work in what we cannot know.
>
> The smallest particle vertiginous exceeds the Mind.[3]

In these lines, Duncan's readers might recognize familiar but disparate trends in his writing expressed in curious unison. The atavistic listing that begins the poem is reminiscent of the opening and closing of "The Fire, Passages 13," while the lilting rhythms, rhymes, and off-rhymes of the following five lines ring with the voice heard in "My Mother Would Be a Falconress." And the adjectival inversion of "vertiginous" in line 6 makes for a peculiarly Duncanian syntactical amplification, something overtly provocative and excessively poetic flaunted at his readers almost as a dare.

I've puzzled often over this poem and the others in "Regulators"—"The Dignities," "Stimmung," and "In Blood's Domaine," in particular—because they resound with the apocalyptic, prophetic voice that Duncan, with a manic clarity, channeled in his later verse. A definitive interpretation of these poems, while undoubtedly useful to our thematic understanding of the work, would not necessarily explain the allure of this prophetic voice, whose call works so persuasively on my imagination, to say the least. Instead, I'd like to try to *read* these poems, to make use of my own readerly intuitions and associations, coaxing them into the kind of formulations that this late sequence of Duncan's authorizes any of his dedicated readers to make.

Even the opening lines of "The Dignities," proposing a metaphoric germination of the powers of the imagination, suggest the appearance of archaic forces that the poem attends to or is directed by. In naming these powers—both in this first passage and throughout the sequence—Duncan invokes angelic properties. The opening line itself, made up of a list of words in Church Latin, gives descriptive names to these angelic beings. The final name in the list is invoked again later in the poem as the angel Gloria, clothed as the morning glory flower:

> *GLORIA* into color flare vermilion petal o'er pale green
> leaf blue star and violet
> deep purple into bronze wing spread into golden
> wing bright yellow spoil
> Spring's prolific patterning and here, a further shade
> within the shade
> the eye draws in where trembling leaf by leaf among a
> slumbering mass light
> strikes its momentary elections the passage or *limen* the
> where-Glory-abounds[4]

That this "Glory," in Duncan's reckoning, thrives in intermediary realities—in shade deepened by an angelic, florid presence or in the liminal existence between divine and earthly matter that angels occupy—serves to make these poems sound litanical, very much like the "Litany of the Saints" in the Tridentine Roman Missal, which is sung on the feast day of Saint Mark (March 25) or at any time the church is seeking to avert a calamity or to implore the mercy of God.[5] The significance of this invocation is made clear earlier in the poem, when Duncan insists, "The Power holds in what we do undoing claim."[6] The capitalized term "Power" refers directly to the traditional name—"Powers"—given by the early Christian theologian Dionysius in his *Celestial Hierarchy* for the fifth rank, or circulation, of angelic beings. Later in "Regulators," the provocation that forms the powerful opening of "In Blood's Domaine"—"The Angel Syphilis in the circle of Signators looses its hosts to swarm / mounting the stem of being to the head"[7]—is followed in the subsequent poem, "After Passage," by the statement, "And if terror be the threshold of Angelic In-Formation, the Masters / of Nuclear Power, malevolent dreamers, knowing and unknowing," which conjures a different kind of destructive angel, related to the arms race and the terrible power of modern science: "the Angel of this Polluting radiance . . . does and undoes the concordances of the DNA helix."[8] What I'm regularly struck by, whenever I read these poems, is the menacing hybridity of traditional conceptions of angelic beings with Duncan's novel, apocalyptic profusions of disease, illness, madness, and the powers of war. Where does this combination come from?

At a talk and reading Duncan gave after the publication of *The Opening of the Field*, he explained, after reading "Often I Am Permitted to Return to a Meadow," that in 1953, following the completion of *Letters*, "I did have in mind, however, starting a book which would have a definite form, but I wasn't sure about around what themes I would build the forms. In the notebook, I had composed several poems concerning angels and their orders that I eventually discarded in the making of the book," by which he means *The Opening of the Field*. Duncan offered these remarks as a way to put the composition of "Often I Am Permitted" in context.[9] When the poem came to him while visiting London in 1956, he must clearly have felt that he had discovered the theme around which to build his "forms." During the talk, he makes no further mention of "angels and their orders," but my suspicion is that this was a poetic concept deeply embedded in his imagination, such that when the apocalyptic themes of "Regulators" began to appear, he must have sensed, at last, that he could make use of this angelic structure. It therefore seems helpful to me, as a way to begin to approach "Regulators," to rehearse the nature of the "celestial hierarchy" and to summon up its place in Western literature, so as to see the texture of the tradition Duncan was invoking in his poems.

TRIADIC ILLUMINATIONS

The *Celestial Hierarchy* is one of the surviving works attributed to Dionysius—or Denys, as he was known in the English tradition—who was believed for many centuries to be the Greek Paul converted to Christianity at the Areopagus at the Parthenon in Athens (Acts 17:34). (Thus was he known as Dionysius the Areopagite.) Dionysius has proven to be more mythic and enigmatic than the scriptural figure whose name he adopted. He's believed to be a Syrian monk who lived in the fifth or sixth century, who wrote in Greek, and who was deeply schooled in Neoplatonism, particularly in the theological speculations of Plotinus. His *Celestial Hierarchy* is what its title suggests: a treatment of each of the rungs, or circulations, of angelic powers surrounding God in heaven, with a discussion of their abilities, orientation, and meaning. More significantly, the hierarchy constitutes a vastly metaphorical conjuration of the cyclic structures the imagination relies on to approach divinity. "In my opinion," writes Dionysius,

> a hierarchy is a sacred order, a state of understanding and an activity approximating as closely as possible to the divine. And it is uplifted to the imitation of God in proportion to the enlightenments divinely given to it. The beauty of God—so simple, so good, so much the source of perfection—is completely uncontaminated by dissimilarity. It reaches out to grant every being, according to merit, a share of light and then through a divine sacrament, in harmony and in peace, it bestows on each of those being perfected its own form.[10]

According to Steven Chase's commentary on this passage, the numerical values of the arrangement are critical to understanding its figurative content: "The concept of hierarchy being arranged triadically—in three sets of threes, hence the nine orders of angels in three groups of three—is . . . important for Dionysius. The famous triad of purgation, illumination, union is a stamp of the angelic hierarchy through which the human soul is led to God."[11]

These angelic orders, though occasionally invoked in our literature (Pound gave the name "Thrones" to a late slab of the *Cantos*, after all), remain mystifying, a condition that oddly reinforces the strength and beauty of Dionysius's triadic vision, which begins at the innermost and most intense core, expanding outward into creation, into the cosmos:

Seraphim
Cherubim
Thrones
(triad of union/sacred order)

Dominions
Powers
Authorities
(triad of illumination/understanding)

Principalities
Archangels
Angels
(triad of purgation/activity)

Many of the greatest minds of the church and the Christian tradition have meditated on the angelic theophany represented in Dionysius's *Celestial Hierarchy*, from Bonaventure to Alan of Lille to Hugh of St. Victor to Gregory the Great to Bernard of Clairvaux. Likewise, the hierarchy became a cornerstone of esoteric lore, providing patterns through which the zodiac might be discerned, as well as insights into the emanating, precipitating energies of God. (Rudolph Steiner, for instance, proposed a sequence of "group rulerships" exhibited by each of the angelic orders, connecting them directly with aspects of the zodiac.)[12] H.D. made ample reference to angelic powers in *Trilogy*, particularly in "Tribute to the Angels," in which she invokes many of the archangels by name, as in the following lines: "I had been thinking of Gabriel, / the moon-regent, the

Angel, // and I had intended to recall him / in the sequence of candle and fire // and the law of the seven."[13] *Trilogy* was extremely important to Duncan's sense of poetic reality. Dionysius's angels, in the words of Hugh of St. Victor, were a "collection of visible forms for the demonstration of invisible realities."[14] And no poet in the Western tradition has attempted this demonstration more clearly and more dynamically than Dante in the *Paradiso.*

DANTE

In Canto 28 of the *Paradiso*, the great inversion that concludes the *Commedia* takes place, and Dante gazes for the first time on the angelic hierarchies, unencumbered by his earthly vision. His initial disorientation is caused by the concentrated intensity of motion with which the three groups of angelic choirs revolve, since this doesn't harmonize with his own sense of the direction of his journey, which up to this point has led him from atop the Mount of Purgatory, on an earth fixed in place, outward through the seven Ptolemaic heavenly spheres. Having reached the Primum Mobile, Dante, with Beatrice's help, recognizes that rather than traveling outward, he has all along been moving toward the center of creation, where God's divinity blooms in a celestial rose. In his commentary on the poem, Charles S. Singleton writes in a scholarly deadpan that this moment of "turning inside-out . . . as it is prepared for and then finally achieved, is one of the most impressive of the whole poem."[15] Once Beatrice explains that the most intense, most sincere circles of heaven, composed entirely of divine fire, are burning so brightly because of their proximity to God, Dante begins to see the angelic orders, which Beatrice then clarifies for him, following Dionysius's vision precisely. "And Dionysius," says Beatrice in Longfellow's translation, "with so great desire / To contemplate these Orders set himself, / He named them and distinguished them as I do."[16]

Dante's likeliest point of contact for Dionysius's *Celestial Hierarchy* was Saint Thomas Aquinas, who discusses Dionysius's work in his *Summa Theologiae*. Aquinas would have known the work through the translation of John Scotus Eriugena, who brought it from Greek into Latin in the ninth century. Beginning with Dante's description of the transformative moment he experiences in the *Commedia*, the celestial hierarchy has acted as a gravitational force in literature, drawing poets into its tightening, gyrating choirs in their hunger and curiosity to represent the vision anew. Part of this attraction must be attributed to the authority and tradition Dante represents in his poem. Peter S. Hawkins usefully discerns Dante's tendency to choose received belief over invention, allowing his poetry, rather than his ideas, to be the conduit of transformation:

> When Dante wrote the *Commedia*, he no doubt searched the Scriptures, weighed received belief, opted for one authority over another, and came up with a response that suited both his convictions and his purposes. This might mean choosing Bonaventure over Aquinas . . . or siding with Dionysius the Areopagite over Gregory the Great when it came to the precise order of the angelic hierarchies. . . . However it was that he actually made these decisions, they are never presented in the *Commedia* as deriving from Scripture or Reason. . . . Rather, the poet gives us what he made up as if it were what he had received through experience.[17]

I think this sense of Dante's presentation of tradition and authority as based in experience—as manifestations of an uplifting and metaphorical (or anagogical, to use Dante's preferred term) reality—is a helpful gauge for approaching Duncan's involvement with and attraction to Dante. In Duncan's derivative poetics, Dante is not merely a figure or archetype but a gushing source, a being through whom "Creation" issues forth in its "fictive certainties." In "The Sweetness and Greatness of Dante's *Divine Comedy*," Duncan writes,

> for it is Creation, it is the Divine Presentation, it is the language of experience whose words are immediate to our senses; from which our own creative life takes fire, *within which* our own creative life takes fire. The creative life is a drive towards the reality of Creation, producing an inner world, an emotional and intellectual fiction, in answer to our awareness of the creative reality of the whole. If the world does not speak to us, we cannot speak with it.[18]

Duncan's "Dante Études," in *Ground Work: Before the War*, are an ingenious elaboration of a poetic indebtedness to Dante's creative vision. The poem that ends the first book of the sequence, "Letting the Beat Go," is an improvisation related at least in feeling to the moment of inversion in the *Paradiso* when Dante gazes upon the circling spherical choirs of angelic powers, baffled by their irradiating glory. Duncan fantasizes himself, as he had famously done before, as a bird of prey:

> Letting the beat go,
> the eagle, we know, does not
> soar to the stars,   he rides
> the boundaries of the air—
>
> but let the "eagle"
> soar to the stars!   there
> where he's "sent"!   The stars
> are blazons then of a high glamor
>   the mind beholds
> —less "real" for that?—
>   a circling power.
> In holding so he flies,   an idea
>   increasing exultation
> we know in the idea of it,   a tower![19]

The three words set apart in the second stanza—"eagle," "sent," and "real"—are marked by the little apostrophic wings of quotation marks to send them flying into the realm of the imagination, in turn sending Duncan into a rapturous, raptorial mode:

> O farflung valiant eagle
>   venturing in immensities,
> wingd hunger   sent amongst starry
>   powers,
> seraphic predator!
>
> I'd hover here,   a wheel of
>   all the real life here below
>   swept up—
>   the glutted cities, choked streams,

  you think I do not know them all,
  the "facts" of this world,   most
    in this mere sweeping-up?

They are the facts from which I fly

    aloft,

beyond our conversation,   imperial,

insensate,   "high,"

  beyond this matter of our speech here,
  into this furthest reach,   this

incidence of a rapacious

  silence,

gnostic invader of the "Sky"![20]

Duncan's approach to these angelic powers is predatory—but the "gnostic" invasion he imagines stains his later work not as a form of knowledge but as one of disease, a recurrent theme in "The Regulators." The migration that occurs from a vision of reality to an internal vision—"the facts from which I fly / aloft"—is something Duncan insists in *The H.D. Book* to be true of the *Divine Comedy*:

> The world-map of Dante is a curiosity, but the poet in the *Paradiso* looking deep into the profound and shining being of God, for all his theological schema of the trinity, sees "one by the second as Iris by Iris seemed reflected, and the third seemed a fire breathed equally from one and from the other" and it is not the theology that lasts but the seeming. . . . This Paradise, like H.D.'s, that once was a place in the physical universe, now is a place in feeling.[21]

RILKE

The other poet besides Dante who figures in any consideration of angelic powers in the Western poetic tradition is Rilke, who (even more than T. S. Eliot) might be called the most influential religious poet of the modern era. Rilke makes an important appearance in "The Regulators," as one of the diseased figures in "In Blood's Domaine":

> —where black the infected
> blood
>
> gushes forth from Rilke's mouth,   from his nose,   from his
> rectal canal
>
> news his whole body bears as its truth   of the septic
> rose[22]

This passage alludes to Rilke's death by the pricking of the thorn of a rose, or so goes the legend, an injury that led to an infection that killed him. The truth was that Rilke had leukemia, which the rose prick revealed. Legend further tells of Rilke's refusal of any palliative aid, and of his desire to feel the end of his life with his senses fully dilated. Elsewhere in the poem, Duncan intones,

> (No, I do not speak of Evils or of Agents of Death   but these Angels
> are attendants of lives raging within life,   under these Wings we
> dread[23]

But Duncan's understanding of Rilke wasn't uncritical. Writing to Denise Levertov in January 1961, Duncan admits, "And Rilke's *Duino Elegies* which once seemd *all*, show up patches now of make-shift,"[24] and nearly a decade later, in December 1969, describing to Levertov a "long unripe, if not dry, period" he found himself in, he mentions that he's been trying to recover his German by translating from Rilke's *Neue Gedichte*. "And these particular poems of Rilke," he explains, "so adverse to my idea of the poem, this ingrown poetry, growing into its confines against its own natural form—like crystals growing within a geode—sets me to work without infecting my own work."[25] Casual as it might seem, Duncan's sense that the *New Poems* wouldn't introduce a virus into his own work is striking, particularly since Duncan's letter continues, "Whereas the Duinos would swamp me out at this time."

Duncan's attraction to the *Duino Elegies* was an attraction to the angelic. In his essay "The Matter of the Bees," which appears as part of the prose epilogue to *Caesar's Gate* (1972), Duncan remarks on what he takes to be the extraordinary perception Rilke mastered in the *Elegies*, as conveyed in the famous letter Rilke wrote shortly before he died to Witold von Hulewitz, his Polish translator. Duncan writes,

> The process of Rilke's poetics is to create a sense in us of the pre-eminence of that other world; but it is also to convert this world into the food of the other. . . . The work of the *Elegies* has to do then with this alchemy in which the elements of our world are transmuted into the honey-gold of an other. The hive of this order may be the skull, and its combs the tissues of the brain, for thought is one of the Invisibles into which the things of our world pass and are stored like honey. Appearing in thought, the "Angel" of the *Elegies* appears in the Invisible.[26]

In his 1925 letter to von Hulewitz, Rilke attempts to paraphrase the angelic powers he summons in the opening of the "First Elegy," whose original inspiration at Duino Castle—with the first words arriving in a "hurricane of the spirit"—sets the tone for the remaining elegies, even as a gap of nearly ten years stood in the way of their completion. "Wer, wenn ich schriee, hörte mich denn aus der Engel / Ordnungen?" the famous first line of the elegy runs in the original German. Along with the strophe that follows, this opening is equally familiar in English translation:

> Who, if I cried, would hear me among the angelic
> orders? And even if one of them suddenly
> pressed me against his heart, I should fade in the strength of his
> stronger existence. For Beauty's nothing
> but beginning of Terror we're still just able to bear,
> and why we adore it so is because it serenely
> disdains to destroy us. Every angel is terrible.[27]

Explaining himself to his Polish translator, Rilke asks, "Transformed? Yes, for it is our task to imprint this provisional, perishable earth so deeply, so patiently and passionately in ourselves that its reality shall arise in us again 'invisibly.' *We are the bees of the invisible.*"[28] This is the passage to which Duncan was responding in *Caesar's Gate*. Improvising in his letter on this sensation of the invisible, Rilke qualifies the nature of these angels who watch over the process of spiritual transformation, "The 'angel' of the *Elegies* has nothing to do with the angel of the Christian heaven (rather with the angel figures of Islam). . . . The angel of the *Elegies* is that creature in whom the transformation of the visible into the invisible, which we are accomplishing, appears already mated."[29] This discernment is powerful, if only because it demonstrates Rilke's understanding of the differences between Christian and Islamic angelology at a time when few others would sense such a thing. For Rilke, angels indicate a lucid intermediary realm hovering between seeing and vision. We use our eyes to see the earth; we use vision to see the divine. The angels of the *Elegies* are beings whose power is apocalyptic, revelatory; they are what Hugh of St. Victor said of them in the twelfth century, "a collection of visible forms for the demonstration of invisible realities."[30]

A reference to this same "matter of the bees" in *The H.D. Book* simultaneously clarifies and confuses what Duncan understands to be the meaning of apocalypse, revealed in the terminology of disease and vehement passions. In his discussion of H.D.'s "The Walls Do Not Fall," Duncan sees a connection between Rilke's recognition that poetry is alienated from what Duncan calls "the commodity culture" and H.D.'s nostalgia for life before the catastrophe of the First World War. Both Rilke and H.D., in Duncan's eyes, implicitly understand the poet as one of the "bees of the invisible":

> The "honey" Rilke and H.D. speak of is such "rapture," the secretion of the life experience of a besieged spirit, part then of a complex that includes the other features we find in apocalyptic statement—anger, outrage, despair, fear, judgment. The flaming cities are not only representations of persecutions suffered or punishments anticipated in heresy, they are also representations of a revenging wrath projected by the heretic, the stored-up sense of injustice and evil will over us raging outward. Within the picture painted or raised in the poem, as in the individual psyche and in the society at large, we see the same symptoms.[31]

Duncan's insistence that the acts of the imagination are symptomatic of cosmic maladies enacted in the body says as much about the mood of the days (this passage was written in 1968) as it does about his chronic, antagonistic conception of creativity as a form of illness. Something he regards as perfectly normal, ordinary. "The artist then," Duncan writes, "is not only psychically at odds but physically at odds."

The crucial term in Rilke's "First Elegy" is the German *Ordnungen*, rightly translated as "orders" by Leishman and Spender. The word could just as easily be rendered as "hierarchies," as in Stephen Mitchell's translation,[32] but what is gained by Mitchell in the allusion to Dionysius is balanced by the loss of the Blakean sense of God as the orderer of the stars and angels. The word *Ordnung* has a commonplace meaning in German, while the verb form, *ordnen*, suggests regulation as much as order. (It means to arrange something, or to tidy up.) My conjecture, then, is that when Duncan was ready to write his own sequence of poems about angelic orders, in such a way that he could withstand Rilke's infectious influence but still memorialize Dante's original vision, he chose "Regulators" as his title to invoke this ordering, this regulation—as deranged and irregular as it was.

TUNING THE DARKNESS

Duncan's conceptualization of angelic orders in the "Passages" sequence was also very likely inspired by a 1974 performance of a Karlheinz Stockhausen piece entitled *Stimmung*. The piece was performed, according to Stephen Fredman, by "the Ballet of the XXth Century, Maurice Béjart artistic director, accompanied by the Collegium Vocale of Cologne, under the direction of Wolfgang Fromme. The entire program consisted of Stockhausen's *Stimmung*, without intermission, and it was performed at the Masonic Auditorium in San Francisco, February 9, 1974, 8:30 P.M., February 10, 2:30 and 8:30 P.M.."[33] This is the performance Duncan attended, with Michael Palmer and Bobbie Creeley.[34] The piece, which has fifty-one sections, grew out of Stockhausen's experimentation with humming, a word alluded to in the meaning of the title, which, in German, can mean both "tuning," in a technical sense, and also "mood" or "feeling," in an atmospheric sense.[35] The piece is composed for six singers who are amplified by microphones and sing in just intonation, keyed to a B-flat drone. According to the liner notes from the 1986 Hyperion Singcircle recording, "In 29 of the sections, 'magic names' are called out. These are the names of gods and goddesses from many cultures—Aztec, aboriginal and Ancient

Greek, for instance—and have to be incorporated into the character of the model."[36] The voices intoning these atavistic presences encouraged Duncan to constellate, to order, his own notions. As he writes in "Stimmung," "The Master Architect has arranged horizons in a renewing design."

"The Dignities" invoked in the opening poem of "Regulators" establish, I think, Duncan's synonym for angelic beings, with entities such as "Gloria," for example, designated as a "Dignity" commanding the design of the poem, presumably a characteristic of the work's Master Architect. Throughout the poem, other Dignities are named and brought forth:

> Veritas.   In truth, Beauty   is a ninth Dignity   hidden
>   in the   fitness.
>
> In a flash   the Lie   seen   truly what it is
>   —driven thru to the very core—
>   to err   is to   find out   anew   this
>   What   we know   persists
>   fitful tho it comes to us   in starts   whose spectral
>   presence underlies
>   —it is the ground of us—
>   every "where" presides   —follow the leader and
>   its music rides as we go.[37]

In "Stimmung," the third poem in "Regulators," Duncan refers to the utterances of the singers in Stockhausen's composition in relation to the Dignities,

> So the Preacher arises again   just when, exalted, we would
>   call upon the Dignities
>   and   luminous   self-evident   transcendent   these,
>   governing,   take their stand[38]

and later in the poem, he more fully describes the performance of Stockhausen's piece:

> All the Time   the Nine actors   stand   "motion-
>   less"   staring   into the

Mind-Space-Time project   the "depth" our perspectives
seek out   hearing

in the grace of a new music   the root the
Preacher thinks to come from

very like the aura of this Falling-in-Love   Stimmung.

Do they countenance the grinding down of lives,   the
poisons pouring out from fortunes and
powers,   Here sound their "A"?

Do they overlook   this ruining of the ways?

As if their faces were flowers   the immoveable masks of the
Dignities

open to the air   lure and regard of a persisting world[39]

In these lines, Duncan echoes a paranoiac mood, anticipative of catastrophe, that he had introduced earlier in *Ground Work II: In the Dark*, in the poem "The Cherubim (I)," which begins with an image of the Ark of the Covenant and the sheltering wings of the scriptural tetramorphs: "Across the ark the wings / commingling / touch in touch until / the will / of each other both close / dark / and dreaming eyes."[40] Later in the poem, which includes yet another figuration of the poetic spirit as a bird of prey, Duncan registers the metaphoric powers of the Cherubim as "rapacious," worrying:

For it is of the stalking I am speaking,
of the tread sinister that follows us thru time,
the attendant wings
surrounding the voice I fear we
begin to hear

and you.[41]

This mood carries forward into what must be regarded as the great induction of angelic pageantry in Duncan's poetry: "In Blood's Domaine."

This is a poem of such exquisite morbidity that, in spite of its grimness, it embodies a great ritual celebration of death and illness and serves as a potent precognition of Duncan's catastrophic demise soon to come.

In his "Commentary on 'The Secret of the Golden Flower,'" a Chinese alchemical text, Carl Jung scolds Europeans for their Enlightenment hauteur:

> We think we can congratulate ourselves on having already reached such a pinnacle of clarity, imagining that we have left all these phantasmal gods far behind. But what we have left behind are only verbal specters, not the psychic facts that were responsible for the birth of the gods. We are still as much possessed by autonomous psychic contents as if they were Olympians. Today they are called phobias, obsessions, and so forth; in a word, neurotic symptoms. The gods have become diseases; Zeus no longer rules Olympus but rather the solar plexus, and produces curious specimens for the doctor's consulting room, or disorders the brains of politicians and journalists who unwittingly let loose psychic epidemics on the world.[42]

As a devoted Freudian, Duncan was, for the most part, skeptical and critical of Jung's ideas. But he made a rapprochement with Jung in his late essay "The Self in Postmodern Poetry," in which he admits, "Freud's intuitions are creative; it is his creative certainty that makes him go too far enough to reveal what cannot be known. Where Jung's reading is always learned and philosophical; he is gnostic. Yet, it is in going back to the texts of Jung, here again, going back to what I thought to disown that I find how striking this knowledge of the Self must have been."[43] Duncan's revelatory innovation in "In Blood's Domaine" is to perceive the Rilkean angelic hierarchies as bearers of disease and of the zodiac. The Angel Syphilis enters the poem in its opening line, bearing the "spirochete invasions that eat at the sublime envelope, not alien, but familiars / Life in the dis-ease radiates"—invasions that consumed Baudelaire, Nietzsche, and Swift. (Spirochetes are infectious bacteria.) Furthermore, "The Angel Cancer crawls across the signs of the Zodiac to reach its / appointed time and bringing down the carnal pride bursts into flower—," a figurative construct that Duncan also refers to in his "Pages from a Notebook": "Only the most fanatic researcher upon cancer could share with the poet the concept that cancer is a flower, an adventure, an intrigue with life."[44] The poem continues to invoke these terrifying angels,

And the pneumatics torn in the secret workings of the Angel
Tuberculosis

(No, I do not speak of Evils or of Agents of Death but these
Angels
are attendants of lives raging within life, under these
Wings we dread[45]

and then concludes with its most menacing gesture,

What Angel, what Gift of the Poem, has brought into my
body

this sickness of living? Into the very Gloria of Life's
theme and variations
my own counterpart of Baudelaire's terrible Ennuie?[46]

Does it sound like a deflection to note, simply, how extraordinary these lines are? In one of his last books, *Words with Power*, Northrop Frye asks, "What kind of language is appropriate for words that do not represent objects or events, or even the totality of them?"[47] I think these final lines of "In Blood's Domaine"—as with the entirety of "Regulators," if revealed in a less crystallized form—are a demonstration of this kind of language, which transcends the representation of objects or events or their totalities and are mythical and metaphorical at their core. To begin to make sense of these poems is to enter into verisimilitude caught from the Penetralium of mystery that Keats elicits from the example of Coleridge. In Duncan's imagination, the body itself becomes a negative capability that the poem, in an act of literary shamanism, ritually dismembers at the hands of the bacterial hosts of angelic beings, "In one way or another to live in the swarm of human speech,"[48] bringing to the poem an "intrigue with life" that is a "sickness with living," such that every angelic disease is a revelation.

In a late chapter of *The H.D. Book*, Duncan insists:

What the dogma of science with its imagination of the world in terms of use and manipulation for profit and the dogma of theology with its view of reality in terms of authority and system oppose in the cult of angels is

> the absolute value given to the individual experience that would imagine the universe in terms of love, desire, devotion, and ecstasy, emotions which men who seek practical ends find most disruptive.[49]

Duncan's poetry seeks impractical, cosmic ends. Despite his frequently strident professions of truth, poetic and religious, and often because of his far-flung intellectual curiosity, Duncan's religiosity found its most vivid expressions in his poetry, experiential at its core, reflecting the onset of his own physical illness in light of the angelic realities he saw in the writings of Dionysius, Dante, and Rilke. The angels inhabiting Duncan's celestial hierarchy are forms of his intellect and experience, expressions of love, desire, devotion, and ecstasy.

8

THE LONG HUTHERED HAJJ

Nathaniel Mackey's Esotericism

What compulsion lies behind the recitation of a text, sacred or poetic? What leads the words into life, clothing them with meaning? In 610 CE, in a cave on Mt. Hira just outside Mecca, the archangel Gabriel revealed himself to Muhammad, an unlettered merchant from the city who, responding to the call of a spiritual vocation, was involved in a month-long period of fasting and meditation. Gabriel urged Muhammad, in the words of the Quran, "Recite! In the name of thy Lord who created!" announcing to him the first verses of the book the meaning of whose name is derived from the Arabic word for recitation. The Islamic scholar Seyyed Hossein Nasr refers to this moment as a sonoral revelation, which in turn would be written down: "When the archangel Gabriel first appeared to the Prophet, the sound of the first verse of the Quran reverberated throughout the space around him."[1] The scholar Karen Armstrong points out that, in what seems comparable to the reverberated sound signaling the beginning of the Quran ("the central theophany of Islam"), Muhammad took the name of God in Arabic, *al-Lah*, and deliberately thickened the sound of the *L* at its center, transforming it into *al-Llah*, to distinguish the uncreated God of Islam from the pagan gods who bore the same name in the Arabian peninsula at the time.[2] One might describe the liturgical art of Quranic recitation as a metaphorical thickening of the sonoral revelation, whose art and variety arise from certain severe restrictions: the inviolability of the text itself, which cannot in any way be altered, expressed through breathing techniques that allow for only one phrase at a time to be vocalized (or, in the case of long phrases, half of a phrase), ornamented by the extension of vowel sounds and the nasalizing of hummed sounds, specific to the Arabic in which the Quran was revealed.[3]

Sacred texts necessarily involve proscriptions about how to tell them, what interpretations of them might be permitted. Robert Duncan, in one of his most authoritative pronouncements, defines the compulsions of recitation in terms of permission and restraint, insisting,

> Myth is the story told of what cannot be told, as mystery is the scene revealed of what cannot be revealed, and the mystic gnosis the thing known that cannot be known. The myth-teller beside himself with the excitement of the dancers sucks in the inspiring breath and moans, muttering against his willful lips; for this is not a story of what he thinks or wishes life to be, it is the story that *comes to him* and forces his telling.[4]

I've always found the pun of the myth teller *beside himself* to be especially telling of Duncan's sense of myth and poetry: It's as much a state of alienation as of involuntary emotion (as in being beside yourself with anger). Myth, whose current is filled with poetry, demands to be told but then forces its teller to reveal things that should never be told. In this sense, Duncan constructs an understanding of myth parallel to Freud's famous understanding of the word "uncanny," when Freud claims that, because of its volatile nature, which is prone to various forms of doubling, its meaning merges with the increasingly ambivalent definition of its opposite (*heimlich*, or familiar, in German). "The uncanny," Freud writes, "is in some way a species of the familiar."[5] Myth, Duncan proposes, is that inexpressible, secret part of the fabric of everyday utterance, as much a license as it is a prohibition.

Nathaniel Mackey is a poet unusually attuned to the thickening of the word that the compulsion to a poetic myth commands and inspires. And in Mackey's mind, this compulsion is as much an imprisonment as it is a liberation. Remarking on the circularity that drives much of his poetic composition, Mackey suggests:

> Recursiveness can mark a sense of deprivation, fostered by failed advance, a sense of alarm and insufficiency pacing a dark, even desperate

> measure, but this dark accent or inflection issues from a large appetite or even a utopic appetite. . . . Recursiveness, incantatory insistence, is liturgy and libation, repeated ritual sip, a form of sonic observance aiming to undo the obstruction it reports.[6]

Splay Anthem, his fourth book of poetry, permits readers to make some important claims about his work, even as it also forces some serious reconsideration of what is happening in that work. Mackey's poetry has been dominated for four decades by two recurring series, "The Song of the Andoumboulou" and "*mu*," both of which, in recent years, have begun more and more to resemble each other. The publisher of *Splay Anthem*, New Directions, wisely compelled the poet to write a preface for the book, presumably to help orient new readers into the labyrinth of these series. I say wisely because the suggestion to write the preface prompted the typically discreet Mackey to make certain of his positions clear. For one, speaking of the two series' involvement with each other, Mackey admits, "Each is the other, each is both, announcedly so in this book by way of number, in earlier books not so announcedly so. By turns visibly and invisibly present, each is the other's twin or contagion, each entwines the other's crabbed advance."[7] In "Song of the Andoumboulou: 46," he puts it this way:

> They lay entwined, asymmetric
> twins, each the other's
> long lost remnant, each
> in what seemed like speaking
> mounted skyward, each
> the
>
> other's complement, coughed
> up a feather, watched it
> float.[8]

Mackey's earlier books of poetry—*Eroding Witness*, in which both of these series originated; *School of Udhra*, which pursued both series in different directions; and *Whatsaid Serif*, devoted entirely to "Song of the Andoumboulou"—are each marked by the poet's obsessive themes: disintegration (erosion), knowledge (witnessing), the transmission of knowledge (schools/esotericism), lore/mythology (West African, Afro-Caribbean,

African American), neology/punning (whatsaying, serif/seraph), and the kinds of hermeneutic, religious systems that provide interpretive structure for fraying, splaying knowledge and its secret transmissions. *Splay Anthem* advances these themes while involving them more deeply in the poet's strange and idiosyncratic mythology and his strategies of esoteric expression. More recently, Mackey has published two additional books, *Nod House* (2011) and *Blue Fasa* (2015), both of which continue to extend and transform these two series ("Song of the Andoumboulou" reaches number 110 in *Blue Fasa*; "*mu*" reaches number 88). "The song of the Andoumboulou," writes Mackey, "is one of burial and rebirth, *mu* momentary utterance extended into ongoing myth, an impulse toward signature, self-elaboration, finding and losing itself. The word for this is *ythm* (clipped rhythm, anagrammatic myth)."[9]

The voice in these poems is characterized by several verbal and rhetorical strategies, and I'd like to emphasize three of them: Undercutting the poems through the act of "whatsaying"; thickening the word of the poems through specific sonic and grammatical wordplay, especially evident in his use of the conditional mood; and expressing an esotericism unique in American poetry. First among these strategies is "whatsaying," a term Mackey borrows from West African storytelling to designate the activity of a jester/fool figure whose duty it is to interrupt the normative narration of a myth with subversive, "paracritical" commentary. In this sense, I equate Mackey's whatsaying with "unsaying," as it has been defined by Michael A. Sells in *Mystical Languages of Unsaying*. There, Sells asserts that unsaying, or apophasis, is "a propositionally unstable and dynamic discourse in which no single statement can rest on its own as true or false, or even as meaningful. In such discourse, a rigorous adherence to the initial logical impasse of ineffability exerts a force that transcends normal logical and semantic structures."[10] Consider, for instance, the following lines from "Song of the Andoumboulou: 50":

Verge that we wanted
verge was the song we sang had there been a
song we sang. No song left our lips.

Nonsonant, we rounded circle's edge,
nonsonant ring shout, verge our muse
and mount.

. . . .
Sparks rose near the well, an
extinguished fire, hung like a signal
or a sign of moving on, a symbol, some
said, showing forth . . . "Post-ecstatic"

was

a word we heard, "copacetic" a word we
heard, "After ecstasy what?" a question
posed in smoke . . .[11]

A crucial term here is "nonsonant," a Mackey coinage, ringing of nonsense and no-sound but also of consonance. Whatsaying, like unsaying's illogical pull, is nonsonant. Norman Finkelstein regards nonsonance as a metonym for Mackey's poetry in and of itself, resonant of its commitments to wordplay and its somatic insistences. "Nonsonance is both prefigurement and warning, a foretold or destined place or experience felt in the body, the blood, to which the poet and his company crosses, toward which we go."[12]

The action of *Splay Anthem*, such as it can be discerned, involves a crew of beings who speak in the first-person plural, the "andoumboulouous we" Mackey mentions in the preface. The Andoumboulou, as initiated readers of Mackey's poetry know, are a mythical species invoked in Dogon funeral song, representing a failed human species, now ghostly, who haunt human memory. "I couldn't help thinking," Mackey confesses, "of the Andoumboulou as not simply a failed, or flawed, earlier form of human being but a rough draft of human being, the work-in-progress we continue to be. The commonplace expression 'man's inhumanity to man' has long acknowledged our andoumboulouousness."[13] Note the flexibility Mackey coaxes from this unusual word, such that it is at once proper noun, adjective, and abstract concept. He takes advantage of this flexibility in the mythical narrative of his poem, such that his "we" finds itself in a perpetually transforming journey of uncertainty. Take the opening of "Spectral Escort" ("*mu*," seventeenth part):

Not exactly a boat or
not only a boat . . .
Weathervane, boat,

flag rolled into
one, furled spur
it
fell to us to
unravel[14]

The figure of a scroll as a vehicle is repeated in "Eye on the Scarecrow" ("*mu*," twentieth part), such that it is Islamic pilgrimage, frayed carpet, and mysterious text simultaneously:

It was a journey we
were on, drawn-out
scrawl we made a road
of, long huthered hajj
we
were on. Raw strip
of cloth we now rode,
wishful, letterless
book
the ride we thumbed.[15]

In "Song of the Andoumboulou: 42," Mackey identifies the vehicle of the journey explicitly as a book,

What we rode was a book. We
fell out of it, scattered[16]

only to revise the book in "Song of the Andoumboulou: 44" into a club where "we" watches a jukebox spinning records:

Wherever we were it was a tavern
we were in, a bar we stepped up
to, ordered . . . Stood in front of
the jukebox, bartender at our backs,
rapture
what before we thought ruin . . .
Whatever we rode it was a record
we spun[17]

Note Mackey's compulsive use of the "w" sound in these selections, ones that permit/force him into a disorienting, conditional indeterminacy, so that "we" is never sure of where it is—wherever, whatever. Mackey's fixation on the sound of the letter *w* signals the second of the strategies mentioned above: *w* is the letter Mackey most frequently uses to thicken the word. "We" is the operative pronoun in his serial epic, an indeterminate collective speaking most often in unison but never in certainty adrift in the world in a way that is plaintive, subjugated, and Gnostic because this condition alludes to a revelation never entirely arrived at. Finkelstein has noted, "Removing pronominal categories to form a collectivity grounded in both history and myth is fundamental to Mackey's poetic."[18] This removal defaults at "we," suggesting that a thickening of the word is a densifying and sacralizing of the collectivity, even as its use removes certainty. Notice what happens in "Sound and Semblance":

> It was the bending of boughs we'd
>   read about, Ibn 'Arabi's reft
> ipseity, soon-come condolence,
>   thetic
>   sough. We saved our breath, barely
>   moved,
>   said nothing, soon-come suzerainty
> volubly afoot,   braided what we'd
>   read and what we heard and what
>   stayed sayless,   giggly wind,
>   wood,
>   riffling wuh . . .[19]

"W," a consonantal sound that drifts into the openness of a vowel, makes the sonic space for reft ipseity—broken selfhood—to be collectively, temporarily constituted in the thetic sough whose note is a sayless "wuh." "Where we were," writes Mackey in "On Antiphon Island" ("*mu*," twenty-eighth part), "not- / withstanding, wasn't there . . ." Collective identity has the property of an erasure or deliberate disorientation. The poem goes on:

>   Where we
>   were was the hold of a ship we were

caught

in. Soaked wood kept us afloat . . . It
wasn't limbo we were in albeit we
limbo'd our way there. Where we
were was what we meant by "mu."

Where

we were was real, reminiscent
arrest we resisted, bodies briefly

had,

held on
to.[20]

To finish with:

Where we were they said likkle for little, lick
ran with trickle, weird what we took it
for . . . The world was ever after, elsewhere,

no

way where we were
was there[21]

The world was ever after: as close to a direct statement of Mackey's Gnosticism as we're likely to find in his work. The ongoing process of testing and contesting reality by thickening its components enables the Gnostic vision as well as the poetry. "To replace waking with realization," as Mackey puts it.[22]

The realm between dream and waking, between vision and realization, is presided over by a demiurge less menacing than obfuscating and disorienting:

Some we

met said it was only a trap, rapt-
anagrammatic diminution we were
shadowed by, mango seed retreat
notwithstanding, demiurgic trick . . .[23]

Here, "trap" and "rapt" make anagrammatic foreshadow of the demiurgic trick of the mango seed (most of the letters of "mango" are there in "anagram"). And the ellipsis serves as Mackey's most characteristic punctuation, a continuance without reference, a provocation for his readers to imagine the endlessness of the journey of "we" forward. Watch all of these features—the repetitions, the "w" sounds, the disorientations and double-takes, the unfinished ellipsis—come together in these lines from the same poem as the lines quoted above, "Song of the Andoumboulou: 50," in which we get a hint of the meaning of the book's title:

> Verge that we wanted verge kept
> insinuating,   song we'd have sung
> had there been one,   anthem
> circling assumed. It was a healing
>
> song
>
> we sang had there been a song we
> sang, swirling water we intimated
> wet our feet . . .[24]

I take the lines "It was a healing / song / we sang had there been a song we / sang" to serve as ideal text for the amulet Mackey makes of his poetry. The poem itself is understood as something lost, something no longer existent but whose memory compels the telling the poet is incapable of ceasing.

Which makes for something very mysterious, to say the least. In Mackey's poetry, mysteriousness gives way to striking but unresolveable esoteric professions. Mackey's esotericism is so rich, so permutative, and so vexing, I'm willing to claim him the most esoteric poet in the American tradition, even more decidedly hermetic than H.D. or Robert Duncan, both poets to whom Mackey is deeply indebted. Mackey's work moves to the limits of reason to engage the transrational phenomena that occupy the peripheries of our perceptions. Think of his work as a sequence of precipitations, in his own words, from "the intuitive, the uncanny, the oneiric, the sympathetic, the coincidental, the ecstatic, the intangible, the paradoxical, the oceanic, the quirky, the psychosomatic, the quixotic, the religioerotic, and so on."[25] In *Splay Anthem*, he fixes these elements into a grand, idiomatic, and catastrophic mythology that is esoteric in a primary sense of the meaning of that word. The historian of hermeticism Antoine Faivre defines esotericism as the theory that makes the practices of occultism possible.[26] He defines occultism as "the homo-analogous principle, or doctrine of correspondences," by which "things that are similar exert an influence on one another by virtue of the correspondences that unite all visible things to one another and to invisible realities as well."[27] Faivre elaborates the definition of esotericism to suggest that it

> has a meaning that is apparent from its etymology, which refers to an "interiorism," an entry into the self through a special knowledge or gnosis, in order to attain a form of enlightenment and individual salvation. This special knowledge concerns the relationships that unite us to God or to the divine world and may also include a knowledge of the mysteries inherent to God himself. . . . To learn these relationships, the individual must enter, or "descend," into himself by means of an initiatory process, progressing along a path that is hierarchically structured by a series of intermediaries.[28]

The Andoumboulou serve, I think, as intermediaries for Mackey's esotericism, just as "*mu*" records the transformation of the initiation, a kind of litany/liturgy invoked as part of a rite of change. In "Song of the Andoumboulou: 50," Mackey recognizes,

> Limbo the book of
>
> the
>
> bent knee . . . Antiphonal thread
> attended by thread. Keening string
> by thrum, inwardness, netherness . . .[29]

The word "netherness" captures something unique about Mackey's esotericism. This word, and the myth of the Andoumboulou more broadly, represent what the historian of Kabbalah Joseph Dan calls "the imperfection of beginnings." Dan uses this provocative phrase to characterize the thought of Isaac Luria, the sixteenth-century Palestinian Jewish mystic who revolutionized the Kabbalah of this period. According to Dan, in answer to the bold but rarely asked question, Why everything?, Luria formulated a mystical perception of catastrophic origination, based on his conviction that "existence does not begin with a perfect Creator bringing into being an imperfect universe; rather, the existence of the universe is the result of an inherent flaw or crisis within the infinite Godhead, and the purpose of creation is to correct it."[30] And at the core of Luria's formulation was the threefold description of catastrophe: *tsimtsum*, or withdrawal at the moment of creative intensity; followed by *shevirah*, or shattering, as a result of the influx of overwhelming divine force exploding into creation; culminating in *tikkun*, or restoration by human intervention of the brokenness of the cosmos. Dan identifies *shevirah* as the esoteric core of Luria's teaching, describing it as "very destructive for religious thought: the supreme divine power undertook an endeavor, and failed to carry it out."[31]

Kabbalah is something only rarely alluded to in Mackey's poetry; it would be inaccurate to ascribe Jewish mystical elements to his work. Nevertheless, I would describe Mackey's poetry as Lurianic, at least partially. It's Lurianic at least in its perception of creation as crisis, in its conviction in poetry's netherness that gestures toward an unrectified inwardness. Mackey's attraction to the Andoumboulou mythos attests to his interest in brokenness, netherness, waywardness, ghostliness, and the unfixable. Just so, his reading of reality is not fixed; rather, it's a revision, a destabilization of the presumptions involved in the imperfection of beginning. I say partially Lurianic because, notably, there is no *tikkun* in Mackey's work. The narrative progress of the reft "we" in *Splay Anthem* offers no consolation of restoration. Rather, there is a crablike, discrepant movement, as signaled by the epigraph from Charles Olson that begins the book: "and all motion / is a crab."

Reading *Splay Anthem*, I'm compelled that Mackey's work is driven by a *negative epistemology*.[32] This means that the hidden truth discovered in Mackey's poetry is, overwhelmingly, disastrous, disintegrating, disabling, and catastrophic. A positive epistemology, by contrast, typically involves a kind of transcendence resulting from the exposure to the hidden truth—a clarity, a gnosis, an imaginal reality perceived and understood. Historical Gnosticism, for instance, presents the prospect of deliverance from the fallen, created world through revelation of its ultimate reality. This is not to say the process of acquiring this knowledge doesn't involve hardships—horrors, even. But it is to say, deliverance is the promise of this sort of epistemology. The relatively recently published *Gospel of Judas* offers many instances or promises of extraordinary, liberating knowledge. Early in the gospel, in a scene typical of the canonical Gospels as well as other Gnostic gospels, Jesus is standing with the disciples, who are struggling to understand him and trying to define who he is. Jesus says to them, "How do you know me? Truly [I] say to you, no generation of the people that are among you will know me." This provocation enrages the disciples, who begin cursing Jesus in their hearts. Jesus provokes them further, challenging them, "[Let] any one of you who is [strong enough] among human beings bring out the perfect human and stand before my face." In spite of their insistence that they have the strength to meet Jesus's challenge, none of the disciples would stand before him "except for Judas Iscariot. He was able to stand before him, but he could not look him in the eyes, and he turned his face away." Then, Judas says, "I know who you are and where you have come from. You are from the immortal realm of Barbelo. And I am not worthy to utter the name of the one who has sent you."[33] The translators of the *Gospel of Judas* helpfully indicate that Barbelo refers to the immortal realm of "the divine Mother of all, who often is said to be the Forethought (*pronoia*) of the Father, the infinite One."[34] For having apprehended this truth, in essence, by revealing the secret name, Judas is rewarded with private teachings from Jesus, who promises, "I shall tell you the mysteries of the kingdom. It is possible for you to reach it, but you will grieve a great deal."[35] This entire exchange fairly characteristically represents a positive epistemology, through which an adept arrives at a greater understanding of reality, albeit typically by way of considerable struggle.

But Mackey's negative epistemology offers no such promise, no such delivery. My intention here isn't to discredit Mackey's Gnostic leanings, ones I've described in the past to characterize and to understand his work.[36] Rather, I'm struck by the nature of the knowledge acquired in this poetic journey, whose expression is various forms of unendingness, as in this under-the-line conclusion to "Song of the Andoumboulou: 51":

> To ride was a well gone to too often, a
> dry world we circumambulated suddenly
> awash, Anuncia's belated largesse.
>
> The
>
> road was all there was and ride was all
> we did.[37]

I sense the circumambulation—reflective of many other circularities in the book, from spinning records to curlicue winds—to refer obliquely to the long huthered hajj identified in "Eye on the Scarecrow." Pilgrims fulfilling the Hajj, the annual Islamic pilgrimage to Mecca, must circumambulate the Ka'ba, the shrine in the center of the Grand Mosque in Mecca, seven times, in an act of sanctification called *tawaf*, initiating them for the holy deeds to follow. Reza Aslan writes that during *tawaf*, "the Ka'ba becomes the axis of the world, and *every* direction is the direction of prayer. It is, one might say, the centrifugal force of praying in the presence of the sacred shrine that compels the worshipper to orbit the sanctuary."[38] The circumambulations of the pilgrims in Mackey's "Song of the Andoumboulou" series seem less focused, less intent on any kind of sanctification. Theirs is an experience of transitoriness without focus, wandering without reprieve. The mysterious word *huther* characterizes something of this drift and uncertainty. "Huther" is a peculiar word, arriving out of the obscure fifteenth-century noun *huther-mother*, or *hudder-mudder*, which means concealment or hiddenness. Mackey's use of the word brings about many questions. For one, where does he get this word? The epigraph for the poem, which comes from Wilson Harris's novel *Black Marsden*, offers a clue. It reads, " . . . that there existed a scout of love from whose effects of grief no one could escape . . ."[39] Mackey draws the word "huther" from the middle of Harris's short novel, which takes place in Edinburgh, Scotland, and in which two characters have the following exchange:

> Mrs. Glenwearie looked away from him and out through one of the windows. "It is not for me to say, sir," she said. "But since you ask me I would say that he's a very unusual gentleman. My dear mother would have called him a kind of hutherer." Goodrich was baffled. "What is a hutherer?" he asked. "It's just," said Mrs. Glenwearie, "och, I don't rightly know how to explain it. Just a hutherer, that's all."[40]

Mackey's transformation of Harris's "hutherer" to "huthered," a participial adjective, is telling. A hutherer, in Harris's use, appears to be an eccentric, perhaps a clairvoyant? Even a mystifier. Certainly someone for whom hiddenness and concealment are operative forces. So why does Mackey use the word in his poem as a modifier? Recall the lines from the poem,

> It was a journey we
> were on, drawn-out
> scrawl we made a road

of, long huthered hajj
                                    we
    were on.[41]

Mackey's huthering is directly related to writing; the pilgrim road is a drawn-out scrawl. Writing is a kind of circumambulation, perhaps an obfuscation. At any rate, it's long, it's huthered, and it's drawn out. In "Sound and Sentience" ("*mu*," thirty-second part), Mackey wonders,

Scales what would once have been
skin . . . Feathers what would once
have been cloth . . . There that
claiming heaven raised hell, fraught
sublimity, exits ever more to
come . . .

and then, later in the same poem, overlooking a

Blent
vista such that splinters reared up
and walked, went remitless . . . Endless
reconnoiter, endless vex, revisitation.[42]

Reconnoiter, vex, revisitation—these characterize the long huthered hajj. (*Blent* appears to be an obscure word for mingled, presumably a compression of *blended*.) Its endlessness invites the metaphors of circulation that repeat but never arrive at a conclusion throughout the book, permitting my sense that an overarching negative epistemology defines Mackey's poetic project.

I think it is fair, even necessary, to link this negative epistemology with Mackey's esotericism. The secret knowledge his work conceals is one of ruinous, catastrophic, vexatious, interminable truth, rather than of transformative liberation. Finkelstein reads Mackey's Gnosticism as nevertheless restorative, if only because the hope for some revelation or truth pervades the work. "History is the record of a gnostic catastrophe," writes Finkelstein, "the violent cosmic upheaval that has led to our current fallen condition. The human community, like the cosmos itself, longs to be ordered and made whole, and I read Mackey's poetry as a shamanic attempt to bring about that order, that cure, despite a nearly irredeemable sense of despair."[43] In Finkelstein's reading, Mackey's poetry itself becomes a "continuous, recursive, sideways movement" between a cataclysmic despair of the actual and the utopian domain of "*Mu*." Mackey's two poetic series "veer between the extremes of catastrophic fall and ecstatic redemption, traveling through landscapes and dream spaces variously shaded by idealism and foreboding."[44]

My sense is that, through the twists, distortions, estrangements, and alienations that mark the progress of his two poetic series, the mythologies out of which "Song of the Andoumboulou" and "*mu*" originate—namely, a Dogon funeral rite that commemorates a disastrous mythology of the antique, sacred past and an etymological exploration of myth and meaning prompted by American jazz and its African American practitioners—serve less as fields of meaning than they do as thematic sources for the work. Over the course of their existence, Mackey's series have proliferated a wild, idiosyncratic, nearly nonsensical set of locations and personas whose variegated names remain steadfastly opaque, even to devoted readers: Ahtt, Nath, N'Ahtt, ythm, Ba, B'Us, Ouab'da, Ouadada, B'Dot, B'Leg, Ra, Stra, C'rib, C'ahtt, Zar, Qu'ahttet, Lag, Nub, Atet, B'Hest, B'Head, the Late Night Lounge, Lone Coast, Dread Lake, Outlantish, Southern California, Los Angeles.[45] What, after all, is the nature of Mackey's esotericism? He's not, like H.D., inscribing a hermetic reading of history nor, like Duncan, insisting on a theosophical, emanative caretaking of Poetry. Nor is he, like Jay Wright, invoking Dogon lore toward suggesting an equation between poetic composition and religious initiation. While it's true that when you read "Song of the Andoumboulou," you do, after all, learn something about the Dogon, I sense increasingly, however, that this learning is auxiliary to the main treasure Mackey's work is protecting, the true knowledge it is hiding at its center. Mackey's true project is an esotericism of the poetry of the Open Field.[46]

Mackey's work has long harbored several clues to his devotion to the poetry of the Open Field, his whatsaying service to its mythology and meaning. Open Field poetry was the subject of his dissertation, for one thing. It's also been the main subject of his critical writings, from his ongoing preoccupation with Charles Olson, Robert Duncan, and LeRoi Jones/Amiri Baraka to his metonymic association of modal- and free-jazz forms with the poetry he writes. It's his creative projects—the serial poetry and the serial fiction—that most compellingly indicate this esotericism of the Open Field. These are two projects Mackey refuses to close. Though *Splay Anthem* ends—with the unpunctuated word "foot"—the two poetic series don't. Were the nature of Mackey's esotericism directed toward a positive epistemology—a deliverance from the world's woes—I suspect the poetic project would, in some form, draw to a conclusion. It's hard to say whether the negative epistemology that I'm arguing now defines the poem is original, which is to say, something there at the start, or whether the compulsion to repeat and to carry on the process of the poem has forced Mackey into increasingly negative epistemological involutions. Whatever the case, this is the poem we keep finding in *Splay Anthem*, gleaned throughout in reference to a mythic book and the interpretation undertaken with it:

Had it been a book *Book*
of the Opening the Book it
would've been called,
kept
under lock and key . . .[47]

(I hear an echo of Duncan's *The Opening of the Field* in Mackey's imaginary, conditional title. There's an equation to be made between book and field.)

Flat realm, no rise,
no resonance, booklessness the
book they thumbed . . . No biblic
aura,

no alternate life, at last they were
only where they were.[48]

(Another Duncan reference: "An Alternate Life" is the sequence that opens *Ground Work II: In the Dark*, Duncan's final poetry collection.) Elsewhere in the same poem, "The Sigh of the Moor" ("*mu*," thirty-third part), he writes,

Beneath a window overlooking Lone
Coast, the sound of waves pounding
salt on the eardrum, a dream of

exegetic sleep. Unbooked but for the
water's ripped edge, frayed page
the rotating earth turned, tore,
one
would someday see . . . So spoke the
oracle, the exegete, dream of
a ceased read read endlessly,
read
annulling omen's end . . .[49]

Unlike the fields of projective verse that Olson and Duncan opened up for American poetry in the 1960s, and even as the password that granted Mackey permission into the Open Field was found in the works of Olson and Duncan, Mackey's poetic range is one of a decidedly restrictive perception, delineated by second guesses, false starts, crabwise movement, and retrogressive whatsaying/unsaying. It's a field, to be sure, but its contours are quantum: a series of mysterious, mythological equations:

It wasn't an epic we sang had
there been a song we sang, heroic
waste
around us though there was. The
beloved's long-distance voice
was what it was. Muse meant lost
in thought it reminded us, erstwhile
epiphany, snuffed . . . It was all
a wrong
turn or we took a wrong turn.

Later, Mackey puts it bluntly, like a latter-day Bogomil: "Heaven it was we were in, / not knowing we were. Hell was not / knowing. / We were in hell . . . So it was in the / kingdom of Nub."[50] In the preface, Mackey defines Nub as a "place name and diagnosis fraught with senses of diminishment: failed extension or falling short but not only that." He confesses, "I don't know everything Nub is or implies or might mean (nubbed version of Numb as well as Nubia but not only that)," but admits he feels himself to be living in a "flailing republic of Nub the United States has become," where (becoming unexpectedly political for a moment), in a "match that seems to have been made in hell, hijacked airliners echo and further entrench a hijacked election, cycles of recriminatory assault further confirming a regime of echo the poem's recourse to echo would cure homeopathically if it could."[51] In the book's last poem, "Song of the Andoumboulou: 60," Mackey resonates familiar themes:

Nonsonant scruff held
on to, sheerness . . . Nothingness
it seemed we grabbed at, gathered,
beginning to be unending it seemed.

We

were beginning to be lured again,
ready to be hectored, huthered, move
on, beginning to be uprooted again.[52]

Whatsaying is the poem's repetitive lure, the project of spelling out—magically and linguistically—the open field in which "we" wander, compulsively attended to, even as it huthers the speaker(s), rendering us connoisseurs of esoteric nonsonance. There is nothing so curious, so strange, so mythically idiomatic being written right now in the United States as this work, and, just so, there is very little else quite so good.

9

APOCALYPTICISM

A Way Forward for Poetry

What does it mean to say a poetry is apocalyptic? Typically, it means that a poetry, or its poet, suggests catastrophe or the quality of conclusion signified in the Book of Revelation, with John the Revelator as apocalyptic model. This can be a helpful designation, but not always. Allusions to Christian omega are inevitable in an apocalyptic poetry, but there is something more at work even in the poems of Blake, for instance, than the revelatory completion of sacred Christian history. Apocalypse is both genre and mode, and each is filled with power. Apocalyptic poetry, then, is language charged with the power to reveal sacred reality, in history and beyond it. "And so there comes a time," writes Norman O. Brown in a potent little essay entitled "Apocalypse," "when civilization has to be renewed by the discovery of new mysteries, by the undemocratic but sovereign power of the imagination, by the undemocratic power which makes poets the unacknowledged legislators of mankind, the power which makes all things new."[1] John in Revelation has the revealed God sitting on the throne say, "Behold, I make all things new . . . I am Alpha and Omega, the beginning and the end" (Rev. 21:5–6). It's the alphabet that makes things new, formed into what Northrop Frye called "words with power." Poetry.

Thinking about Revelation, Frye identifies two aspects of apocalyptic vision. The first he calls "panoramic apocalypse," which is "the vision of staggering marvels placed in a near future and just before the end of time. As a panorama, we look at it passively, which means that it is objective to us."[2] This connects the Book of Revelation to generic understandings of apocalypse and apocalypticism, namely, "social movements emphasizing the evilness of the present age and the imminent coming of a new age of righteousness."[3] Apocalypse as a genre began to appear as early as the third century BCE, at the hands of Jewish rebel-visionaries, as "ways of making God accessible to a world in which the divine was no longer present in its traditional form."[4] As it worked in the Jewish imagination, it suffused early Christian theology, carrying over into Islamic thought as it began to develop in the eighth century CE. The Book of Revelation is perhaps the apex of this literary tradition, one of whose functions was to propose a kind of hope for a hopeless world, written for people disenfranchised from power, who could reseize it in this energetic writing—finding power, making all things new.[5]

Frye contends that the panoramic apocalypse of Revelation yields to a second, transformative aspect, one analogous to the aspect of the apocalyptic poetry in the discussion that follows. "The panoramic apocalypse," claims Frye, "ends with the restoration of the tree and water of life, the two elements of the original creation." But this restoration seems to be a type of "upward metamorphosis to a new beginning that is now present," a kind of mental-physical abolishing of categories that begins when the reader finishes reading, closing the book and putting it down, passing into what Frye identifies as a "second life." "In this second life," he insists, "the creator-creature, divine-human antithetical tension has ceased to exist, and the sense of the transcendent person and the split of subject and object no longer limit our vision."[6] Writing about eschatology in *The HarperCollins Dictionary of Religion*, Jonathan Z. Smith puts it this way: "The substance of salvation (God's forgiveness and eternal life) is available now, in virtue of Christ. But the full expression of salvation can only occur beyond history, where God is all in all, and so does not yet exist."[7] The peculiar power of a truly apocalyptic poetry is its expression of the vitality of a God all in all, beyond history but knowable somehow in it, who does not yet exist but who pulsates a profound, irrefutable influence from an unforeseen future obliquely but entirely recognized in an exegetical totalization of language. Put another way: Apocalyptic poetry is a power load of words. Today, two poets writing such apocalyptic poetry are Joseph Donahue and Pam Rehm.

Donahue and Rehm are different poets at root, even as they belong in the same company. Donahue has spent years mastering long serial poems that combine elements of mysticism, esotericism, protest, and the alienation of the urban experience, exemplified in two early sequences—"Spectral Evidence" and "Christ Enters Manhattan"—but most especially in *Terra Lucida*, his still-in-process vatic cataclysm. This work places him in a lineage that includes Pound, H.D., Olson, Duncan, and especially Nathaniel Mackey as direct ancestors. Rehm also writes poems in sequence, albeit series typically shorter and more concerned with dilations and contractions of scenes of domestic mysticism, such as the joys and tedium of taking care of her family, than with the esoteric and apocryphal histories that legislate Donahue's poetry. Rehm's masters are Dickinson and Niedecker among poets, and the Gospel writers and epistolarians of the New Testament among others. I take her work principally to be an act of protest against the incarcerating concerns of the age, especially material concerns, as well as a gesture of defiance in her insistence that poetry can be a kind of privacy, even as it is secured in a public space.

Apocalypse links these two poets together, giving their work its power. We can see these links in both poets through their connections to *apex of the M*, a literary journal that ran for six issues in the mid-1990s, and to H.D. Rehm was one of the founding editors of *apex of the M*, along with Lew Daly (her husband), Alan Gilbert, and Kristen Prevallet, all three of whom were enrolled at the time as graduate students at the State University of New York at Buffalo in its poetics program. (Rehm alone was not a student at Buffalo.) *Apex of the M* was an unusual and spirited journal to have emerged from this place at this time, which was then best known as one of the primary stations of then-emergent academic Language poetry, led by Charles Bernstein. In contrast to the prevailing Marxist ideology and notions of the fragmentation of language and subject in the time of late capitalism that one attributes to Language poetry, the editors of *apex of the M* wanted conspicuously to connect their enterprise to notions of the spirit, claiming in the provocative editorial that opened the inaugural issue: "Of primary importance in this shift [away from the current state of the art] is a commitment to heterogeneity and alterity, to the unknown and the unspeakable as material influx leading to love."[8] Defiantly romantic in tenor, the editors excoriated mainstream "workshop" poetry as "deplorable" and insisted that avant-garde poets, in giving priority to language itself, had committed themselves emptily to the conventions of innovation, "leading to the socially inept dead-end of autonomous forms." "Why, then, should we not resist equally," asked the editors, "both the suburban vacuity of mainstream poetics and verse, and the avant-garde's poetics of 'language itself,' with its forcefield-like purgation of radical alterity and non-linguistic, material influx and receptivity from what we heed and write?"[9] Instead of these, the editors called for a "radical transparency of language" that would resist solipsism or the incorporation of the other into the problem of the poem, instead seeking a poetry of the "Conscious Ear," one of Dickinson's definitions of "spirit."[10]

Devin Johnston, writing at the time about *apex of the M* in *Chicago Review*, noted how the journal espoused an expressivist poetics and a return to romanticism, in which the poet "finds forms of spiritual synthesis in the world,"[11] identifying notions of religious concern that set off the journal distinctly from the theoretical and material concerns that seemed to define Language poetry at the time. As the editors claimed:

> We feel that perhaps Modernism and probably post-Modernism will be seen as having been but footnotes between, if not two phases of Romanticism—the Platonic and the eschatological, then between Romanticism and the poetries of the approaching millennium, and we hope that, following Dickinson, Melville, Stevens, and others, a new understanding of our task as iconoclasts and not innovators will emerge.[12]

This first issue of the journal included work by Bernadette Mayer, John Taggart, Nathaniel Mackey, and Will Alexander, alongside that of Elizabeth Willis, Peter Gizzi, and Benjamin Friedlander, all three of whom were also at the time students in the poetics program at SUNY-Buffalo. While I find the work in this issue of the journal—as well as that in the other five of its short run—compelling, it doesn't as a whole approach the forcefulness and the memorable quality of the editorials that appeared in the first three issues, each of whose romantic spirit was stoked by the insurrectionary language of apocalypse. The first (and best) editorial concludes with this claim:

> Only in direct proportion to the way in which speaking disarms us, making us irreplaceable on the path of an urgency by which we must

> each in our own way remain overcome, will the faint strains of an apocalypse of utterance guide all hierarchy and mediacy into place, overwhelmed by a spiritual force rendering them powerless against a destruction more irreversible than any fall, in the future of a suffusion almost immediately indistinguishable from peace.[13]

Rehm recalls that the initial editorial in *apex of the M* was written mainly by Lew Daly and Alan Gilbert. For his part, Daly claims that at the time of writing it, he was involved in reading "a strange mix of Levinas, Captain Ahab, and Mark and Matthew on the end of the world."[14] Daly regards apocalypse as an essentially political genre exposing divine intent, asking, "isn't apocalypse a cosmic event but also an act of God and a matter of God's judgment? And God's judgment is not against the whole world but against the jurisdictions of the world, the dominions of man over man. Perhaps the cosmic part of apocalyptic justice reflects a literature borne of righteous disempowerment."[15] This accords with something Daly wrote in an essay published in 1994, from a series of answers to questions posed to him by Rehm:

> This is the remaining mission of the writing act: to each in our own way retain in ourselves the experience of loneliness, to keep it from reaching the world, from exceeding in pointlessness even the furthest field from a point of reference common to all. It will remain my own only when my attention is, as in a way unknown to me which poems convey, transformed into a capacity to become in a sense collaborated with the life of God, and to bring forth into signs all manner of responsibility to the principle of life.[16]

Questions of divine reality pervade the poetry of Donahue and Rehm, just as they direct Daly's thought. Is it a surprise that the initial editorial in *apex of the M* caused controversy among avant-garde poets?[17] Contemporary poets, with a few notable exceptions, tend to shun expressions and affirmations of religious realities. Ron Silliman, who can usefully be seen to represent the opinions of avant-garde poets, both at the time this editorial was written and presently, has stated that the death of Charles Olson in 1970 "signaled the end of an ardent interest by many poets in all matters of the occult [and the 'mystical' in general], including say historical investigations of earlier religious models." What replaced this interest was "theory."[18] Even if a few poets and readers would take up the call of the editors of *apex of the M*, most would reject it.

After the third issue of the journal, no additional editorials were written. By the fifth issue, Daly and Rehm were no longer listed as editors but rather as associate editors. After six issues, *apex of the M* appeared no more. In the meantime, Daly concluded his academic work at Buffalo, leaving that institution to pursue a master of divinity degree at Union Theological Seminary in New York City, more or less leaving the poetry world behind for good.[19] What does this say about apocalypticism in contemporary poetry? Not necessarily that it's impossible, or not worth doing, but that it's a difficult path to take, particularly in a poetry world secularizing at least as rapidly as the rest of the world, where making claims for the spirit and for "the unknown and the unspeakable as material influx leading to love" have become simply too unsettling to take without preparatory ironizing.

Donahue had two poems published in the third issue of *apex of the M*, one of them, "Canto Escondito," an early iteration of *Terra Lucida*. Donahue clearly took the editorial call of those first issues to heart, or, rather, they reflected what was already in his heart: "I remember very well and with a good deal of excitement the early issues of *Apex*. I remember feeling, finally! Someone is saying it out loud! I don't remember the particulars of the opening salvo, but essentially feeling in deep sympathy with it."[20] Rehm had work included in the second issue of the journal. To the initial editorial, for her part, she contributed "the quote, it's either by H.D. or E.D. and maybe a sentence of two around it but nothing else."[21] She's referring to a phrase by H.D., quoted in the editorial: "our awareness leaves us defenseless,"[22] which comes from section 29 of "The Walls Do Not Fall." In the way Donahue's poetic authority arises from an ongoing, permutative questioning of revelation's capacities, Rehm's begins from a vulnerable openness arising from the awareness she vitalizes in her writing, typically through questioning and second-guessing. For both poets, I think H.D. can be shown to have provided useful models for revelation and awareness.

The H.D. I'm imagining for thinking about the apocalypticism in Donahue's and Rehm's poetry provides two models. The first is the poet who devised a means of projecting mysterious interior realities into poems that involve a kind of direct, oracular speech, psychological masks, and verisimilar biblical pronouncements. This is the poet who lived in the Hotel Regina not far from the Ringstrasse in Vienna in 1933 to be psychoanalyzed by Freud, the poet for whom psychoanalysis and occultism were an equivalency because they activated a universal symbolism, the poet who transformed her experiences of emotional chaos and "war-terror" into an astrological pageant with anagrammatic riddles. This H.D. is the poet who, in a letter to her companion Bryher, in which she relates a dream she had already related to Freud, nevertheless reinterprets that dream, writing to Bryher: "But the exquisite part of the dream is that it expands and contracts and one can see new combinations, all founded on the most trivial incident yet with a universal or astrological symbolism."[23]

The second model is the poet who wrote the sequences in *Trilogy*, whose work brings forth manifestations of angels and the zodiac, on the one hand, and a war-torn, prophetic hopefulness, on the other. Angels serve in Judaism, Christianity, Gnosticism, and Islam as intervening agents, superhuman but subservient to the divine. The angelic hierarchies invoked by H.D. in "Tribute to the Angels" are rooted as much in the Dionysian tradition—presented in the sixth century by Dionysius the Areopagite in *The Celestial Hierarchy*—as in biblical tradition. Bernard McGinn relates that "the function of the celestial hierarchy in our uplifting is not that we try to become angels or even that we reach God through angelic mediation, but that the proper interpretation and understanding of the angels as multiple manifestations of the divine beauty is anagogic and divinizing."[24] Anagogy is a Neoplatonic term meaning "uplifting," adapted by Dionysius to signify the act of projecting the mind into the imaginal ranks of angels or realms of scripture toward creating this recognition of the divine nature of the creation within oneself. Though perhaps complicated to conceive of in terms of the typical practices of modernist poetry, it's nevertheless an apt description of what happens in H.D.'s poem, in that the tribute to the angels that the poet invokes depends on the receptivity of human beings to this divine immanence.

"Tribute to the Angels," the second part of *Trilogy*, sequences an angelic summons amid the fallout from the Second World War in England; H.D. explicitly compares her witnessing of this catastrophe with the apocalypse seen by John the Revelator. The third section of the sequence reads:

I John saw. I testify;
if any man shall add

God shall add unto him the plagues,
but he that sat upon the throne said,

I make all things new.
I John saw. I testify,

but *I make all things new,*
said He of the seven stars,

he of the seventy-times-seven
passionate, bitter wrongs,

He of the seventy-times-seven
bitter, unending wars.[25]

Though she elsewhere in the poem invokes several angels by name—"Gabriel: // Raphael, Gabriel, Azrael, / three of seven—what is War / to Birth, to Change, to Death?"[26]—she works a mysterious purpose throughout, suggesting that this procession of angelic beings leads the way for a manifestation of the Goddess archetype: Mary, the Mother of God, Venus, and the ocean all in one, but angelophanic nevertheless—an intermediating messenger clothed in visionary transience:

Now polish the crucible
and in the bowl distill

a word most bitter, *marah*,
a word bitterer still, *mar*,

sea, brine, breaker, seducer,
giver of life, giver of tears;

now polish the crucible
and set the jet of flame

under, till *marah-mar*
are melted, fuse and join

and change and alter,
mer, mere, mere, mater, Maia, Mary,

Star of the Sea,
Mother.[27]

Much of H.D.'s poem can be seen as an elaboration and articulation of this Goddess, such that "venerate" pulsates with the name of Venus, and the Lady she names is incarnate the world over as "the flowering of the rood," a sign of life and an affirmation of "thanks that we rise again from death and live."

I want to stress that I take H.D. not as a source for Donahue's and Rehm's poetry but as a model. Donahue's *Terra Lucida*, like H.D.'s *Trilogy*, is written in a procession of free-verse couplets, both poems relating an esoteric geography of the imagination, mapped by an alluring crypto-Christian symbolism. Rehm's concision of expression and condensation of thought and idea bear more than a passing resemblance to H.D.'s imagist poems, but I think more importantly the tactic of wordplay, anagram, and sense excavation from the sounds of words, as exhibited in the passages from "Tribute to the Angels" quoted above, reinforces Rehm's own witnessing tendency, her desire to see and to testify in her poems to the awareness that leaves her defenseless.

Donahue appears to have begun writing the sequence of poems in *Terra Lucida* as early as 1995, when "Canto Escondito" was published in *apex of the M*. Since then, he has published sections of the poem in a series of chapbooks, first culminating in 2009 with the book publication of *Terra Lucida* and continuing onward in 2012 with the publication of *Dissolves: Terra Lucida IV–VIII*, both by Talisman House, and forward to 2015, with the publication of *Dark Church*, by Verge Books. Since the time that these earlier parts of the poem were published, the sequence has undergone editorial changes as the dimensions of the larger project have become clearer. Through 2004, for instance, when Carolina Wren Press published

In This Paradise: Terra Lucida XXI–XL, each section of the poem was given a Roman numeral. With the appearance of *The Copper Scroll: From Terra Lucida* with Dos Madres Press in 2007, the numbering system was dropped, but with the appearance of *Dissolves*, it's clear that the larger groupings within the book are being designated by Roman numerals. In the first Talisman House book, *Terra Lucida*, the parts of the poem are introduced by double zeros: "00." But section names—"trifle alm omen," "in this paradise," and "the copper scroll"—have been maintained, as have subtitles. (For instance, "canto escondito" opens "in this paradise.") My sense is that as Donahue registered the detonations and after-echoes of mythohistorical and personal-psychological material in his poems, the process of numerically sequencing his poem began to limit both the associations among the parts of the poem and the imagination by which he was conjuring them. It's a "disordered devotion," to borrow a phrase from Duncan, that Donahue presents to us in *Terra Lucida*. With the publication of *Dark Church*, the double zeros opening each new section have been dropped as well.

The title means "earth of light" or "land of light."[28] The Islamic scholar and self-declared visionary Henry Corbin used the name *terra lucida* in a few instances; Donahue is likeliest to have gotten his title from Corbin's book *The Man of Light in Iranian Sufism*, where Corbin, speaking of the *mundus imaginalis*, which is an intermediary realm in which the worldly self confronts its angelic self, "a concrete world of archetype-Figures, apparitional Forms, Angels of species and of individuals,"[29] declares that in Manicheanism "there is the Earth of Light, *Terra lucida*, situated in the kingdom of light. It is governed by a divinity of eternal light, surrounded by twelve Splendors."[30] To see this realm, claims Corbin, is an actuality "vouched to the apperception of the active Imagination."[31] Corbin's memorable coinage for qualifying the productions of the active imagination is *imaginal*. It's a useful term to invoke in the light of the considerable esoteric, scriptural, and heretical lore Donahue brings to his poem. For Corbin, the imaginal signifies all that we come upon in the realm of "the Angel," which is the realm of vision, a transcendent dimension humans can enter through the cultivation of this vision: "Its growth is concomitant with a visionary apperception, giving shape to the supersensory perceptions and constituting that totality of ways of knowing that can be grouped under the term *hierognosis*."[32]

Donahue's is a decidedly hierognostic poem, revealing "knowledge of the holy." The sacred knowledge he reveals, however, is only visible to us in the intermediary realm of the *terra lucida*. In this sense, Donahue seems to be intuiting, if not in fact borrowing, Corbin's application of the heresy of Docetism to Islamic mysticism. Put somewhat simply, Docetism is the heresy claiming that Christ had merely the appearance of a physical body but not any material or human nature. Some Gnostics in the early centuries were allied to this doctrine. But this heresy was more or less eliminated from early Christianity by Saint Irenaeus of Lyons in the late second century.[33] Corbin has argued that the principles of Docetism were incorporated into emergent Islamic mysticism not to discern the true nature of Christ but to understand the visionary realm of the angels. In "The Prophetic Tradition," his essay on apocalypticism in Islam, Norman O. Brown, defending Corbin's claim, insists:

> The truth is that Docetism is an alternative to the Incarnationalism inherent in Christianity from the start, an undercurrent which became the mainstream in Islam, which is not inspired by the idea that the flesh is evil and that salvation consists in evading the consequences of having a body. . . . Docetism, as the Greek root of the word indicates, is devotion to appearances, to apparitions, to visionary experience, to vision.[34]

Reality is angelophanic: When we enter the realm in which we can see angelic presences, we enter the realm in which we can see the divine. But inasmuch as we might strive to tune our vision to see the *terra lucida*, this very realm is already interfering with the material realm, bringing the havoc of its vision upon us.

Consider this hierophany from Donahue, framed by doubts and meditations on doubt, on the one side, and by a description of early Christian heresy, on the other side:

> A mortal is about to see
> the majesty of the throne . . .
>
> Though in the stream of clouds
> it may be only the foot of the throne,

or a snarl of white mist in the field
in the first of the sunlight.

Nonetheless, an heretical beauty
floods the ranks of the world.

The black still pours down
but the peaks break free.

Branches aglow with a wet flame . . .
Sky, a deep violet, surges

behind the charcoal mountain
where the rain is still falling

on a single gorge of brightness
after the sudden storm of

the first night of my death.
Angelic tormentors are silent

The archive of what is stands open.
While in the ruins of an orchard

with its stretch of tree-stumps
like the broken guards

of a once sublime palace,
birds lie quietly on the grass.[35]

Nonetheless, an heretical beauty / floods the ranks of a world. An interesting pun whiffs from "ranks": Donahue is invoking the ranks of the angelic hierarchy imagined by Dionysius (and Rilke), just as he is alluding to the rank and file of the world below. But isn't there a smell here, the rank odor of the human world below, which, despite its stench, streams with a beauty from the light emanating from God's eternal throne? In *Major Trends in Jewish Mysticism*, Gershom Scholem points out that "the earliest form of Jewish mysticism was throne-mysticism."[36] Unlike the forms of absorbed contemplation elaborated in theosophical Kabbalah, the subject of much of Scholem's book, throne mysticism is characterized by "perception of [God's] appearance on the throne, as described by Ezekiel, and cognition of the mysteries of the celestial throne-world."[37] Scholem goes on to compare throne mysticism to early Christian mystical and Gnostic practices, comparable to what Corbin identified as the active Imagination in Islamic mysticism, or what we might think of nowadays as creative visualization.[38] The silent angelic tormentors Donahue summons in this part of his poem stand perhaps for the interferences this visionary realm works on our consciousness: whether we seek this earth of light ourselves or find ourselves suddenly staring at the blinding throne of God, insight combines with anguish to give us the archive of what is in the ruined grounds of a once-sublime palace.

Like Nathaniel Mackey's "Song of the Andoumboulou," Donahue's *Terra Lucida* follows the course of an oblique plot in which a questing subject transforms at times into a collective subjectivity, moving through "*A world dark as anthracite / & lit by flames of an invisible war,*"[39] gaining insight, suffering sadness, finding death and resurrection, and battling evil: "And during those two days / when our souls were elsewhere, // dazzled in pavilions of the spirit, / with angels, martyrs, and rock stars, // what evil slipped into me? What curse got me?"[40] Similar to Mackey's series as well, *Terra Lucida* gives the sense that the phantasmal world the poem takes place in is as untrustworthy as it is revelatory:

> Then will all
> be nothing?
>
> Then will every
> death be a delusion?
>
> Then will our lives
> be ways of shade
>
> in the roaring core of
> the sun at night,
>
> be shadows
> in the dazzle?[41]

Shadows in the dazzle: this could stand as a statement for Donahue's hierognostic conclusions about reality.

If one thing characterizes the active imagination Donahue brings to bear on his poem, it's his desire that the visionary reality he has entered not be merely some dream but a place of absolute reality. His skill at conveying this feeling seems unmatched by any other contemporary American poet, such that parts of his poem exhibit a simultaneous lightness of touch and gravitational pull, where surrealistic follies vie with imaginal intensities. One of the best examples of Donahue's mastery appears in the midst of "in this paradise," in lines that combine throne mysticism with the look and feel of a Richard Diebenkorn painting:

> One heaven for optics, one
> for mysticism, & down the hall,
>
> idling, on a stage, a string quartet.
> A hawk shakes the trees as the sun falls
>
> over these houses, over these hills
> where, since this is California,
>
> a father tells his son: there are
> two kinds of infinities,
>
> those that can be counted,
> & those that cannot. And later,
>
> at bedtime, the mother will add
> and there are those crossed
>
> by souls once they have drunk
> from white cups of magnolia
>
> blossom over a sunlit deck, in
> a forest, where festive guests toast
>
> the abracadabra of zero,
> as, at a low-limbed tree where

the path meets the stream,
the ghosts of two girls wait in

the shade for a passerby, purer
than you, from whom to slice

the heart, & read in its red
the whim of the stars.

I'm drowsy, but I don't want
to sleep, one girl says to the other.

I don't want our marvelous
death to be only a dream.

The abracadabra of zero: it's that quality of inevitability Donahue manages in these lines, the expression of death as marvelous, and the sense that the heart has in it the whim of the stars that both ventilates and intensifies the apocalypse we get glimpses from in his poetry.

Where Donahue's apocalypticism is dazzling, literary, and esoteric, Rehm's is more sober and melancholic, expressing the anxieties of the Gospels themselves or the urgencies of Paul's letters, with their sense that "the form of this world is passing away" (1 Cor. 7:31). Like Emily Dickinson, Rehm combines audacity and rue in her poems in equal measure. Consider this poem by Dickinson:

One Crucifixion is recorded—only—
How many be
Is not affirmed of Mathematics—
Or History—

One Calvary—exhibited to stranger—
As many be
As Persons—or Peninsulas—
Gethsemane—

Is but a Province—in the Being's Centre—
Judea—
For Journey—or Crusade's Achieving—
Too near—

Our Lord—indeed—made Compound Witness—
And yet—
There's newer—nearer Crucifixion
Than That—[42]

The poem hinges on the striking phrase that Gethsemane is but a province in the center of our being, which opens the door to the wild claim that Christ's "Compound Witness" looks into her own being, where a newer, nearer, and presumably equally harrowing crucifixion is happening. As Harold Bloom notes, "Dickinson's Jesus did not love her, nor she him: she believed neither in the Resurrection nor the Atonement. Yet she shared in the sufferings of Jesus, and in what she took to be his triumph over them."[43] What Bloom appears to miss in his assessment of Dickinson's religion is the sense of regret that stains her claims of one Calvary for each sufferer. It's a bold claim, but a rueful one, too.

Compare Dickinson's poem to one of Rehm's:

A roof is no guarantee
that you'll sleep

The unease of premises
pins together the curtains
at night

Waiting for a clearness
of purpose

Eating 3 meals a day
we go to bed hungry

Privacy is not a remedy

We've become separated
by "efficiencies"
Nobody can do anything with

A kind of machine person
Floundering in the dark

It's hard to believe
5 sparrows were sold for this[44]

Like Dickinson's, Rehm's poem hinges on a claim whose critique stems from perception: here, the sense that our lives are filled with things that make it easier but worse. And also like Dickinson, Rehm works in her poems through aphorisms—"a roof is no guarantee that you'll sleep"—but ones she modulates with a resigned disdain that verges on despair: "It's hard to believe 5 sparrows were sold for this." "This poem," writes Rehm, "is about the frustration of living in a culture that separates humans from the natural world. It's a poem that wonders what it means to live among things that I wouldn't consider to be essential to living." It's hard not to hear echoes of the opening of George Oppen's "Of Being Numerous" here: "There are things / We live among 'and to see them / Is to know ourselves.'"[45] The self-knowledge Rehm's poem elicits, however, is, to make use of H.D.'s phrase from "The Walls Do Not Fall" again, *an awareness that leaves her defenseless.* "The sparrows," continues Rehm, "are a reference to Luke 12:6."[46]

The twelfth chapter of Luke finds Jesus defending himself against the Pharisees, who are "lying in wait for him and seeking to catch something out of his mouth, that they might accuse him" (Luke 11:54). He begins to speak—there's a sense of cunning to his oratory because he has a huge audience of followers, "many thousands," so many that they are beginning to crowd each other and step upon one another. When Jesus begins to speak, he points an argumentative finger at the Pharisees themselves: "Beware ye of the leaven of the Pharisees, which is hypocrisy. For there is nothing covered that shall not be revealed nor hidden that shall not be known. For whatsoever things you have spoken in darkness shall be published in the light, and that which you have spoken in the ear in the chambers shall be proclaimed upon the housetops" (Luke 12:1–3). *For there is nothing covered that shall not be revealed.* This is the essence of the Gospels' apocalypticism: Unlike the flamboyant witnessing of John the Revelator, reflected so vividly in Donahue's poetry, here in Luke, revelation is soothsaying. As Jesus continues, having accused the Pharisees of their hidden agenda, he tells the crowd whom they should truly fear:

> And I say to you, my friends, be not afraid of them that kill the body and after that have no more that they can do. But I will shew you whom ye shall fear: fear ye him who after he hath killed hath power to cast into hell. Yea I say to you: fear him. Are not five sparrows sold for two farthings, and not one of them is forgotten before God? But even the very hairs of your head are all numbered. Fear not therefore; you are of more value than many sparrows.
>
> (Luke 12:4–7)

In *The Historical Jesus*, John Dominic Crossan refers to "the message of an open secret" in reference to the mission of Jesus and his disciples: "The missionaries have a message that is neither private nor clandestine, neither hidden nor occult, neither secret nor mysterious."[47] One way to look at this passage in Luke is to see that Jesus, arguing that nothing that is hidden will not one day be revealed, is calling for full and open confession. The sparrows stand for a currency in this economy of the open secret: God is aware that these sparrows are being sold in the market as a good deal; he's also aware of every hair and blemish on your body. And he wants to reassure you that you are worth more than these sparrows.

Rehm, in a curious but potent inversion of Jesus's teaching, uses the buying and the selling of the sparrows to stand for something more troubling: The realization that we live in a culture that disastrously separates humans from the natural world, placing worth on creatures we intend to use for our own ends, and that none of Christ's radical teaching has had much of an impact on this exchange. Rehm's genius is to focus on the sparrows in her poem. Trading for these efficiencies leads only to false comforts, without guarantees, and eventual despair. "It's hard to believe / 5 sparrows were sold for this." Reading Luke, she seems to tell us, our thoughts shouldn't be focused on the evil one who might cast us into hell after we die; rather, our thoughts should be on the poor sparrows, worth much more than the sad world we live in with them. Rehm's sympathies for the animal world are as keen as they are revelatory. In "Acts of Fiction," from *Small Works*, she writes:

> I turned. I saw a door open
> between my confessions.
> On it were written these words:
>
> *The animals are angels*
>
> I then drew near the earth with
> bended knee. The flowers were
> so small and bright.
> The birds were glowing like stars.[48]

In Rehm's poetry, animals intermediate our knowledge of the world.

Rehm's principal tool of revelation in her poetry is the anagram. Typically, she identifies a word with some significance to her poem, from out of which she seeks hidden meanings and associations. Certainly, there's a playfulness to her rearrangements of the letters in a word, but there's also a gravity she seems to locate, connecting her practice, for me, to the exercise of *notarikon*, the practice in ecstatic Kabbalah of rearranging the letters in the name of God—or in other things—to uplift one's praying mind to a transcendent realm of meaning. Words of power in Rehm's poetry yield kinetic meaning as they modulate from one arrangement of letters to another. In the *Sefer Yetsirah*, a work of Jewish mysticism compiled between the third and sixth centuries, we read: "Twenty-two elemental letters. God engraved them, carved them, weighed them, permuted them, and transposed them, forming them with everything formed and everything destined to be formed."[49] For comparison, take these lines from "When Poverty Is Unobtainable":

> Behold
> a wilderness of voices
> crying within one
>
> Pursuit

> The tension created between proof
> and devotion
>
> When reveal becomes a lever
> and you press it
>
> your heart will feel gallantly
> recreated[50]

In a sense, the exhortation to behold in these lines prompts the poet and reader to look to see that there is a lever hidden in the letters of "reveal." Rehm's anagrammatic process is premised on consequence: It's not so much that there is "a lever" in "reveal" if you can find it. It's that a lever in reveal will be revealed—"When"—at which point it must be pressed.

Elsewhere in *Small Works*, her book from 2005, we find in the poem "A Charm for Sleep" claims such as "Fear has an ear / in it," "My balm was a lamb," and "To ward something off / draw it."[51] But Rehm's poem "Eden" might be read as an *ars poetica* for her anagrammatic technique as well as a demonstration of her skills with this method:

> Endure has an end
> you may rue
> at the outset
>
> But it also has need
>
> and need is an Eden
> (if you know what I mean)
>
> Eden = Need
>
> One and the same
> the same
>
> How I hold it.[52]

Endure is one of these words of power in Rehm's body of work: It locates her feelings of frustration with the world of getting and spending she tolerates and suffers in, but it also suggests the ability to bear something difficult without breaking—the definition of virtue in Rehm's world. But even endurance has an end, one manifested in need. The hinge of this poem is the ironic intensity of her declaration/discovery that "need is an Eden," underscored by the parenthetical aside, which we can read as something said under the breath and meant to be funny or, more likely, as something deadly serious. (Do we really know what she means? Probably not.) To reinforce her point, she makes plain the equation Eden = Need, which then allows her to finish the poem with a repetition—"the same"—and an assertion—"How I hold it"—calling the whole poem into momentary question, in that it sounds suddenly as resolved as it does desperate.

The mysterious word in "Eden" is rue, a word I've used already to characterize Rehm's (and Dickinson's) poetry. In this poem, it's the residue of letters/sounds left behind after "end" has been extracted from "endure." Ruefulness is sorrow, regret, and grief: an unusual feeling to drive one's work. Rehm uses rueful feelings in her poetry the way the fathers of the early Christian church elaborated the concept of *penthos*. These early Christian thinkers borrowed from paganism the idea of *penthos*—which is a specialized kind of mourning, typically for relatives or friends, or even lamentation for a dead god (the word shares an etymological root with *pathos*)—which they refined further into the special feeling of compunction that offers the possibility of comfort. This notion derives from the beatitudes, in which Matthew has Jesus say, "Blessed are those who mourn, for they shall be comforted" (Matt. 5:4). (One Greek word—*penthountes*—stands for "those who mourn.") For the desert fathers, *penthos* was a blessing because it required so much discernment: It was believed to strike suddenly and to plant itself deep within the soul. Saint Gregory of Nyssa wrote, "*Penthos* (in general) is a sorrowful disposition of the soul, caused by the privation of something desirable." Irénée Hausherr explains that "there is one word that expresses all that is desirable: salvation. . . . Here then is the first concept of *penthos: mourning for lost salvation*, whether one's own or that of others."[53]

I don't necessarily think in these poems Rehm is mourning for the lost salvation of herself or anyone else, though I do think the binary of woundedness/healing stands for the problem of salvation in her work, wrapped up in the problem of worthiness that similarly pervades her poetry. Nevertheless, the conceptualization of something like *penthos* is helpful for imagining the kind of rue that works in Rehm's poetry, a plaintiveness arising from connections made, connections lost, and the sense of the importance of recognizing these connections even as they cannot satisfy the Edenic needs that trigger them. In one poem, Rehm describes "A paradise of loneliness // incurred."[54] That a paradise of loneliness exists in the human soul is a distinct possibility; Rehm qualifies that phrase to make sure we understand that human solitude is both punishment and debt, even as its reality is like that of the primordial garden longed for since the dawn of human consciousness.

We can look to a selection from an earlier poem to see the apocalyptic qualities the ruefulness in Rehm's poetry elicits. "Where Oh Where Has My Little God Gone?" appears in *Gone to Earth*, published in 2001, though the poem first appeared in 1996 in *LVNG* 6. The poem, which is a sequence of eight unnumbered parts, seeks to address its own opening question, "By what are you thwarted?," cataloguing spiritual, material, emotional, and actual impingements. The second part of the poem depicts existential hardship in the face of market realities:

Economic life
will run down blind alleys
a specter

"Eternity's curtain"
pulled by purse strings

Once apprehended
the coin becomes a relic
diminished by the number
of deaths in our time

The gibbering shades of the departed

It is absurd to speak
of the spirit presenting itself
to make us live again

The body is an echo
in the shadow-image of Pantheism[55]

This section of the poem resounds with several words of power: specter, coin/relic, gibbering shades, absurd, body/echo, shadow-image, Pantheism. Each word facilitates what feels to be an excoriating meditation on the *deus absconditus* of the poem's title. Rehm's clarification of the specters and gibbering shades as something like the body itself—echoes in the shadow image of an earlier, unified, but superstitious religious reality—is, well, haunting. There's no better word for it. For Rehm, apocalypticism is not an anticipation as much as it is a means of expressing the oppressing realities of the present. In this sense, her approach to apocalypse accords with Daly's sense that as a genre, apocalypse is embroiled with political economy; he calls it "a literature of complete yet coded protest against worldly domination structures."[56] For Rehm, more so than for John the Revelator or for Donahue, in whom the spectacle of apocalypse resides, apocalypse is an actuality once apprehended that shows eternity's curtain pulled open not by religious longing but by purse strings. And what do we see in eternity? Shadow images. Spirits presenting themselves absurdly, speaking of salvation and resurrection. Here, it's a sobering vision. For Rehm—who can be an intensely joyful poet—salvation comes at the hands of connections to loved ones, to beloved figures from myth and history, and to books. Her poem "Acts of Knowledge" reads:

> As if a book
> were a kind of
> voluntary nurse
>
> looking for the wound
> inside you
>
> Words and senses
> Terror and delicacy
>
> Wisdom
>
> The leaves on the tree
> grew[57]

A WAY FORWARD IN POETRY

Blake's "Night the Ninth Being the Last Judgment," the cataclysmic finale to "The Four Zoas," begins:

> And Los & Enitharmon builded Jerusalem weeping
> Over the Sepulcher & over the Crucified body
> Which to their Phantom Eyes appear'd Still in the Sepulcher
> But Jesus stood beside them in the Spirit Separating
> Their spirit from their body. Terrified at Non Existence
> For such they deemd the death of the body. Los his vegetable hands
> Outstretchd his right hand branching out in fibrous strength
> Siezd the Sun. His left hand like dark roots coverd the Moon
> And tore them down cracking the heavens across from immense
>   to immense
> Then fell the fires of Eternity with loud & shrill
> Sound of Loud Trumpet thundering along from heaven to
>   heaven
> A mighty sound articulate Awake ye dead & come
> To Judgment from the four winds! Awake & Come away[58]

There is no creative explosion comparable to the one Blake enacts in "The Four Zoas," according to Northrop Frye. "In this ninth Night," he claims, "Blake seems to have found his way back to the very headwaters of Western imagination, to the crystalline purity of vision of the *Völuspa* or *Muspilli*, where the end of time is perceived, not as a vague hope, an allegory or an indigestible dogma, but as a physical fact as literal as a battle and as imminent as death."[59] Blake's visionary eruption models infinity as theophanic fact—the actuality of God perceived in an eternal present. Donahue's poetry presents apocalyptic theophany as imaginal *summa*: an Earth of Light intermediating the eyesight of insight poetic vision enables. Rehm's poetry presents apocalyptic fact as a battle as imminent as death, as the awareness that leaves us defenseless. Both extend Blake's aims. Ruminating on the potency of Blake's commanding poem, Frye continues:

> For the whole point about an apocalypse is that the darkening sun and the falling stars and the rest of the fireworks represent a kind of vision

> that is disappearing because it is unreal, whereas what takes place is permanent because it is real, and if real, familiar. With a deafening clangor of trumpets and a blinding flash of light, Man comes awake with the sun in his eyes and his alarm clock ringing beside him, and finds himself in what he now sees to have been all the time his own home.[60]

Where is our own home now? More than two decades since the editors of *apex of the M* issued their call for an apocalyptic poetry of radical transparency, what has ensued? Where do we find ourselves? For one thing, there has been the institutionalization of Language poetry, which might be characterized as antiapocalyptic (nonrevelatory). Language poetry currently represents a default mode for experimentation in poetry, in contrast to the vatic/apocalyptic mode that characterized some of the innovative poetry of the mid–twentieth century, especially in San Francisco (Duncan, Blaser, Everson, and Ginsberg, for instance). In some senses, Language poetry displaced this vatic mode, which was what the editors of *apex of the M* strove nevertheless to represent in the pages of their magazine.

For another thing, we've seen the institutionalization of creative writing programs for poets to attend. There are many things to say about this, probably best done by someone more qualified than myself. But it's hard to repress the sense that this trend represents a general drift from poetry as a kind of awakening to poetry as a kind of complacency.

Most prominently, we have seen the rise of the Internet in relation to the lives of poets, initially in the form of listservs, then in the form of poetry blogs and places like the Poetry Foundation website, and more recently in the telegraphic modes of social media, such as Facebook and Twitter, good places for promoting poetry but bad places for appreciating and understanding it. As much as I value and make daily use of the archival element of poetry on the Internet, I don't believe the shift of poetry to the Internet has done poetry much discernible good. That may still come, but at the present, the Internet has encouraged the rise to prominence of the opinionater and the curator as poetry's primary spokespeople and of opinion making and curation as poets' primary activities.

A poetry of apocalypse is no easier to find today than it was twenty years ago. It's no coincidence that both Donahue and Rehm are obscure poets whose work is attended to by small but dedicated audiences. In their work, they carry forward the achievements of what is for me the most compelling strain in American poetry, practiced in the past century by H.D., Charles Olson, Robert Duncan, Ronald Johnson, Susan Howe, Fanny Howe, John Taggart, Lissa Wolsak, and Nathaniel Mackey. Nevertheless, an apocalyptic poetry remains something difficult to write for a poetry world filled with allergies to the spirit. But if poetry has a way forward through the glaring electronic darkness of the present, if there is a poet who will stretch a vegetable hand, flexing it in fibrous strength to seize the sun, it will be a poet who has attended to the apocalyptic clarion sounded in Donahue's and Rehm's words of power, telling that poet clearly and plainly, "Awake & Come away."

CONCLUSION

WHY NOT BE TOTALLY CHANGED INTO FIRE?

Describing the symbolic saturation he experienced while writing some of his early poems, William Butler Yeats remarked,

> I had sometimes when awake, but more often in sleep, moments of vision, a state very unlike dreaming, when these images [from Irish folklore] took upon themselves what seemed an independent life and became a part of a mystic language, which seemed always as if it would bring me some strange revelation.[1]

Much as the religious poet has Moses backing into the great dazzle of God's darkness as a model for retrieving and revealing a religious language, the poet also has Orpheus to guide the project of encountering mysteries. For Yeats, the visionary drowse of falling sleep (or waking up) enables revelation, eventually prophetic, in a Mosaic sense, but initially Orphic in the sense of descending into and returning from an underworld inhabited by mysterious forms and even stranger language. Though Yeats could make it seem easy, this is hard work, and not always effective. Writing about a stay in a monastery, Fanny Howe remarks:

> On Ascension Day in the middle of May 1999, I went on a retreat hoping for a revelation. I hoped that I would find better words for spiritual phenomena than I was finding in the Catholic Church during the Eucharistic prayer and the homilies. I prayed the doors of heaven would fly open

> and I would see at last; I prayed because I did not believe any of it would happen.[2]

Sometimes it doesn't happen. In truth, most of the time it doesn't. In this regard, the religious poet is more like Moses wandering in the desert for forty years than the prophet of God speaking to a burning bush on an upslope of the holy mountain.

Yet sometimes it does happen. The burning bush is real. Ronald Johnson believed the burning bush to be the preeminent symbol of the imagination, authorizing the entire poetic and visionary process. The scene in Exodus with the burning bush stands for what F. C. Happold describes as "the sudden moments of intuitive perception, elusive, fading quickly, but of deep significance, illuminations which . . . reveal . . . new facets of reality."[3] This is a vision of light and darkness at once, arising out of long, often dull struggle and sudden, revivifying flashes of insight. My work in *Thick and Dazzling Darkness* arises from that scene in chapter 20 of Exodus in which Moses, having received the Ten Commandments, begins to bring the Law down from the mountain to the people, who have been watching in fear and trembling. "And all the people saw the voices and the flames and the sound of the trumpet and the mount smoking and, being terrified and struck with fear, they stood afar off. . . . But Moses went to the dark cloud wherein God was" (Exod. 20:19, 21).[4] Elliot R. Wolfson, a scholar of Jewish mysticism, lucidly expands on this passage from Exodus by way of an argument put forth by Saint Gregory of Nyssa, a fourth-century Cappadocian bishop and theologian. Gregory, Wolfson explains, describes three levels on which the invisible God might be envisioned: the cosmological, the anthropological, and the theophanic. The cosmological level is, for all practical purposes, the Orphic level, in which things seen—hidden things and revealed things—make manifest divine powers. The anthropological level shows that the image of God lies at the center of the person, to be awakened in the mind and bodied forth in the world. The theophanic level is exemplified by the unconsuming fire of the burning bush, its "ineffable and mysterious illumination." Gregory, according to Wolfson, reads the "dark cloud" Moses enters

> as an expression of the view that contemplation is a progression to what cannot be contemplated: the pinnacle of the mind's ascent consists of

> beholding the "luminous darkness," an oxymoron that resolves the exegetical problem with which Gregory began his exposition; the ostensible conflict between the theophany at the bush where God appears in the light and the later statement that Moses enters the cloud of darkness to encounter God is no clash at all, as the mystic vision is a seeing of *luminous darkness*, a vision of unseeing through the mirror of the infinite, the image of God mysteriously embodied in the person of Christ and to some degree in each human being, that is, a seeing through which one comes to see that one cannot see, the blindness that is true insight.[5]

There is seeing, and there is not seeing. In the religious imagination, both are forms of vision, of insight.

This puts me in mind of one of my favorite passages in Thomas Merton's *The Wisdom of the Desert*, which consists of his versions of the sayings of the desert fathers:

> Abbot Lot came to Abbot Joseph and said: Father, according as I am able, I keep my little rule, and my little fast, my prayer, meditation and contemplative silence; and according as I am able I strive to cleanse my heart of thoughts: now what more should I do? The elder rose up in reply and stretched out his hands to heaven, and his fingers became like ten lamps of fire. He said: Why not be totally changed into fire?[6]

Something about the work of the religious poet aligns with Merton's early Christian anecdote: Long and typically thankless labor done in obscurity inflected by grace into sudden, epiphanic illumination. Both burning bush and dark cloud. Both desert wandering and alpine ascent. Both enduring confusion and ecstatic confidence. Early in *The Flowering of the Rod*, the third part of *Trilogy*, H.D. writes:

> I am so happy,
> I am the first or the last
>
> of a flock or a swarm;
> I am *full of new wine*;
>
> I am branded with a word,
> I am burnt with wood,

drawn from glowing ember,
not cut, not marked with steel;

I am the first or the last to renounce
iron, steel, metal;

I have gone forward,
I have gone backward,

I have gone onward from bronze and iron,
into the Golden Age.[7]

The religious poet is full of new wine, totally changed to fire, moving onward into the golden age. As long as there are readers of poetry, there will be religious poets performing this work. Why?

In the "Conclusions" to *The Varieties of Religious Experience*, having presented extensive case studies that validate the pathological and mystical aspects of his subject, but in a moment of exultant resignation, William James confesses,

> The whole drift of my education goes to persuade me that the world of our present consciousness is only one out of many worlds of consciousness that exist, and that those other worlds must contain experiences which have a meaning for our life also; and that although in the main their experiences and those of this world keep discrete, yet the two become continuous at certain points, and higher energies filter in.[8]

Religious poetry filters the higher energies in. As readers, we seek these energies, drawing power from what this poetry releases into us. No matter what the age declares of itself, no matter how absent of spiritual truth and tendency you operate, there is beneath the loquacious level that your rationalism inhabits a deeper level to your nature where intuitions and occult convolutions gather and where, even deeper, a darkness emanates the material of creation. It's poetry that narrates and demonstrates that dark energy, an unconsuming fire in which our imaginations come most intensely to life.

PERMISSIONS

To write a book about modern and contemporary poetry is to participate in a vital conversation enabled by the quotation of poetry throughout. Quoting poetry in a book of this sort is an area of publishing where the principles of fair use are baffled by sometimes extravagant permissions fees. Therefore, I would like to extend sincere thanks to those publishers—small, commercial, and university presses alike—that waived permissions fees or requested token fees instead to make it easier for this book to come to print. Thank you, Flood Editions, Graywolf Press, New Directions, Palgrave Macmillan, Skysill Press, Stanford University Press, Station Hill Press, Talisman House, and the University of California Press.

For permission to reprint "Prophetic Frustrations: Robert Duncan's Tribunals," thanks to Stanford University Press. For permission to reprint " 'What Lies Beneath My Copy of Eternity?': Religious Language in the Poetry of Lissa Wolsak," thanks to Nate Dorward and the Gig Press. For permission to reprint "Robert Duncan's Celestial Hierarchy," thanks to Palgrave Macmillan.

For permission to reprint "The Walls Do Not Fall," by H.D. (Hilda Doolittle), from *Collected Poems, 1912–1944*, copyright © 1982 by The Estate of Hilda Doolittle. Reprinted by permission of New Directions Publishing Corp.

For permission to reprint "Tribute to the Angels," by H.D. (Hilda Doolittle), from *Trilogy*, copyright © 1945 by Oxford University Press;

copyright renewed 1973 by Norman Holmes Pearson. Reprinted by permission of New Directions Publishing Corp.

Poetry by Frank Samperi is reprinted by permission of Skysill Press, copyright © 2013 by the Estate of Frank Samperi.

Poetry by Emily Dickinson is reprinted by permission of the publishers and the Trustees of Amherst College from *The Poems of Emily Dickinson: Variorum Edition*, edited by Ralph W. Franklin, Cambridge, Mass.: The Belknap Press of Harvard University Press, copyright © 1988 by the President and Fellows of Harvard College. Copyright © 1951, 1955 by the President and Fellows of Harvard College. Copyright © renewed 1979, 1983 by the President and Fellows of Harvard College. Copyright © 1914, 1918, 1919, 1924, 1929, 1930, 1932, 1935, 1937, 1942 by Martha Dickinson Bianchi. Copyright © 1952, 1957, 1958, 1963, 1965 by Mary L. Hampson.

Excerpt from "People and a Heron," by Robinson Jeffers from *The Collected Poetry of Robinson Jeffers*, volume 1, *1920–1928*, edited by Tim Hunt, copyright © 1938 and renewed by Donnan and Garth Jeffers. All rights reserved. Used with permission of Stanford University Press, www.sup.org.

Excerpts from "The Inhumanist" and "The Deer Lay Down Their Bones," by Robinson Jeffers from *The Collected Poetry of Robinson Jeffers*, volume 3, *1939–1962*, edited by Tim Hunt, copyright © 1938 and renewed by Donnan and Garth Jeffers. All rights reserved. Used with permission of Stanford University Press, www.sup.org.

Excerpts from "Hurt Hawks," copyright © 1928 and renewed 1956 by Robinson Jeffers; "The Deer Lay Down Their Bones" and "Roan Stallion," copyright © 1925, 1929 and renewed 1953, 1957 by Robinson Jeffers, from *The Selected Poetry of Robinson Jeffers* by Robinson Jeffers. Used by permission of Random House, an imprint and division of Random House LLC. All rights reserved.

For permission to reprint from "Cawdor" by Robinson Jeffers from *Cawdor and Medea*, copyright © 1928, 1956 by Robinson Jeffers. Copyright © 1970 by Donnan Call Jeffers & Garth Sherwood Jeffers. Reprinted by permission of New Directions Publishing Corp.

Poetry by Geoffrey Hill is reprinted by permission of Oxford University Press, from *Broken Hierarchies: Poems 1952–2012*, edited by Kenneth Haynes copyright © 2013.

Excerpts from "Passages 31: The Concert," by Robert Duncan, from *Bending the Bow*, copyright © 1968 by Robert Duncan. Reprinted by permission of New Directions Publishing Corp. Excerpts from "In Blood's Domaine," by Robert Duncan, from *Ground Work II: In the Dark*, copyright © 1987 by Robert Duncan. Reprinted by permission of New Directions Publishing Corp. Excerpts from "After Passage," "Letting the Beat Go," and "Passages 35: Before the Judgment" by Robert Duncan, from *Ground Work: Before the War / In the Dark*, copyright © 1984 by Robert Duncan. Reprinted by permission of New Directions Publishing Corp. Excerpts from "Stimmung," "The Cherubim," and "The Dignities" by Robert Duncan, from *Ground Work: Before the War / In the Dark*, copyright © 1987 by Robert Duncan. Reprinted by permission of New Directions Publishing Corp.

Poetry by Fanny Howe from *One Crossed Out* (1997), copyright © 1997, reprinted by permission of the Permissions Company, on behalf of Graywolf Press.

Poetry by Fanny Howe from *Selected Poems* (2000), copyright © 2000, and *Gone* (2003), copyright © 2003, reprinted by permission of the University of California Press.

Poetry by Lissa Wolsak from *Squeezed Light: Collected Poems 1994–2005*, copyright © 2010, reprinted by permission of Station Hill Press.

Poetry by Nathaniel Mackey from *Splay Anthem*, copyright © 2002 by Nathaniel Mackey. Reprinted by permission of New Directions Publishing Corp.

Poetry by Joseph Donahue from *Terra Lucida* (2009), copyright © 2009, reprinted by permission of the poet.

Poetry by Pam Rehm from *Gone to Earth* (2001) and *Small Works* (2005), copyright © 2001, 2005, reprinted by permission of Flood Editions.

NOTES

INTRODUCTION: RELIGIOUS POETRY IN A SECULAR AGE

1. Richard Eliot Friedman, *Commentary on the Torah* (San Francisco: HarperSanFrancisco, 2001), 240. Friedman numbers the verse as Exodus 20:18.
2. *The Five Books of Moses*, trans. Everett Fox (New York: Schocken, 1995), 373. Fox also numbers the verse Exodus 20:18.
3. In Henry Vaughan, *The Complete Poems*, ed. Alan Rudrum (New York: Penguin), 629.
4. Ibid., 290. I've reproduced these lines using original spelling and punctuation.
5. Kenneth Burke, *The Rhetoric of Religion* (Berkeley: University of California Press, 1970), 1.
6. Dionysius, "The Mystical Theology," in *The Essential Writings of Christian Mysticism*, ed. Bernard McGinn (New York: Modern Library, 2006), 286.
7. Robert Duncan, *Collected Essays and Other Prose*, ed. James Maynard (Berkeley: University of California Press, 2014), 145.
8. Robert von Hallberg, *Lyric Powers* (Chicago: University of Chicago Press, 2008), 9.
9. Ibid., 42.
10. "Secularism," in *The HarperCollins Dictionary of Religion*, ed. Jonathan Z. Smith (San Francisco: HarperSanFrancisco, 1995), 970.
11. Fanny Howe, *The Wedding Dress* (Berkeley: University of California Press, 2003), 10.
12. By "esotericism" I mean the system of correspondences that reveal hidden or inward truths, often experiential in nature, that relate to some of the initiatic and intellectual currents typically ascribed to Western esotericism. Antoine Faivre refers to this as a form of "interiorism," "an entry into the self through a special knowledge or gnosis, in order to attain a form of enlightenment and individual salvation." See Antoine Faivre, "Esotericism," in *Hidden Truths: Magic, Alchemy, and the Occult*, ed. Lawrence E. Sullivan (New York: Macmillan, 1989), 38–39.

13. Peter O'Leary, introduction to *Trilogy*, by Frank Samperi (Nottingham: Skysill, 2013), unpaginated.
14. "Religion, definition of," in *The HarperCollins Dictionary of Religion*, ed. Jonathan Z. Smith (San Francisco: HarperSanFrancisco, 1995), 893. Smith authored the various entries on religion and the study of religion in this dictionary.
15. In *Luminous Epinoia*, a book of my poetry, I include a poem called "Chemical," which rewrites Celan's poem "Chemisch," which takes alchemy as its theme. See *Luminous Epinoia* (Brooklyn, N.Y.: Cultural Society, 2010), 75.
16. Paul Celan, *Gedichte II* (Frankfurt: Suhrkamp Verlag 1997), 196–202. Translations mine.
17. Ibid., 196. My poem "Celan," in *Depth Theology* (Athens: University of Georgia Press, 2006), 36, includes a slightly more extravagant version of this poem of Celan's.
18. Bernard McGinn, *The Foundations of Mysticism* (New York: Crossroad, 1991), 171.
19. Gerard Manley Hopkins, *The Journals and Papers of Gerard Manley Hopkins*, ed. Humphrey House (Oxford: Oxford University Press, 1959), 127.
20. See, for instance, Northrop Frye, *Words with Power: Being a Second Study of the Bible and Literature* (New York: Harcourt Brace Jovanovich, 1990), 63–96.
21. It's worth noting that the theory of secularization that Berger put forward in *The Sacred Canopy* has been challenged repeatedly in the decades that have followed its publication, not the least by Berger himself, who came to find its central premise, that modernity invariably produces a decline in religion, to be inaccurate. See, for instance, Gregor Thuswaldner, "A Conversation with Peter Berger," *Cresset* 77, no. 3 (Lent 2014): 16–21.
22. Diarmaid MacCulloch, *The Reformation: A History* (New York: Penguin, 2003), 99.
23. Talal Asad, *Formations of the Secular: Christianity, Islam, Modernity* (Stanford, Calif.: Stanford University Press, 2003), 1, 2.
24. Charles Taylor, *The Secular Age* (Cambridge, Mass.: Harvard University Press, 2006), 1.
25. Peter L. Berger, *The Sacred Canopy* (Garden City, NY: Anchor, 1969), 1.
26. Ibid., 24–25.
27. Ibid., 25.
28. Ibid., 28.
29. Ibid., 111, 112.
30. Ibid., 124–125.
31. Robert Duncan, *Fictive Certainties* (New York: New Directions, 1985), 91.
32. Walt Whitman, *Selected Poems 1855–1992*, ed. Gary Schmidgall (New York: St. Martin's Press), 20. (These are lines 127–129 and 136–139 of the 1855 "Song of Myself.")
33. Susan Howe, *My Emily Dickinson* (Berkeley: North Atlantic Books, 1985), 21.
34. Emily Dickinson, poem 285, *The Poems of Emily Dickinson*, ed. R. W. Franklin (Cambridge, Mass.: Harvard University Press, 1998), 127.
35. Northrop Frye, *T. S. Eliot* (New York: Grove, 1963), 24.
36. Ibid.
37. T. S. Eliot, "Burnt Norton," in *Collected Poems 1909–1935* (New York: Harcourt, Brace, and Company, 1936), 219, 220.

38. Sigmund Freud, *Civilization and Its Discontents*, trans. David McClintock (London: Penguin, 2002), 3–4.
39. Typically, Freud's relation to organized religion is regarded on a spectrum running from critical to hostile. Mainly, his approach was reductive. This was true of his understanding of the oceanic feeling as well. William B. Parsons summarizes: "As many would have it, the oceanic feeling is but the psychoanalytic version of the perennialist claim that mysticism is 'one and the same everywhere,' and the occasional regression to the preverbal, pre-Oedipal 'memory' of unity . . . is the explanation behind the transient, ineffable experience of oneness with the universe." William B. Parsons, *The Enigma of the Oceanic Feeling: Revisioning the Psychoanalytic Theory of Mysticism* (Oxford: Oxford University Press, 1999), 35–36. But Parsons also goes to lengths to demonstrate that Freud's perception of the oceanic feeling was far subtler, "considerably richer, less pejorative, and more suggestive than has been traditionally thought to be the case" (51). Put another way, it's not coincidental that Freud's supposedly reductive study of religion and culture has provided a language for studying religious states and mysticism that continues to be viable.
40. Susan Stanford Friedman, introduction to *Analyzing Freud: Letters of H.D., Bryher, and Their Circle*, ed. Susan Stanford Friedman (New York: New Directions, 2002), xxix–xxx.
41. Albert Gelpi, "The Thistle and the Serpent" in H.D., *Notes on Thought & Vision* (San Francisco: City Lights, 1982), 11.
42. H.D., *Notes on Thought & Vision*, 18–19.
43. Ibid., 20.
44. H.D., *Tribute to Freud* (New York: New Directions, 1984), 44, 45, 46.
45. Ibid., 51.
46. H.D., *Collected Poems 1912–1944* (New York: New Directions, 1986), 532–533.
47. Fred Gettings, *The Arkana Dictionary of Astrology* (London: Arkana, 1990), 397.
48. Ibid., 30.
49. T. S. Eliot, *Collected Poems 1909–1935* (New York: Harcourt, Brace and Company, 1936), 70–71.
50. Ibid., 91.
51. Frye, *T. S. Eliot*, 48.
52. Ibid., 51.
53. Robert Duncan, *The H.D. Book*, ed. Michael Boughn and Victor Coleman (Berkeley: University of California Press, 2011), 77–78.
54. Ibid., 79.
55. William James, *The Varieties of Religious Experience* (New York: Penguin, 1985), 173.
56. Ibid., 189.
57. Duncan, *The H.D. Book*, 79.
58. Ibid.

1. A MYSTICAL THEOLOGY OF ANGELIC DESPAIR: WRITING RELIGIOUS POETRY AND THE *TRILOGY* OF FRANK SAMPERI

1. See Mark Scroggins, *The Poem of a Life: A Biography of Louis Zukofsky* (n.p.: Shoemaker & Hoard, 2007), 321.
2. When originally published, *The Prefiguration*, *Quadrifariam*, and *Lumen Gloriae* had not yet been given the overall title *Trilogy*. Since the books have recently been reissued under that title, and since this title is how readers have generally referred to the book, I have opted to refer anachronistically throughout this chapter to *Trilogy* in reference to the whole work.
3. Peter O'Leary, introduction to *Trilogy*, by Frank Samperi (Nottingham: Skysill, 2013), unpaginated.
4. Frank Samperi, "Anti-Hero," *Quadrifarium* (New York: Grossman/Mushinsha, 1973), unpaginated.
5. John Taggart, "A Spiritual Definition of Poetry," *Songs of Degrees* (Tuscaloosa: University of Alabama Press, 1993), 23–24.
6. Ibid., 24.
7. Michael A. Sells, *Mystical Languages of Unsaying* (Chicago: University of Chicago Press, 1994), 4–5.
8. Henry Corbin, *Alone with the Alone: Creative Imagination in the Sufism of Ibn 'Arabi*, trans. Ralph Manheim, Bollingen Series 91 (Princeton, N.J.: Princeton University Press, 1997), 389.
9. Frank Samperi, *Lumen Gloriae* (New York: Grossman/Mushinsha, 1973), unpaginated.
10. Ibid.
11. *Catechism of the Catholic Church*, Libraria Editrice Vaticana (Liguori: Liguori Publications, 1994), 2809 (references by paragraph number).
12. Quoted in Vladimir Lossky, *The Mystical Theology of the Eastern Church* (New York: St. Vladimir's Seminary Press, 1976), 69.
13. William Blake, "Jerusalem," in *The Complete Poems* (New York: Penguin, 1977), 53:24 (referred to by plate and line number).
14. Ibid., 96:20–28.
15. Gershom Scholem, *On the Kabbalah and Its Symbolism*, trans. Ralph Manheim (New York: Schocken, 1965), 112.
16. Ibid., 113.
17. Patrick S. Diehl, *The Medieval European Religious Lyric: An Ars Poetica* (Berkeley: University of California Press, 1984), 5.
18. Samperi, *Lumen Gloriae*, unpaginated.
19. Samperi, *Quadrifarium*, unpaginated.
20. Ibid.
21. Ibid.
22. Ibid.
23. Ibid.

24. Ibid.
25. Ibid. When John Martone edited a selection of Samperi's poetry for Station Hill Press in 2004, he entitled it *Spiritual Necessity*.
26. John Martone, e-mail to the author, September 15, 2003.
27. Samperi, *Quadrifariam*, unpaginated.
28. Frank Samperi, *The Prefiguration* (New York: Grossman/Mushinsha, 1971), unpaginated.
29. Ibid.
30. See Diehl, *The Medieval European Religious Lyric*, 7.
31. Ewart Cousins, introduction to Bonaventure, *The Soul's Journey Into God / The Tree of Life / The Life of St. Francis*, trans. Ewart Cousins, Classics of Western Spirituality (Mahwah, N.J.: Paulist Press, 1978), 24–25.
32. Ibid., 26.
33. Ibid.
34. Bonaventure, *The Soul's Journey Into God*, section 7.4, p. 113.
35. Samperi, *Quadrifariam*, unpaginated.
36. Ibid.
37. Taggart, "A Spiritual Definition of Poetry," 21.
38. Samperi, *Quadrifarium*, unpaginated.
39. Taggart, "A Spiritual Definition of Poetry," 21.
40. Diehl, *The Medieval European Religious Lyric*, 13.
41. Ibid., 14.
42. Samperi, *Quadrifarium*, unpaginated.
43. O'Leary, introduction to *Trilogy*, unpaginated.
44. Samperi, *Quadrifariam*, unpaginated.
45. Samperi, *The Prefiguration*, unpaginated.
46. Ibid.
47. Ibid.
48. *Catechism*, 293 (referred to by paragraph number).
49. Plotinus, *The Enneads*, trans. Stephen MacKenna (New York: Penguin, 1991), V.1.6, p. 354 (references by Ennead, tractate, and chapter; also by page number).
50. Ibid., VI.9.9, 545–546.
51. Samperi, *Lumen Gloriae*, unpaginated.
52. Samperi, *Quadrifariam*, unpaginated.

2. ROBINSON JEFFERS, THE MAN FROM WHOM GOD HID EVERYTHING

1. William Everson, *The Excesses of God: Robinson Jeffers as a Religious Figure* (Stanford, Calif.: Stanford University Press, 1988), 168.
2. Albert Gelpi, foreword to Everson, *The Excesses of God*, ix.
3. Everson, *The Excesses of God*, 168.
4. Robinson Jeffers, *The Selected Poetry of Robinson Jeffers*, ed. Tim Hunt (Stanford, Calif.: Stanford University Press, 2001), 106.

5. Ibid., 594–595.
6. Ibid., 719.
7. Krista Walters, "Robinson Jeffers," *Encyclopedia of American Poetry*, ed. Eric L. Haralson (Chicago: FitzRoy Dearborn, 2001), 329–330.
8. Jeffers, *Selected Poetry*, 591.
9. Ibid., 126–127.
10. Robert Hass, introduction to *Rock and Hawk: A Selection of Shorter Poems by Robinson Jeffers* (New York: Random House, 1987), xxxvi.
11. See Charles Simic, "Divine, Superfluous Beauty," *New York Review of Books* 49, no. 6 (April 2002): 49.
12. Written by Brother Antoninus, Everson's adopted identity when he was a *donatus*, or lay brother, of the Order of Dominicans at St. Albert's in Oakland, California.
13. In this list, greatness can be understood as a recognizable quality in the poetry of intrinsic power and lasting influence.
14. Sigmund Freud, "The Uncanny," in *The Uncanny*, trans. David McClintock (New York: Penguin), 134.
15. See John Seabrook, "It Came from Hollywood," *New Yorker*, December 1, 2003.
16. Poems 285 and 670, respectively, in *The Poems of Emily Dickinson*, ed. R. W. Franklin (Cambridge, Mass.: Belknap/Harvard, 1999). Poem 285 is discussed in its entirety in the introduction; poem 670, again in its entirety, in chapter 9.
17. See my discussion of Duncan's poem "My Mother Would Be a Falconress," in *Gnostic Contagion: Robert Duncan and the Poetry of Illness* (Middletown, Conn.: Wesleyan, 2002), for a treatment of the predatory nature of Duncan's religious poetics.
18. Jeffers, *Selected Poetry*, 165.
19. Ibid., 680.
20. Ibid., 681.
21. Ibid., 194.
22. Ibid., 214.
23. Ibid., 242.
24. Ibid., 241.
25. Ibid., 243.

3. SPIRITUAL OSMOSIS: ABSORBING THE INFLUENCE IN GEOFFREY HILL'S LATER POETRY

1. Geoffrey Hill, *Broken Hierarchies: Poems 1952–2012* (Oxford: Oxford University Press, 2013), 298; Geoffrey Hill, *Speech! Speech!* (Washington, D.C.: Counterpoint, 2000), 10. A note about citations from Hill's poetry: in *Broken Hierarchies*, Hill has revised some of the poems quoted in this chapter from the versions as they appeared in their initial book publication. Primarily, he has downplayed the orthographical innovations that mark the earlier versions. Since these innovations play a role in my argument, poems as quoted will reflect those initial book-publication versions. For ease of reference, I will include citations to both sources, as above.

2. Mark Scroggins, *Louis Zukofsky and the Poetry of Knowledge* (Tuscaloosa: University of Alabama Press, 1997), 323.
3. Robert Potts, "The Praise Singer," *Guardian*, August 10, 2002.
4. The original version of this chapter was written to address the trilogy of *The Triumph of Love*, *Speech! Speech!*, and *The Orchards of Syon*.
5. Hill, *Broken Hierarchies*, 243; *The Triumph of Love* (Boston: Houghton Mifflin, 2000), 9.
6. Hill, *Broken Hierarchies*, 216; *Canaan* (Boston: Houghton Mifflin, 1998), 51.
7. Hill, *Broken Hierarchies*, 3.
8. There are the precedents of the blank-verse "Funeral Music" and "The Songbook of Sebastian Arrarruz," in *King Log* from 1968, and then *Mercian Hymns* from 1971, Hill's prose-poem remythologization of the rule of King Offa, the eighth-century monarch of the kingdom of Mercia, which comprised much of southern England at the time. Which is all to say, Hill's early work shouldn't be strictly understood as that of a formalist. Rather, it's that the early work he was best known for was largely formal in character.
9. These headpieces are abandoned in *Broken Hierarchies*, replaced with a Latin phrase, "Tempus aedificandi tempus destruendi," which inverts Ecclesiastes 3:3 and which means "a time to build up and a time to break down."
10. Among the revisions to *The Triumph of Love* to be found in *Broken Hierarchies* is a reduction in the number of these snide editorial intrusions. See, for instance, section 28, already quoted above, in which the "[possibly a lacuna—ED]" is removed.
11. Hill, *Broken Hierarchies*, 347; *Speech! Speech!*, 59.
12. Hill, *Broken Hierarchies*, 277; *The Triumph of Love*, 67.
13. Ibid., 68.
14. The Brigettines, or the Order of the Most Holy Savior, were founded in 1344 by Saint Brigid of Sweden, a widow and mother of eight who devoted herself to contemplation, liturgical worship, and the restoration of the pope at Avignon to Rome, which, not incidentally, was precisely the mission of Saint Catherine of Siena (*The HarperCollins Encyclopedia of Catholicism*, 196).
15. See *The Orcherd of Syon*, ed. Phyllis Hodgson and Gabriel M. Liegey (Oxford: Oxford University Press, 1966), especially the "Preface" and "The Translator's Prologue."
16. Hill, *Broken Hierarchies*, 384; *The Orchards of Syon* (Washington D.C.: Counterpoint, 2002), 34.
17. Hill, *Broken Hierarchies*, 270–271; *The Triumph of Love*, 56.
18. Geoffrey Hill, "The Art of Poetry No. 80," interviewed by Carl Phillips, *Paris Review* 154 (Spring 2000): 288, 289. Emphasis added.
19. Hill, *Broken Hierarchies*, 290; *Speech! Speech!*, 2.
20. See, for instance, William Logan's review of *Speech! Speech!* in *New Criterion* (December 2000).
21. Hill, "The Art of Poetry No. 80," 290.
22. See Robert Potts, "The Praise Singer," *Guardian*, August 10, 2002.
23. See, again, William Logan's review of *Speech! Speech!* in *New Criterion* (December 2000).
24. Denis Donoghue, *Words Alone* (New Haven, Conn.: Yale University Press, 2000), 129.

25. Geoffrey Hill, *Collected Critical Writings*, ed. Kenneth Haynes (Oxford: Oxford University Press, 2008), 366.
26. Ibid., 371.
27. Ibid., 273.
28. Ibid., 248.
29. Ezra Pound, *The Spirit of Romance* (New York: New Directions, 1968), 153.
30. Hill, *Broken Hierarchies*, 264–265; *The Triumph of Love*, 46.
31. Geoffrey Hill, "Rhetorics of Value," Tanner Lectures on Human Values, delivered at Brasenose College, Oxford, March 6 and 7, 2000, http://www.tannerlectures.utah.edu/lectures/index.html.
32. Hill, *Broken Hierarchies*, 276–277; *The Triumph of Love*, 67.
33. Hill, Tanner Lectures, 283.
34. Hill, "The Art of Poetry No. 80," 283.
35. As Elaine Pagels early on indicated, in Gnostic theology and practice, self-knowledge is knowledge of God. See *The Gnostic Gospels* (New York: Random House, 1979), 119ff.
36. Hill, *Collected Critical Writings*, 327.
37. Henry Vaughan, "The Night," in *The Meditative Poem*, ed. Louis L. Martz (New York: Anchor, 1963), 436.
38. Hill, *Collected Critical Writings*, 318.
39. Ibid., 319.
40. Published in the summer of 1989, "A Pharisee of Pharisees" was presumably written sometime soon beforehand, which is around the same time that he was writing "Envoi (1919)," his essay on Pound.
41. Hill, *Collected Critical Writings*, 321.
42. Ibid., 282.
43. Philip Sherrard, "Presuppositions of the Sacred," in *The Sacred in Life and Art* (Ipswich: Golgonooza, 1990), 1.
44. Michael A. Sells, *Mystical Languages of Unsaying* (Chicago: University of Chicago Press, 1994), 3.
45. Hill, *Broken Hierarchies*, 395; *The Orchards of Syon*, 45.
46. Hill, *Broken Hierarchies*, 397; *The Orchards of Syon*, 47.
47. Hill, *Broken Hierarchies*, 382; *The Orchards of Syon*, 32.

4. PROPHETIC FRUSTRATIONS: ROBERT DUNCAN'S *TRIBUNALS*

1. Robert Duncan, *The H.D. Book*, ed. Michael Boughn and Victor Coleman (Berkeley: University of California Press, 2010), 66.
2. Ibid., 168.
3. Ibid., 188.
4. Though Duncan's reaction to *Tribunals* most certainly informed his decision not to publish, Duncan did not state this intention until he wrote the preface for *Caesar's Gate*, published by Sand Dollar Press in 1972. It's worth noting here that Duncan's sense

of this publishing silence is complex, especially in the light of the ongoing publication of his earlier poetry during this period, as well as the small-press editions and numerous journal publications he managed during this time, including books such as *The Years as Catches*, *Caesar's Gate* (as already mentioned), and the two Fulcrum editions of his work in the United Kingdom. What he intended with this declaration is that he wouldn't publish a "new" book of poetry, one made up of poems written since the time of his decision. Nonetheless, he also published fine editions of some of the poems that would enter into *Ground Work: Before the War*, including an edition of "Achilles' Song," as well as photocopied editions of his work he sent out to friends, for which he collected money. See, for instance, letter 448 from Denise Levertov to Duncan in *The Letters of Robert Duncan and Denise Levertov*, ed. Robert J. Bertholf and Albert Gelpi (Stanford, Calif.: Stanford University Press, 2003), 660, in which Levertov tells Duncan she will be sending him a check for "*ground work*." Duncan responds in the next letter by telling her not to worry about sending any money. This period would also see the publication of previously unpublished but earlier work, including especially *Book of Resemblances*, in a holograph of Duncan's calligraphy and Jess's drawings. This is not so much a criticism—none of these publications was with a major press, some were decidedly ephemeral—as it is a reflection that Duncan's sense of this silence needs to be examined with some readerly care. As with so much else in his creative life, I suspect he made this declaration as much for the tensions it would generate in his writing as for the criticism of publishing and publishers that it implied.

5. Duncan to Levertov, *Letters*, 552.
6. Robert Duncan, "Man's Fulfillment in Order and Strife," in *Collected Essays and Other Prose*, ed. James Maynard (Berkeley: University of California Press, 2014), 202.
7. See Duncan's essay "A Critical Difference of View," in the appendix of *The Letters of Robert Duncan and Denise Levertov*, 729–733. The essay was originally published in *Stony Brook*.
8. Duncan to Levertov, March 18, 1970, letter 441, in *Letters*, 651.
9. Duncan to Levertov, December 16, 1966, letter 383, in *Letters*, 563.
10. Duncan to Levertov, October 4, 1971, letter 449, in *Letters*, 661.
11. The disintegration of Duncan's and Levertov's friendship is spelled out in one of the striking features of their correspondence: Of the 720 pages of surviving correspondence, 700 of them are filled with letters prior to their dispute in 1971, covering a period of eighteen years. The last twenty pages cover the same period, eighteen years up to the point of Duncan's death in 1988. I discuss the Duncan-Blaser dispute in some detail in my *Gnostic Contagion: Robert Duncan and the Poetry of Illness* (Middletown, Conn.: Wesleyan University Press, 2002), 151–160. See also Andrew Mossin, "In the Shadow of Nerval: Robert Duncan, Robin Blaser, and the Poetics of (Mis)Translation," *Contemporary Literature* 38, no. 4 (1997): 673–704.
12. See Sayyed Hossein Nasr, *The Heart of Islam* (San Francisco: HarperSanFrancisco, 2002), esp. chap. 1, "One God, Many Prophets," 1–55. It's also worth mentioning here the fatwa issued against Salman Rushdie for invoking the so-called Satanic Verses, Quranic revelations Muslims believed to have been inspired by Satan, in which Muhammad approves the worship of three idols, verses subsequently rejected by Muhammad.

Rushdie, then, was believed to be a satanic agent because his use of these verses suggests the human, i.e., violable, character of the prophecy. For this reason, without ever reading a word of *The Satanic Verses*, it was "permissible" for the Ayatollah Khomeini to issue the fatwa against Rushdie.

13. George Butterick, "Seraphic Predator: A First Reading of Robert Duncan's *Ground Work*," *Sagetrieb* 4, no. 2–3 (Fall–Winter 1985): 273–274.
14. E-mail to the author, March 26, 2003.
15. Duncan to Levertov, October 4, 1971, letter 449, in *Letters*, 660.
16. The evidence suggests that while Duncan understood the work involved in typesetting, he so mistrusted his printers that he was never able to accept typesetting as an art in its own right. See, for instance, in "A Narrative of Memos," the letters from Duncan to Fredericks, on January 17 and July 15, 1958, in Duncan, *Letters: Poems, 1953–1956*, ed. Robert J. Bertholf (Chicago: Flood, 2003), 68–70.
17. Robert Duncan, front note, "Facsimile of the holograph notebook and of final typescript," in Robert Duncan, *Tribunals: Passages 31–35* (Los Angeles: Black Sparrow, 1970).
18. Ibid.
19. Robert Bringhurst, *Elements of Typographic Style*, version 2.4 (Point Roberts, Wash.: Hartley and Marks, 2001), 84.
20. Robert Duncan, "A Preface Prepared for *MAPS* #6: The Issue," *MAPS* 6 (1974): 1. Duncan didn't always feel bellicose toward Martin. In a letter of July 17, 1967, Duncan urges Levertov to contribute to a Black Sparrow series Martin was planning, praising him as a "true *amateur*: i.e., one who has the care that comes from the love of what he works in or studies." *Letters of Robert Duncan and Denise Levertov*, 580.
21. It's worth noting that this typescript version is not the same one that appears in *Ground Work: Before the War* and that, indeed, there are some few slight differences between these typescripts.
22. Bringhurst, *Elements of Typographic Style*, 19, 18.
23. *MAPS*, 5.
24. Robert Duncan, *Collected Later Poems and Plays*, ed. Peter Quartermain (Berkeley: University of California Press, 2014), 444.
25. Lew Daly, *Swallowing the Scroll: Late in the Prophetic Tradition with the Poetry of Susan Howe and John Taggart* (Buffalo, N.Y.: M Press, 1994), 56. In speaking of Howe's and Taggart's work, Daly places them as direct descendants of a Duncanian prophetic tradition in poetry.
26. Ibid., 37.
27. Ibid., 61.
28. Moshe Idel, *Absorbing Perfections: Kabbalah and Interpretation* (New Haven, Conn.: Yale University Press, 2002), 187.
29. Duncan, *Collected Later Poems and Plays*, 463.
30. See Genesis 6:1–6.
31. Hesiod, "Works and Days," in *The Homeric Hymns and Homerica*, trans. by Hugh G. Evelyn-White (London: William Heinemann; New York: Macmillan, 1914), 11.
32. Duncan, *Collected Later Poems and Plays*, 461.

33. Dante, *Inferno* 21, lines 22–23, trans. Henry Wadsworth Longfellow (New York: Modern Library, 2003), 101.
34. Duncan, *Collected Later Poems and Plays*, 462.
35. Robert Hollander, "Notes, *Inferno XXX*," in Dante, *The Inferno*, trans. by Robert Hollander and Jean Hollander (New York: Anchor, 2000), 562.
36. Duncan, *Collected Later Poems and Plays*, 466.
37. See ibid., 470–482.
38. Lewis Hyde, "Prophetic Excursions," in *The Essays of Henry D. Thoreau* (New York: North Point, 2002), ix.
39. Duncan, *The H.D. Book*, 168.
40. Duncan, *Collected Later Poems and Plays*, 468.
41. Ibid.
42. Ibid., 468–469.

5. WHAT LIES BENEATH MY COPY OF ETERNITY? RELIGIOUS LANGUAGE IN THE POETRY OF LISSA WOLSAK

1. Ben Friedlander, "Philip Jenks and the Poetry of Experience," *Chicago Review* 48, no. 8 (Winter 2002–2003): 66. Lest it appear that I am trying to co-opt Friedlander's terms here—he is interested in defusing notions of any native difficulty in his subject's poetry while preserving the experience of reading work that is manifestly confusing—I want to say that Friedlander's essay has been helpful to me in constructing ways of thinking about Wolsak's poetry in relation to other so-called experimental work of the past ten years. It's helpful as well that Wolsak's poetry resembles Jenks's.
2. Dante, "Epistle XIII" [Letter to Can Grande], in *The Letters of Dante*, trans. Padgett Toynbee (Oxford: Clarendon, 1920), accessible through the Princeton Dante Project 2.0, http://etcweb.princeton.edu/dante/pdp/.
3. Consider Elaine Pagels, *The Gnostic Gospels* (New York: Random House, 1979); Elaine Pagels, *Beyond Belief: The Secret Gospel of Thomas* (New York: Random House, 2003); Karen King, *What Is Gnosticism* (Cambridge, Mass.: Harvard University Press, 2003); Robert Eisenman, *James the Brother of Jesus* (New York: Penguin, 1997); and Marvin Meyer, *Secret Gospels* (Harrisburg, Penn.: Trinity Press International, 2003).
4. Northrop Frye, *Words with Power: Being a Second Study of the Bible as Literature* (New York: Harcourt Brace Jovanovich, 1990), 112.
5. Lissa Wolsak, *Squeezed Light: Collected Poems, 1994–2005* (Barrytown, N.Y.: Station Hill, 2010), 146.
6. Ibid., 79.
7. I found this citation in the *OED* online, 2nd ed., under the definition for "indwelling."
8. Wolsak, *Squeezed Light*, 87.
9. Bernard McGinn, *The Foundations of Mysticism* (New York: Crossroad, 1992), 31.
10. Ibid., xviii–xix.
11. Vladimir Lossky, *The Mystical Theology of the Eastern Church*, trans. the Fellowship of St. Alban and St. Sergius (London: James Clarke, 1957), 38–39.

12. Ibid., 42.
13. Wolsak, *Squeezed Light*, 155.
14. Jean-Luc Marion, *God Without Being*, trans. Thomas A. Carlson (Chicago: University of Chicago Press, 1991), 11.
15. Ibid., 12.
16. Ibid., 17.
17. Ibid., 22.
18. Elaine Pagels writes that *epinoia* conveys genuine insight and might be translated as "imagination." The term appears in *The Secret Book of John*, a work of early Christian Gnosticism, which speaks of this "luminous *epinoia*" as a creative force virtually endowed with consciousness. Pagels describes that "*epinoia* conveys hints and glimpses, images and stories, that imperfectly point beyond themselves toward what we cannot now fully understand." Pagels, *Beyond Belief*, 165.
19. Wolsak, *Squeezed Light*, 130.
20. Ibid., 74.
21. Ibid., 83.
22. Ibid., 82.
23. See, for instance, Mircea Eliade, *Shamanism: Archaic Techniques Toward Ecstasy* (Princeton, N.J.: Bollingen, 1964); and I. M. Lewis, *Ecstatic Religion: A Study of Shamanism and Spirit Possession*, 2nd ed. (New York: Routledge, 1989).
24. Wolsak, *Squeezed Light*, 96.
25. Because of the popularity of this novel, originally published in 1961, "grok" continues to have something of a countercultural aura to it.
26. Wolsak, *Squeezed Light*, 252.
27. Ibid., 256.
28. Ibid., 34.
29. Ibid., 143.
30. "The passing beyond humanity may not be set forth in words: therefore let the example suffice any for whom grace reserves that experience." Dante, *Paradiso* 1:70–72, trans. Charles S. Singleton (Princeton, N.J.: Bollingen, 1975), 7. Dante, having ascended from the Garden of Eden at the end of *Purgatorio* is ascending from earth into the heavenly spheres. Commenting on this word, Singleton writes: "As a verb, the coined term is striking enough; but it is the more so in being, in this context, a verb of motion." He goes on to equate this verb with the *lumen gratiae* of Beatrice, which he compares to the light of Virgil's guidance, which he calls "*umanar*," or "within the proportion of our human nature." Charles S. Singleton, *Journey to Beatrice* (Baltimore, Md.: Johns Hopkins University Press, 1958), 26, 33. Making my own comparison: Wolsak's transhumance is Dante's *transumanar*; her co-mercy is Virgil's *umanar.*
31. Lissa Wolsak, e-mail to the author, August 14, 2004.
32. Lissa Wolsak, e-mail to the author, August 26, 2004.
33. Wolsak, *Squeezed Light*, 188–189.
34. Lissa Wolsak, e-mail to the author, September 13, 2004.
35. "The unthought known" is the psychoanalyst Christopher Bollas's concept for the instinctive knowledge—which he separates from acquired knowledge—that character-

izes the thought and feeling of the "true self," a notion Bollas borrows and amplifies from the writings of D. W. Winnicott. See, for instance, Christopher Bollas, *Forces of Destiny: Psychoanalysis and Human Idiom* (London: Free Association Books, 1991), 10; and D. W. Winnicott, "The Theory of the Parent-Infant Relationship," in *The Maturational Process and the Facilitating Environment* (London: Hogarth, 1972).

36. Wolsak, *Squeezed Light*, 226.
37. "Differences and discrepancies between accounts and versions are not due primarily to vagaries of memory or divergences in emphasis but to quite deliberate theological interpretations of Jesus." John Dominic Crossan, *The Historical Jesus* (HarperSanFrancisco, 1991), xxx. Elsewhere, he writes, "It is precisely that *fourfold* record that constitutes the core problem. If you read the four gospels vertically and consecutively, from start to finish and one after another, you get a generally persuasive impression of unity, harmony, and agreement. But if you read them horizontally and comparatively, focusing on this or that unit and comparing it across two, three, or four versions, it is disagreement rather than agreement that strikes you most forcibly." John Dominic Crossan, *Jesus: A Revolutionary Biography* (HarperSanFrancisco, 1994), x.
38. Lissa Wolsak, e-mail to the author, August 1, 2004.
39. I'm indebted to Robert von Hallberg for this idea, who passed it along to me in an e-mail, August 11, 2004.

6. CATHOLICS: READING FANNY HOWE

1. Czeslaw Milosz, who lived much of his adult life in California, was Catholic (though complexly so) but remains nonetheless identified as a Polish poet. Denise Levertov converted to Catholicism late in her life (in the 1990s); while her new faith undoubtedly influenced her late work, none of it has inspired as much interest as the work she wrote in the 1960s. Other U.S. Catholic poets include Marie Ponsot, Lawrence Joseph, the former NEA chairman Dana Gioia, and the biographer and poet Paul Mariani. Robert Lowell famously converted to Catholicism as a young man—his book *Lord Weary's Castle* was written under the influence of his conversion—but then just as famously let his faith lapse, much to the disappointment and consternation of his friend Flannery O'Connor. Hopelessly obscure, but devoutly Catholic, Robert Lax, who attended Columbia with Merton and like his famous friend was a convert to the faith, deserves to be mentioned here as well. A study of the fruitful intersection of Lax's experimentalism and his Catholicism remains to be written; in the meantime, readers can investigate Robert Lax's *Poems (1962–1997)*, ed. John Beer (Seattle: Wave, 2013). Beer's introduction, which puts Lax's work, among other things, in its religious context, is excellent.
2. In 2009, Howe won the prestigious Ruth Lilly Poetry Prize from the Poetry Foundation. In announcing the award, *Poetry* magazine editor Christian Wiman said, "Fanny Howe is a religious writer whose work makes you more alert and alive to the earth, an experimental writer who can break your heart. Live in her world for a while, and it can change the way you think of yours." http://www.poetryfoundation.org/foundation/release_041409.html.

3. Fanny Howe, *The Winter Sun: Notes on a Vocation* (St. Paul, Minn.: Graywolf, 2009), 122.
4. Fanny Howe, "In Conversation with Leonard Schwartz," *Jacket* 28, http://jacketmagazine.com/28/schwartz-iv-howe.html.
5. The problem this statement alludes to is best captured in the indeterminate type of writing "Catholic" is, as discussed later in the chapter.
6. Fanny Howe, *The Wedding Dress* (Berkeley: University of California Press, 2003), 126.
7. Simone Weil, "*The Iliad*, or a Poem of Force," in Simone Weil and Rachel Bespaloff, *War and the Iliad*, trans. Mary McCarthy (New York: NYRB, 2005), 35.
8. Ibid., 34.
9. Fanny Howe, *One Crossed Out* (St. Paul, Minn.: Graywolf Press, 1997), 15.
10. Ibid., 15–16.
11. Fanny Howe, *Gone* (Berkeley: University of California Press, 2003), 65.
12. Howe, *One Crossed Out*, 11.
13. Howe, *Gone*, 67.
14. Ibid., 94.
15. This sequence first appeared in Fanny Howe, *The Vineyard* (Providence, R.I.: Lost Roads, 1988).
16. Fanny Howe, *Selected Poems* (Berkeley: University of California Press, 2000), 121.
17. Howe, *Gone*, 71.
18. Brian Phillips, "Ten Takes," *Poetry* 185, no. 5 (February 2005): 397.
19. Steve Evans, "Field Notes, October 2003–June 2004," *The Poker* 4 (Summer 2004): 78, emphasis added.
20. Phillips, "Ten Takes," 397.
21. Ibid.
22. Ibid., 397–398.
23. Ibid., 398.
24. Ibid.
25. Christian Wiman, introductory remarks to Fanny's Howe's receipt of the Ruth Lilly Poetry Prize and subsequent reading, archived at the Poetry Foundation website, http://www.poetryfoundation.org/journal/audioitem.html?id=1624.
26. Many of Merton's New Directions titles remain in print, including a recently released new selected poems, *In the Dark Before Dawn*, ed. Lynn R. Szabo (New York: New Directions, 2005).
27. Lay brothers to monastic orders are fully incorporated into the community but are not ordained. Historically, lay brotherhoods arose to relieve clerical monks of tasks that would keep them from their study and ministry. Typically, lay brothers were less educated and fulfilled duties of manual labor. In Everson's case, this meant he could live at St. Albert's and participate in the communal life of the order but, because not bound by vows of ordination, could also pursue his life as a poet in the outside world, giving readings and publishing his work without requiring church permission. See Richard McBrien, ed., *The HarperCollins Encyclopedia of Catholicism* (San Francisco: HarperSanFrancisco, 1995), 760.
28. Albert Gelpi's edition of Everson's selected writings, *Dark God of Eros: A William Everson Reader* (Berkeley: Heyday, 2003), representing his poetry, autobiographical and

critical prose, and letters and interviews, is a helpful place to survey Everson's accomplishments.

29. Eve Grubin, "Theology and Poetry: An Interview with Fanny Howe." *Lyric* 7 (2005): 69.
30. Howe, *The Winter Sun*, 122.
31. Grubin, "Theology and Poetry," 72.
32. Ibid., 73.
33. Fanny Howe, "Christianity and Poetry: A Symposium," with Jennifer Atkinson, Scott Cairns, Fanny Howe, Paul Mariani, and Eric Pankey, *Pleiades* 24, no. 7 (2004): 42.
34. Howe, *The Wedding Dress*, xii.
35. Ibid.
36. Ibid., xiii–xvi.
37. Ibid., xvii.
38. Ibid., xviii.
39. Ibid.
40. Ibid., xix.
41. Ibid., xx.
42. Ibid., xxvi.
43. Howe, *Gone*, 122.
44. See Pew Forum on Religion and Public Life, *U.S. Religious Landscape Survey*, chap. 3: "Religious Affiliation and Demographic Groups," 40, http://religions.pewforum.org/pdf/report-religious-landscape-study-chapter-3.pdf.
45. See Danzy Senna, *Where Did You Sleep Last Night?* (New York: Farrar, Straus and Giroux, 2009), esp. 90–96.
46. Howe, *The Wedding Dress*, 107–108.
47. David B. Burrell, "Apologetics," in *The HarperCollins Encyclopedia of Catholicism*, 72–73.
48. Howe, *The Wedding Dress*, 114.
49. Ibid., 66.
50. Ibid., 109.
51. Ibid., 112.
52. Ibid., 113.
53. Ibid., 116.
54. Ibid.
55. Dante, *The Inferno*, trans. Henry Wadsworth Longfellow (New York: Modern Library, 2003), 1.7.
56. Howe, *The Wedding Dress*, 119.
57. Ibid., 120.
58. Ibid., 121.
59. Ibid., 121–122.
60. Ibid., 122.
61. Grubin, "Theology and Poetry," 73.
62. Howe, *The Wedding Dress*, 122.
63. Howe, "Christianity and Poetry: A Symposium," 51.

64. Simone Weil, *Gravity and Grace* (London: Routledge & Taylor, 1963), 103–104.
65. Ibid., 28.

7. ROBERT DUNCAN'S CELESTIAL HIERARCHY

1. Robert Duncan, *The H.D. Book*, ed. Michael Boughn and Victor Coleman (Berkeley: University of California Press, 2010), 240–241.
2. Clément Oudart, "Genreading and Underwriting (in) Robert Duncan's *Ground Work*," in *(Re:)Working the Ground: Essays on the Late Writings of Robert Duncan*, ed. James Maynard (New York: Palgrave Macmillan, 2011), 151–168.
3. Robert Duncan, *Collected Later Poems and Plays*, ed. Peter Quartermain (Berkeley: University of California Press, 2014), 697.
4. Ibid., 699–700.
5. See *The Roman Missal in Latin and English for Every Day of the Year* (New York: P. J. Kennedy & Sons, 1934). In "The Dignities," Duncan invokes the final prayer of the Mass with the words "*ite, missa est*," or, "Go, you are dismissed."
6. Duncan, *Collected Later Poems and Plays*, 698.
7. Ibid., 708.
8. Ibid., 711.
9. This talk was formerly archived at the Factory School website (www.factoryschool.org) but is no longer available.
10. Pseudo-Dionysius, *The Complete Works*, trans. Colm Luibheid (Mahwah, N.Y.: Paulist Press, 1987), 153–154.
11. Steven Chase, *Angelic Spirituality: Medieval Perspectives on the Ways of Angels* (Mahwah, N.Y.: Paulist Press, 2002), 257.
12. See Fred Gettings, *The Arkana Dictionary of Astrology* (London: Arkana, 1990), 90–91.
13. H.D., *Collected Poems* (New York: New Directions, 1986), 563. More provocative even than this passage from "Tribute to the Angels" is a passage from "The Walls Do Not Fall," in which H.D. ingeniously connects angelic presence to a superfluity of unconscious, chaotic insight: "Depth of the sub-conscious spews forth / too many incongruent monsters // and fixed indigestible matter / such as shell . . . we were caught up by the tornado / and deposited on no pleasant ground, // but we found the angle of incidence / equals the angle of reflection; // separated from the wandering stars / and the habits of the lordly fixed ones, // we noted that even the erratic burnt-out comet / has its peculiar orbit" (534–535).
14. Chase, *Angelic Spirituality*, 189.
15. Dante, *Paradiso*, trans. Charles Singleton (Princeton, N.J.: Bollingen, 1975), 2:450.
16. Dante, *Paradiso*, Canto 28, ll. 130–132, trans. Henry Wadsworth Longfellow (New York: Barnes & Noble Classics, 2006), 150–151.
17. Peter S. Hawkins, *Dante's Testaments: Essays in Scriptural Imagination* (Stanford, Calif.: Stanford University Press, 1999), 93.
18. Robert Duncan, *Collected Essays and Other Prose*, ed. James Maynard (Berkeley: University of California Press, 2014), 107.

19. Duncan, *Collected Later Poems and Plays*, 556.
20. Ibid., 556–557.
21. Duncan, *The H.D. Book*, 589.
22. Duncan, *Collected Later Poetry and Plays*, 709.
23. Ibid., 710.
24. Robert Duncan and Denise Levertov, *The Letters of Robert Duncan and Denise Levertov*, ed. Robert J. Bertholf and Albert Gelpi (Stanford, Calif.: Stanford University Press, 2003), 270.
25. Ibid., 644.
26. Robert Duncan, *Caesar's Gate: Poems, 1949–50* (Berkeley: Sand Dollar, 1972), 65.
27. Rainer Maria Rilke, *Poems*, trans. J. B. Leishman and Stephen Spender (New York: Everyman's Library, 1996), 165.
28. Rainer Maria Rilke, *Selected Letters*, ed. Harry T. Moore (Garden City, N.Y.: Anchor, 1960), 389.
29. Ibid., 390–391.
30. In *The H.D. Book*, Duncan proposes an understanding of the angels of Rilke and H.D. as dedications, in that both poets dedicated their works to their patron angels. "Just as when we wake at some hour of the night and find ourselves not disoriented, in the dark, but in the thought of some attribute of God, a particular angel, to see things in that light; so we may find ourselves in the course of a poem also in the thought of some attribute of our Life, a particular person, having also his or her particular time" (241).
31. Ibid., 337.
32. Rainer Maria Rilke, *The Selected Poetry of Rainer Maria Rilke*, trans. Stephen Mitchell (New York: Random House, 1982), 151.
33. Stephen Fredman, e-mail to the author, January 25, 2007.
34. According to Michael Palmer, in an e-mail to the author, January 29, 2007.
35. On March 5, 1934, Freud wrote a letter to H.D. in which he recounted the events of the recent weeks in Vienna, in which Bolshevist rebels had staged a brief civil war against the increasingly reactionary Austrian government. Freud was in no mood to leave Vienna, in spite of the abjurations of his friends. ("It is unpleasant to go into exile at the age of seventy-eight—but now we have escaped at least this danger.") Writing to H.D. in English, he described the experience of this conflict: "We passed a week of civil war. Not much personal suffering, just one day without electric light, but the 'stimmung' was awful and the feeling as of an earthquake." This letter appears in H.D., *Tribute to Freud* (New York: New Directions, 1984), in the appendix of letters at the end of the book, which was originally published in the United States in 1974, by David S. Godine Books. It is highly likely that Duncan had read this letter and was registering, consciously or not, an echo of Freud's sense of "stimmung" when he used the word to title a poem in "Regulators."
36. Wikipedia, "Stimmung," https://en.wikipedia.org/wiki/Stimmung.
37. Duncan, *Collected Later Poetry and Prose*, 699.
38. Ibid., 703.
39. Ibid., 704–705.
40. Ibid., 675.

41. Ibid., 675–676.
42. C. G. Jung, *Collected Works* (Princeton, N.J.: Bollingen, 1967), 13:37. Ross Hair has remarked to me in an e-mail that serotonin is the Mercurius of our age.
43. Duncan, *Collected Essays and Other Prose*, 231.
44. Ibid., 39.
45. Duncan, *Collected Later Poetry and Plays*, 710.
46. Ibid.
47. Northrop Frye, *Words with Power* (New York: Harcourt, Brace, Jovanovich, 1990), 109.
48. Duncan, *Collected Essays and Other Prose*, 37.
49. Duncan, *The H.D. Book*, 520.

8. THE LONG HUTHERED HAJJ: NATHANIEL MACKEY'S ESOTERICISM

1. Seyyed Hossein Nasr, "Islam," in *Our Religions*, ed. Arvind Sharma (San Francisco: HarperSanFrancisco, 1993), 446.
2. Karen Armstrong, *Muhammad: A Biography of the Prophet* (San Francisco: HarperSanFrancisco, 1992), 268.
3. For a discussion of these techniques, see Michael A. Sells's essay "Hearing the Qur'an," in *Approaching the Qur'an* (Ashland, Ore.: White Cloud, 1999), 145–180.
4. Robert Duncan, "The Truth and Life of Myth," in *Collected Essays and Other Prose*, ed. James Maynard (Berkeley: University of California Press, 2014), 140.
5. Sigmund Freud, "The Uncanny," in *The Uncanny*, trans. David McClintock (New York: Penguin, 2003), 134.
6. Nathaniel Mackey, preface to *Splay Anthem* (New York: New Directions, 2006), x.
7. Ibid., ix.
8. Ibid., 46.
9. Ibid., xiii.
10. Michael A. Sells, *Mystical Languages of Unsaying* (Chicago: University of Chicago Press, 1994), 3. In an interview collected in his *Paracritical Hinge*, Mackey admits that Sells's book exerted an influence on his thinking. See "Interview by Paul Naylor," in *Paracritical Hinge: Essays, Talks, Notes, Interviews* (Madison: University of Wisconsin Press, 2005), 327.
11. Mackey, *Splay Anthem*, 70–71.
12. Norman Finkelstein, *On Mount Vision: Forms of the Sacred in Contemporary American Poetry* (Iowa City: University of Iowa Press, 2010), 199.
13. Mackey, *Splay Anthem*, xi.
14. Ibid., 14.
15. Ibid., 25.
16. Ibid., 29.
17. Ibid., 36.
18. Finkelstein, *On Mount Vision*, 185.
19. Mackey, *Splay Anthem*, 55.

20. Ibid., 64.
21. Ibid., 65.
22. Ibid., xiii.
23. Ibid., 68.
24. Ibid., 72.
25. Mackey, *Paracritical Hinge*, 327.
26. Though Faivre prefers the name "hermetism," I've opted to use the slightly more common term "hermeticism" instead.
27. Antoine Faivre, "What Is Occultism?" in *Hidden Truths: Magic, Alchemy, and the Occult*, ed. Lawrence E. Sullivan (New York: Macmillan, 1989), 3.
28. Antoine Faivre, "Esotericism," in *Hidden Truths: Magic, Alchemy, and the Occult*, ed. Lawrence E. Sullivan (New York: Macmillan, 1989), 39.
29. Mackey, *Splay Anthem*, 67.
30. Joseph Dan, *Kabbalah: A Very Short Introduction* (Oxford: Oxford University Press, 2006), 74.
31. Ibid., 75.
32. This term is borrowed from Marco Pasi, a professor in the History of Hermetic Philosophy Program at the University of Amsterdam. He coined this term in a presentation entitled "Arthur Machen's Panic Fears: Western Esotericism and the Irruption of Negative Epistemology," given at the Esalen Institute's Center for Theory and Research, during a conference on Western esotericism and fiction, May 15–18, 2006.
33. *The Gospel of Judas*, ed. Rodolphe Kasser, Marvin Meyer, and Gregor Wurst (Washington, D.C.: National Geographic, 2006), 21–23.
34. Ibid., 23.
35. Ibid.
36. I devoted a chapter to Mackey's poetry—focused primarily on his Gnosticism—in *Gnostic Contagion: Robert Duncan and the Poetry of Illness* (Middletown, Conn.: Wesleyan University Press, 2002).
37. Mackey, *Splay Anthem*, 80.
38. Reza Aslan, *No God but God: The Origin, Evolution, and Future of Islam* (New York: Random House, 2005), 149.
39. Mackey, *Splay Anthem*, 25.
40. Wilson Harris, *Black Marsden* (London: Faber and Faber, 1972), 52.
41. Mackey, *Splay Anthem*, 25.
42. Ibid., 86, 87.
43. Finkelstein, *On Mount Vision*, 187.
44. Ibid., 193.
45. Listing these names prompts another comparison: Mackey's personal mythology bears curious resemblance to that of H. P. Lovecraft's Cthulhu mythos, which likewise relies on a negative epistemology and whose stories portray characters who intuit, sometimes unwittingly, that horrible nature of the suprareality surrounding them, in which the veneer of "normal" reality hides the hideous truth of alien realities inhabited by unspeakable beings—with names such as Yog-Sothoth, Shub-Niggurath, and Nyarlathotep—too much for any human to bear without going irredeemably mad.

46. This is not to suggest that Mackey's poetry doesn't include considerable esoteric and occult material, from alchemical formulae to Dogon secret rites to Sufi and Shi'ite mysticism (thanks, in part, to readings of Sells and Henry Corbin), nor is it to suggest that Open Field poetry/projective verse as conceptualized by Olson and Duncan isn't derived from or performed through esoteric doctrines and procedures. Olson, as is widely known, was considerably affected by Jung's alchemical writings, just as Duncan's breakthrough in *The Opening of the Field* occurred, in part, as a result of his intensive study of the Zohar. An analogy for what Mackey is doing in relation to the Open Field is perhaps to think of what Mircea Eliade, Gershom Scholem, and Henry Corbin accomplished in the study of religion in the twentieth century: they made the practice of their scholarship cultic, worshipful. Religion (the study of it) became their religion. This is a simplified version of the argument Steven Wasserstrom puts forth in his book *Religion After Religion* (Princeton, N.J.: Princeton University Press, 1999).
47. Mackey, *Splay Anthem*, 26.
48. Ibid., 88.
49. Ibid., 91.
50. Ibid., 115, 117. The Bogomils were a heretical dualist cult in the Balkans in the tenth century who abhorred matter and despised its creator as evil. As dualists, Bogomils bear some resemblance to historical Gnostics, but they are not the same thing. Just as I don't think it's entirely accurate to call Mackey a Gnostic, it's unfair to call him a Bogomil, too. My use of the term here is somewhat flippant. Mackey is, however, in ways that are utterly peculiar, a dualist, such that this world seems commanded and controlled by evasive, vexing powers, and the next world exists entirely in the premonitions of dream and vision, precipitated by some process the controlling power of which is completely elusive. And in this regard, he resembles no other American poets, not even the ones most deeply influenced by him or working in the same lineage. (I'm thinking of Joseph Donahue and Norman Finkelstein.)
51. Ibid., xv.
52. Ibid., 120.

9. APOCALYPTICISM: A WAY FORWARD FOR POETRY

1. Norman O. Brown, "Apocalypse: The Place and Mystery in the Life of the Mind," in *Apocalypse and/or Metamorphosis* (Berkeley: University of California Press, 1991), 4.
2. Northrop Frye, *The Great Code: The Bible and Literature* (San Diego: Harcourt Brace, 1982), 136.
3. "Apocalypticism," in *HarperCollins Dictionary of Religion*, edited by J. Z. Smith (San Francisco: HarperCollins, 1997), 55.
4. Bernard McGinn, *The Foundations of Mysticism* (New York: Crossroad, 1992), 6.
5. The theologian Oliver O'Donovan provides a helpful overview of the argument that Revelation is "the most powerful piece of resistance literature from the period of the early empire" in his essay "History and Politics in the Book of Revelation," in Oliver O'Donovan and Joan Lockwood O'Donovan, *Bonds of Imperfection: Christian Politics,*

Past and Present (Grand Rapids, Mich.: Eerdmans, 2004), 25–47. In his essay, he describes Revelation as John's insistence that "Empire is not simply an extreme case of unified rule; it is the coalescence of powers that drains integrity from all but the dominant partner. . . . But this general thesis about the end of empire is woven together with an eschatological narrative of the disclosure of evil as messianic pretension" (41).

6. Frye, *The Great Code*, 137.
7. "Eschatology," in *HarperCollins Dictionary of Religion*, 342.
8. "State of the Art," *apex of the M* 1 (1994): 5.
9. Ibid., 7.
10. Ibid., 6.
11. Devin Johnston, "*apex of the M* #1–3," *Chicago Review* 41, no. 4 (1995): 131.
12. "State of the Art," 7.
13. Ibid.
14. Lew Daly, e-mail to the author, July 22, 2009.
15. Lew Daly, e-mail to the author, July 26, 2009.
16. Lew Daly, "From Ends Irrespective of (the Limits of) Their Means, or: Further From Closure Than Any Process, Freeing the Other From Form (an ongoing essay in response to questions posed by Pam Rehm)," in *A Poetics of Criticism*, ed. Juliana Spahr, Mark Wallace, Kristin Prevallet, and Pam Rehm (Buffalo: Leave Books, 1994), 189.
17. Some of the fallout from the appearance of the journal is archived in the chronicle of the early years of the Buffalo Poetics Listserv, *Poetics@*, ed. Joel Kuszai (New York: Roof Books, 1999), 92–103. Responses and invectives from Marjorie Perloff, Tom Mandel, James Sherry, and Leslie Scalapino are included.
18. Ron Silliman to Tom Cheetham, posted at Cheetham's blog, *The Legacy of Henry Corbin*, December 5, 2009, http://henrycorbinproject.blogspot.com/2009/12/notes-on-mysticism-in-20th-century.html. Notice characteristic scare quotes around the word mysticism. Brackets in the original.
19. Lew Daly presently works in the area of public policy. Among his activities, he has published a book analyzing connections between faith-based initiatives and social welfare; see his *God and the Welfare State* (Cambridge, Mass.: Boston Review/MIT Press, 2006).
20. Joseph Donahue, e-mail to the author, February 10, 2010.
21. Pam Rehm, e-mail to the author, June 23, 2009.
22. "State of the Art," 5.
23. H.D. to Bryher, April 28, 1933, in *Analyzing Freud: Letters of H.D., Bryher, and Their Circle*, ed. Susan Stanford Friedman (New York: New Directions, 2002), 212.
24. McGinn, *The Foundations of Mysticism*, 165.
25. H.D., "Tribute to the Angels," in *Collected Poems 1912–1944* (New York: New Directions, 1986), 549.
26. Ibid., 550.
27. Ibid., 552.
28. In 1998, the poet sent me a copy of the initial chapbook publication of this poem: Joseph Donahue, *Terra Lucida* (Chester, N.Y.: Heaven Bone Press, 1998); under the title, he inscribed "Latin for 'scattered sunbeams.'"

29. Henry Corbin, *The Man of Light in Iranian Sufism*, trans. Nancy Pearson (Boulder, Colo.: Shambhala, 1978), 42.
30. Ibid., 57.
31. Ibid., 42–43. In another essay, "The *Imago Templi* in Contemplation," Corbin adduces the *terra lucida* to the "intermediary Orient" in which the Temple of the Grail would momentarily appear to its questors, such as Parsifal's coming upon the Castle of the Fisher King, for instance. See Henry Corbin, "The *Imago Templi* in Contemplation," in *Temple and Contemplation* (London: Keegan Paul, 1986), 367.
32. Corbin, *The Man of Light*, 6.
33. See "Docetism," in *The HarperCollins Encyclopedia of Catholicism*, ed. Richard McBrien (San Francisco: HarperSanFrancisco, 1995), 423.
34. Brown, *Apocalypse and/or Metamorphosis*, 55.
35. Joseph Donahue, *Terra Lucida* (Jersey City, N.J.: Talisman House, 2009), 84.
36. Gershom Scholem, *Major Trends in Jewish Mysticism* (New York: Schocken, 1961), 44.
37. Ibid.
38. I suspect there is also a connection, if not an equivalency, to Jung's notion of the "transcendent function," in which the unconscious is temporarily unified by the conscious mind.
39. Joseph Donahue, *In This Paradise: Terra Lucida XXI–XL* (Durham, N.C.: Carolina Wren Press, 2004), 19.
40. Ibid., 22.
41. Donahue, *Terra Lucida* (Talisman House), 97.
42. Emily Dickinson, poem 670, *The Poems of Emily Dickinson*, ed. R. W. Franklin (Cambridge, Mass.: Harvard University Press, 1998), 299.
43. Harold Bloom, introduction to *American Religious Poems*, ed. Harold Bloom and Jesse Zuba (New York: Library of America, 2006), xxxviii.
44. Pam Rehm, "a roof is no guarantee," in *Gone to Earth* (Chicago: Flood Editions, 2001), 1.
45. George Oppen, "Of Being Numerous," in *Collected Poems* (New York: New Directions, 1975), 147.
46. Pam Rehm, note, in *Best American Poetry 2002*, ed. Robert Creeley and David Lehman (New York: Scribner, 2002), 215.
47. John Dominic Crossan, *The Historical Jesus* (San Francisco: HarperSanFrancisco, 1991), 347.
48. Pam Rehm, *Small Works*, 54–55.
49. Daniel C. Matt, *The Essential Kabbalah* (San Francisco: HarperSanFrancisco, 1996), 102.
50. Rehm, *Small Works*, 4. This title has always struck me as echoing Niedecker's early poem "When Ecstasy Is Inconvenient."
51. Ibid., 6, 8, 9.
52. Ibid., 25.
53. Irénée Hausherr, *Penthos: The Doctrine of Compunction in the Christian East*, trans. Anselm Hufstader OSB (Kalamazoo, Mich.: Cistercian Publications, 1982), 18.
54. Rehm, *Small Works*, 60.

55. Rehm, *Gone to Earth*, 32.
56. Daly, e-mail to the author, July 22, 2009.
57. Rehm, *Small Works*, 62.
58. William Blake, *The Complete Poems*, ed. Alicia Ostriker (New York: Penguin, 1977), 436.
59. Northrop Frye, *Fearful Symmetry* (Princeton, N.J.: Princeton University Press,1957), 305–306.
60. Ibid., 306.

CONCLUSION: WHY NOT BE TOTALLY CHANGED INTO FIRE?

1. In *The Poems of W. B. Yeats*, ed. Richard J. Finneran (New York: Macmillan, 1983), 622.
2. Fanny Howe, *The Winter Sun* (Saint Paul, Minn.: Graywolf, 2009), 174.
3. F. C. Happold, *Mysticism: A Study and an Anthology* (London: Penguin, 1970), 39.
4. In the Douay-Rheims translation.
5. Elliot R. Wolfson, *Language, Eros, Being: Kabbalistic Hermeneutics and Poetic Imagination* (New York: Fordham University Press, 2005), 216, 217.
6. Thomas Merton, *The Wisdom of the Desert* (New York: New Directions, 1960), 50.
7. H.D., *Collected Poems 1912–1944*, ed. Louis L. Martz (New York: New Directions, 1986), 583–584.
8. William James, *Varieties of Religious Experience* (New York: Penguin, 1982), 519.

BIBLIOGRAPHY

Armstrong, Karen. *Muhammad: A Biography of the Prophet*. San Francisco: HarperSan-Francisco, 1992.

Asad, Talal. *Formations of the Secular: Christianity, Islam, Modernity*. Stanford, Calif.: Stanford University Press, 2003.

Aslan, Reza. *No god but God: The Origin, Evolution, and Future of Islam*. New York: Random House, 2005.

Berger, Peter L. *The Sacred Canopy*. Garden City, N.Y.: Anchor, 1969.

Bertholf, Robert J. "A Narrative of Memos." In *Letters: Poems, 1953–1956*, ed. Robert J. Bertholf, 59–71. Chicago: Flood Editions, 2003.

Bertholf, Robert J., and Albert Gelpi, eds. *The Letters of Robert Duncan and Denise Levertov*. Stanford, Calif.: Stanford University Press, 2003.

Blake, William. *The Complete Poems*. New York: Penguin, 1977.

Bloom, Harold. Introduction to *American Religious Poems*, ed. Harold Bloom and Jesse Zuba, xxv–xlvi. New York: Library of America, 2006.

Bollas, Christopher. *Forces of Destiny: Psychoanalysis and Human Idiom*. London: Free Association Books, 1991.

Bonaventure. *The Soul's Journey Into God / The Tree of Life / The Life of St. Francis*. Trans. Ewart Cousins. Classics of Western Spirituality. Mahwah, N.J.: Paulist Press, 1978.

Bringhurst, Robert. *Elements of Typographic Style*. Version 2.4. Point Roberts, Wash.: Hartley & Marks, 2001.

Brown, Norman O. *Apocalypse and/or Metamorphosis*. Berkeley: University of California Press, 1991.

Burke, Kenneth. *The Rhetoric of Religion*. Berkeley: University of California Press, 1970.

Burrell, David B. "Apologetics." In *The HarperCollins Encyclopedia of Catholicism*, ed. Richard P. McBride, 72–73. San Francisco: HarperSanFrancisco, 1995.

Butterick, George. "Seraphic Predator: A First Reading of Robert Duncan's *Ground Work*." *Sagetrieb* 4, no. 2–3 (Fall–Winter 1985): 273–284.

Catechism of the Catholic Church. Libraria Editrice Vaticana. Liguori: Liguori Publications, 1994.

"Christianity and Poetry: A Symposium." With Jennifer Atkinson, Scott Cairns, Fanny Howe, Paul Mariani, and Eric Pankey. *Pleiades* 24, no. 1 (2004): 38–53.

Celan, Paul. *Gedichte II*. Frankfurt: Suhrkamp Verlag 1997.

Chase, Steven. *Angelic Spirituality: Medieval Perspectives on the Ways of Angels*. Classics of Western Spirituality. Mahwah, N.Y.: Paulist Press, 2002.

Corbin, Henry. *Alone with the Alone: Creative Imagination in the Sufism of Ibn 'Arabi*. Trans. Ralph Manheim. Bollingen Series 91. Princeton, N.J.: Princeton University Press, 1997.

——. *The Man of Light in Iranian Sufism*. Translated by Nancy Pearson. Boulder, Colo.: Shambhala, 1978.

——. *Temple and Contemplation*. Trans. Philip Sherrard. London: Kegan Paul, 1986.

Couliano, Ioan P. *The Tree of Gnosis*. San Francisco: HarperSanFrancisco, 1990.

Cousins, Ewart. Introduction to Bonaventure, *The Soul's Journey Into God / The Tree of Life / The Life of St. Francis*, trans. Ewart Cousins, 1–48. Classics of Western Spirituality. Mahwah, N.J.: Paulist Press, 1978.

Crossan, John Dominic. *The Historical Jesus: The Life of a Mediterranean Peasant*. San Francisco: HarperSanFrancisco, 1991.

——. *Jesus: A Revolutionary Biography*. San Francisco: HarperSanFrancisco, 1994.

Daly, Lew. "From Ends Irrespective of (the Limits of) Their Means, or: Further from Closure Than Any Process, Freeing the Other from Form (an ongoing essay in response to questions posed by Pam Rehm)." In *A Poetics of Criticism*, ed. Juliana Spahr, Mark Wallace, Kristin Prevallet, and Pam Rehm, 187–196. Buffalo: Leave Books, 1994.

——. *God and the Welfare State*. Cambridge, Mass.: Boston Review/MIT Press, 2006.

——. *Swallowing the Scroll: Late in the Prophetic Tradition with the Poetry of Susan Howe and John Taggart*. Buffalo, N.Y.: M Press, 1994.

Dan, Joseph. *Kabbalah: A Very Short Introduction*. Oxford: Oxford University Press, 2006.

Dante. "Epistle XIII" [Letter to Can Grande]." In *The Letters of Dante*, trans. Padgett Toynbee. Oxford: Clarendon, 1920. Accessed at the Princeton Dante Project 2.0, http://etcweb.princeton.edu/dante/pdp/.

——. *The Inferno*. Trans. Henry Wadsworth Longfellow. New York: Modern Library, 2003.

——. *The Inferno*. Trans. Robert Hollander and Jean Hollander. Notes by Robert Hollander. New York: Anchor, 2000.

——. *The Paradiso*. Trans. Henry Wadsworth Longfellow. New York: Barnes & Noble, 2006.

——. *Paradiso*. Trans., with a commentary, by Charles Singleton. Vol. 2. Princeton, N.J.: Bollingen, 1975.

Dickinson, Emily. *The Poems of Emily Dickinson*. Ed. R. W. Franklin. Cambridge, Mass.: Harvard University Press, 1998.

Diehl, Patrick S. *The Medieval European Religious Lyric: An Ars Poetica*. Berkeley: University of California Press, 1984.

Dionysius. "The Mystical Theology." In *The Essential Writings of Christian Mysticism*, ed. Bernard McGinn, 283–289. New York: Modern Library, 2006.

Donoghue, Denis. *Words Alone*. New Haven, Conn.: Yale University Press, 2000.

Donahue, Joseph. *In This Paradise: Terra Lucida XXI–XL*. Durham, N.C.: Carolina Wren, 2004.

——. *Terra Lucida*. Chester, N.Y.: Heaven Bone, 1998.

——. *Terra Lucida.* Jersey City, N.J.: Talisman House, 2009.

Duncan, Robert. *Bending the Bow.* New York: New Directions, 1968.

——. *Caesar's Gate: Poems, 1949–50.* Berkeley: Sand Dollar, 1972.

——. *Collected Essays and Other Prose.* Ed. James Maynard. Berkeley: University of California Press, 2014.

——. *The Collected Later Poems and Plays.* Ed. Peter Quartermain. Berkeley: University of California Press, 2014.

——. "Facsimile of the holograph notebook and of final typescript." In *Tribunals: Passages 31–35.*

——. "The Feast, *Passages* 34." Booklet. Included in *Tribunals.*

——. *Fictive Certainties.* New York: New Directions, 1985.

——. *Ground Work: Before the War.* New York: New Directions, 1984.

——. *The H.D. Book.* Ed. Michael Boughn and Victor Coleman. Berkeley: University of California Press, 2011.

——. "A Preface prepared for MAPS #6: THE ISSUE." *MAPS 6* (1974): 1–16.

——. *A Selected Prose.* Ed. Robert J. Bertholf. New York: New Directions, 1995.

——. *Tribunals: Passages 31–35.* Santa Barbara, Calif.: Black Sparrow, 1970.

Eliade, Mircea. *The Sacred and the Profane.* Trans. Willard R. Trask. San Diego, Calif.: Harcourt, Brace, Jovanovich, 1959.

——. *Shamanism: Archaic Techniques of Ecstasy.* Trans. Willard R. Trask. Bollingen Series 77. Princeton, N.J.: Princeton University Press, 1964.

Eliot, T. S. *Collected Poems 1909–1935.* New York: Harcourt, Brace, and Company, 1936.

Evans, Steve. "Field Notes, October 2003—June 2004." *The Poker* 4 (Summer 2004): 66–87.

Everson, William. *Dark God of Eros: A William Everson Reader.* Ed. Albert Gelpi. Berkeley: Heyday, 2003.

Faivre, Antoine. "Esotericism." In *Hidden Truths: Magic, Alchemy, and the Occult,* ed. Lawrence E. Sullivan, 38–39. New York: Macmillan, 1989.

——. "What Is Occultism?" In *Hidden Truths: Magic, Alchemy, and the Occult,* ed. Lawrence E. Sullivan, 3–9. New York: Macmillan, 1989.

Finkelstein, Norman. *On Mount Vision: Forms of the Sacred in Contemporary American Poetry.* Iowa City: University of Iowa Press, 2010.

Fox, Everett, trans. *The Five Books of Moses.* New York: Schocken, 1995.

Friedlander, Ben. "Philip Jenks and the Poetry of Experience." *Chicago Review* 48, no. 4 (Winter 2002–2003): 65–81.

Friedman, Richard Eliot. *Commentary on the Torah.* San Francisco: HarperSanFrancisco, 2001.

Friedman, Susan Stanford, ed. *Analyzing Freud: Letters of H.D., Bryher, and Their Circle.* New York: New Directions, 2002.

Freud, Sigmund. *Civilization and Its Discontents.* Trans. David McClintock. London: Penguin, 2002.

——. "The Uncanny." In *The Uncanny,* trans. David McClintock, 121–161. New York: Penguin, 2003.

Frye, Northrop. *Fearful Symmetry.* Princeton, N.J.: Princeton University Press, 1957.

——. *The Great Code: The Bible and Literature.* San Diego, Calif.: Harcourt Brace Jovanovich, 1982.

——. *T. S. Eliot.* New York: Grove, 1963.

——. *Words with Power: Being a Second Study of the Bible as Literature.* New York: Harcourt Brace Jovanovich, 1990.

Gelpi, Albert. "The Thistle and the Serpent." In H.D., *Notes on Thought & Vision.* San Francisco: City Lights, 1982.

Gettings, Fred. *The Arkana Dictionary of Astrology.* London: Arkana, 1990.

The Gospel of Judas. Ed. Rodolphe Kasser, Marvin Meyer, and Gregor Wurst. Washington, D.C.: National Geographic, 2006.

Grubin, Eve. "Theology and Poetry: An Interview with Fanny Howe." *Lyric* 7 (2005): 69–74.

Happold, F. C. *Mysticism: A Study and an Anthology.* London: Penguin, 1970.

Harris, Wilson. *Black Marsden.* London: Faber, 1972.

Hass, Robert. "Introduction." In *Rock and Hawk: A Selection of Shorter Poems by Robinson Jeffers,* ed. Robert Hass, xv–xliii. New York: Random House, 1987.

Hausherr, Irénée. *Penthos: The Doctrine of Compunction in the Christian East.* Trans. Anselm Hufstader OSB. Kalamazoo, Mich.: Cistercian Publications, 1982.

H.D. *Collected Poems 1912–1944.* New York: New Directions, 1986.

——. *Notes on Thought & Vision.* San Francisco: City Lights, 1982.

——. *Tribute to Freud.* New York: New Directions, 1984.

Hawkins, Peter S. *Dante's Testaments: Essays in Scriptural Imagination.* Stanford, Calif.: Stanford University Press, 1999.

Hesiod. "Works and Days." Trans. Hugh G. Evelyn-White. New York: Macmillan, 1914.

Hill, Geoffrey. "The Art of Poetry No. 80." Interviewed by Carl Phillips. *Paris Review* 154 (Spring 2000): 272–299.

——. *Broken Hierarchies: Poems 1952–2012.* Ed. Kenneth Haynes. Oxford: Oxford University Press, 2013.

——. *Canaan.* New York: Houghton Mifflin, 1996.

——. *Collected Critical Writings.* Ed. Kenneth Haynes. Oxford: Oxford University Press, 2008.

——. *The Enemy's Country.* Stanford, Calif.: Stanford University Press, 1991.

——. "A Matter of Timing." *Guardian,* Sept. 21, 2002.

——. *The Orchard of Syon.* Washington, D.C.: Counterpoint, 2002.

——. "Rhetorics of Value." Tanner Lectures on Human Values. Delivered at Brasenose College, Oxford, March 6 and 7, 2000. http://www.tannerlectures.utah.edu/lectures/index.html.

——. *Speech! Speech!* Washington, D.C.: Counterpoint, 2000.

——. *Style and Faith.* Washington, D.C.: Counterpoint, 2003.

——. *The Triumph of Love.* New York: Houghton Mifflin, 1998.

Hollander, Robert. "Notes, *Inferno XXX.*" In Dante, *The Inferno,* trans. Robert Hollander and Jean Hollander, 558–563. New York: Anchor, 2000.

Hopkins, Gerard Manley. *The Journals and Papers of Gerard Manley Hopkins.* Ed. Humphrey House. Oxford: Oxford University Press, 1959.

Howe, Fanny. *Gone.* Berkeley: University of California Press, 2003.

——. "In Conversation with Leonard Schwartz," *Jacket* 28, http://jacketmagazine.com/28/schwartz-iv-howe.html.

——. *One Crossed Out.* St. Paul, Minn.: Graywolf, 1997.

——. *Selected Poems.* Berkeley: University of California Press, 2000.

——. *The Wedding Dress: Meditations on Word and Life*. Berkeley: University of California Press, 2003.

——. *The Winter Sun: Notes on a Vocation*. St. Paul, Minn.: Graywolf, 2009.

Howe, Susan. *My Emily Dickinson*. Berkeley: North Atlantic Books, 1985.

Hyde, Lewis. "Prophetic Excursions." In *The Essays of Henry D. Thoreau*. New York: North Point, 2002.

Idel, Moshe. *Absorbing Perfections: Kabbalah and Interpretation*. New Haven, Conn.: Yale University Press, 2002.

James, William. *The Varieties of Religious Experience*. New York: Penguin, 1985.

Jeffers, Robinson. *Rock and Hawk: A Selection of Shorter Poems by Robinson Jeffers*. Ed. Robert Hass. New York: Random House, 1987.

——. *The Selected Poetry of Robinson Jeffers*. Ed. Tim Hunt. Stanford, Calif.: Stanford University Press, 2001.

Johnston, Devin. "*apex of the M #1–3*." *Chicago Review* 41, no. 4 (1995): 131–135.

Jung, C. G. *Collected Works*. Vol. 13. Trans. R. F. C. Hull. Bollingen Series 20. Princeton: Bollingen, 1967.

Kuszai, Joel, ed. *Poetics@*. New York: Roof, 1999.

Lewis, I. M. *Ecstatic Religion: A Study of Shamanism and Spirit Possession*. 2nd ed. London: Routledge, 1989.

Logan, William. Review of *The Orchards of Syon*. *New Criterion*, June 2002.

——. Review of *Speech! Speech! New Criterion*, December 2000.

Lossky, Vladimir. *The Mystical Theology of the Eastern Church*. Trans. Members of the Fellowship of St. Alban & St. Sergius. Crestwood, N.Y.: St. Vladimir's Seminary Press, 1976.

Mandelstam, Osip. "Conversation About Dante." In *The Poet's Dante*, ed. Peter S. Hawkins and Rachel Jacoff, trans. Jane Gary Harris and Constance Link, 40–93. New York: FSG, 2001.

MacCulloch, Diarmaid. *The Reformation: A History*. New York: Penguin, 2003.

Mackey, Nathaniel. *Paracritical Hinge: Essays, Talks, Notes, Interviews*. Madison: University of Wisconsin Press, 2005.

——. *Splay Anthem*. New York: New Directions, 2006.

Marion, Jean-Luc. *God Without Being*. Trans. Thomas Carlson. Chicago: University of Chicago Press, 1991.

Matt, Daniel C. *The Essential Kabbalah*. San Francisco: HarperSanFrancisco, 1996.

McBrien, Richard P., ed. *The HarperCollins Encyclopedia of Catholicism*. San Francisco: HarperSanFrancisco, 1995.

McGinn, Bernard. *The Foundations of Mysticism*. New York: Crossroad, 1991.

Meister Eckhart: Teacher and Preacher. Ed. Bernard McGinn. Classics of Western Spirituality. Mahwah, N.J.: Paulist Press, 1986.

Merton, Thomas. *In the Dark Before Dawn*. Ed. Lynn R. Szabo. New York: New Directions, 2005.

——. *The Wisdom of the Desert*. New York: New Directions, 1960.

Mossin, Andrew. "In the Shadow of Nerval: Robert Duncan, Robin Blaser, and the Poetics of (Mis)Translation." *Contemporary Literature* 38, no. 4 (1997): 673–704.

Nasr, Sayyed Hossein. *The Heart of Islam*. San Francisco: HarperSanFrancisco, 2002.

——. "Islam." In *Our Religions*, ed. Arvind Sharma, 425–532. San Francisco: HarperSanFrancisco, 1993.

O'Donovan, Oliver, and Joan Lockwood O'Donovan. *Bonds of Imperfection: Christian Politics, Past and Present*. Grand Rapids, Mich.: Eerdmans, 2004.

O'Leary, Peter. *Gnostic Contagion: Robert Duncan and the Poetry of Illness*. Middletown, Conn.: Wesleyan University Press, 2002.

——. "Introduction." In Frank Samperi, *Trilogy*, ix–xv. Nottingham: Skysill, 2013.

——. *Luminous Epinoia*. Brooklyn: Cultural Society, 2010.

Oppen, George. *Collected Poems*. New York: New Directions, 1975.

The Orcherd of Syon. Ed. Phyllis Hodgson and Gabriel M. Liegey. Oxford: Oxford University Press, 1966.

Otto, Rudolf. *The Idea of the Holy*. Trans. J. W. Harvey. Oxford: Oxford University Press, 1958.

Oudart, Clément. "Genreading and Underwriting (in) Robert Duncan's *Ground Work*." In *(Re:)Working the Ground: Essays on the Late Writings of Robert Duncan*, ed. James Maynard, 151–168. New York: Palgrave Macmillan, 2011.

Pagels, Elaine. *Beyond Belief: The Secret Gospel of Thomas*. New York: Random House, 2003.

——. *The Gnostic Gospels*. New York: Random House, 1979.

Parsons, Williams B. *The Enigma of the Oceanic Feeling: Revisioning the Psychoanalytic Theory of Mysticism*. New York: Oxford University Press, 1999.

Pew Forum on Religion & Public Life/U.S. Religious Landscape Survey. http://religions.pewforum.org/pdf/report-religious-landscape-study-chapter-3.pdf.

Phillips, Brian. "Ten Takes." *Poetry* 185, no. 5 (February 2005): 392–404.

Plotinus. *The Enneads*. Trans. Stephan MacKenna. New York: Penguin, 1991.

Potts, Robert. "The Praise Singer." *Guardian*, August 10, 2002.

Pound, Ezra. *The Spirit of Romance*. New York: New Directions, 1968.

Pseudo-Dionysius. *The Complete Works*. Trans. Colm Luibheid. Classics of Western Spirituality. Mahwah, N.J.: Paulist Press, 1987.

Rehm, Pam. *Gone to Earth*. Chicago: Flood Editions, 2001.

——. "Note." In *Best American Poetry 2002*, ed. Robert Creeley and David Lehman, 215. New York: Scribner Poetry, 2002.

——. *Small Works*. Chicago: Flood Editions, 2005.

Rilke, Rainer Maria. *Poems*. Trans. J. B. Leishman and Stephen Spender. New York: Everyman's Library, 1996.

——. *Selected Letters*. Ed. Harry T. Moore. Garden City, N.Y.: Anchor, 1960.

——. *The Selected Poetry of Rainer Maria Rilke*. Trans. Stephen Mitchell. New York: Random House, 1982.

The Roman Missal in Latin and English for Every Day of the Year. New York: P. J. Kennedy & Sons, 1934.

Samperi, Frank. *Lumen Gloriae*. New York: Grossman/Mushinsha, 1973.

———. *The Prefiguration*. New York: Grossman/Mushinsha, 1971.

———. *Quadrifariam*. New York: Grossman/Mushinsha, 1973.

Scholem, Gershom. *Major Trends in Jewish Mysticism*. New York: Schocken, 1961.

——. *On the Kabbalah and Its Symbolism*. Trans. Ralph Manheim. New York: Schocken, 1965.

Scroggins, Mark. *Louis Zukofsky and the Poetry of Knowledge*. Tuscaloosa: University of Alabama Press, 1998.

——. *The Poem of a Life: A Biography of Louis Zukofsky*. Berkeley: Shoemaker & Hoard, 2007.

Seabrook, John. "It Came from Hollywood." *New Yorker*, December 1, 2003.

Sells, Michael A. *Approaching the Qur'an*. Ashland, Ore.: White Cloud, 1999.

——. *Mystical Languages of Unsaying*. Chicago: University of Chicago Press, 1994.

Senna, Danzy. *Where Did You Sleep Last Night?* New York: FSG, 2009.

Sherrard, Philip. *The Sacred in Life and Art*. Ipswich: Golgonooza, 1990.

Silliman, Ron. "To Tom Cheetham." Posted at Cheetham's blog "The Legacy of Henry Corbin." December 5, 2009. http://henrycorbinproject.blogspot.com/2009/12/notes-on-mysticism-in-20th-century.html.

Simic, Charles. "Divine, Superfluous Beauty." *New York Review of Books* 49, no. 6 (April 11, 2002): 48–50.

Singleton, Charles S. *Journey to Beatrice*. Baltimore, Md.: Johns Hopkins University Press, 1981.

Smith, Jonathan Z., ed. *The HarperCollins Dictionary of Religion*. San Francisco: HarperSanFrancisco, 1995.

Taggart, John. "A Spiritual Definition of Poetry." *Songs of Degrees*. Tuscaloosa: University of Alabama Press, 1993.

Taylor, Charles. *The Secular Age*. Cambridge, Mass.: Harvard University Press, 2006.

Thuswaldner, Gregor. "A Conversation with Peter Berger." *Cresset* 77, no. 3 (Lent 2014): 16–21.

Vaughan, Henry. *The Complete Poems*. Ed. Alan Rudrum. New York: Penguin, 1995.

——. "The Night." In *The Meditative Poem*, ed. Louis L. Martz, 434–436. New York: Anchor, 1963.

von Hallberg, Robert. *Lyric Powers*. Chicago: University of Chicago Press, 2008.

Walters, Krista. "Robinson Jeffers." In *Encyclopedia of American Poetry*, ed. Eric L. Haralson, 329–330. Chicago: FitzRoy Dearborn, 2001.

Wasserstrom, Steven. *Religion After Religion: Gershom Scholem, Mircea Eliade, and Henry Corbin at Eranos*. Princeton, N.J.: Princeton University Press, 1999.

Weil, Simone. *Gravity and Grace*. London: Routledge & Taylor, 1963.

Weil, Simone, and Rachel Bespaloff. *War and the Iliad*. Trans. Mary McCarthy. New York: NYRB, 2005.

Whitman, Walt. *Selected Poems 1855–1992*. Ed. Gary Schmidgall. New York: St. Martin's Press, 2000.

Wiman, Christian. Introductory remarks to Fanny's Howe's receipt of the Ruth Lilly Poetry Prize and subsequent reading. The Poetry Foundation. http://www.poetryfoundation.org/journal/audioitem.html?id=1624.

Winnicott, D. W. *Human Nature*. New York: Schocken, 1988.

——. "The Theory of the Parent-Infant Relationship." In *The Maturational Process and the Facilitating Environment*, 37–55. London: Hogarth, 1972.

Wolfson, Elliot. *Language, Eros, Being: Kabbalistic Hermeneutics and Poetic Imagination*. New York: Fordham University Press, 2005.

Wolsak, Lissa. *Pen Chants or nth or 12 spirit-like impermanences*. New York: Roof, 2000.

——. *Squeezed Light: Collected Poems 1994–2005*. Barrytown, N.Y.: Station Hill, 2010.

Wolsak, Melissa. *The Garcia Family Co-Mercy*. Vancouver: Tsunami Editions, 1994.

Yeats, William Butler. *The Poems of W. B. Yeats*. Ed. Richard J. Finneran. New York: Macmillan, 1983.

INDEX